MOVIE
LUST

MOVIE LUST

MAITLAND McDONAGH

RECOMMENDED VIEWING FOR EVERY MOOD, MOMENT, AND REASON

SASQUATCH BOOKS
SEATTLE

To My Mother

Printed in the United States of America
Published by Sasquatch Books
Distributed by Publishers Group West
15 14 13 12 11 10 09 08 07 06   9 8 7 6 5 4 3 2 1

Cover photograph: PhotoAlto
Author photograph: Country Lane Photography
Cover design: Bob Suh
Interior design: Rowen Scott
Interior illustrations: Bob Suh
Interior composition: William Quinby

Library of Congress Cataloging-in-Publication Data is available.

ISBN 1-57061-478-4

Sasquatch Books
119 South Main Street, Suite 400
Seattle, WA 98104
(206) 467-4300
www.sasquatchbooks.com
custserv@sasquatchbooks.com

Contents

INTRODUCTION

My earliest movie memories involve gloomy little black-and-white sci-fi/horror pictures about missing girls and melancholy aliens from dying worlds, movies my babysitter left on in the background while she read fashion magazines. We weren't a "round up the kids and go to the drive-in" family (we don't have drive-ins in Manhattan) and rumors of perverts, junkies, and sundry bad influences lurking in theaters ensured that my parents didn't let us go alone. I didn't watch much TV, because I was the kind of gluttonous little bookworm who inhaled *Gods, Graves & Scholars: The Story of Archeology* and Herbert van Thal's notoriously grisly *Pan Book of Horror Story* anthologies with equal enthusiasm. I don't even remember actually watching *Not of This Earth* (1957) and *Night Caller from Outer Space* (1965), but they crept into my brain and lodged themselves somewhere cozy. Years later, when I was in college and a wan girl who came to class in a tatty '50s party dress with her hair swept up into a chignon remarked nonchalantly that she edited a fanzine called *Bikini Girl*, the words "*Night Caller from Outer Space?*" slithered straight from my unconscious to my mouth. *Night Caller*'s mutated alien, Mr. Medra (I don't think I've ever typed that name before, and never noticed it was an anagram for "dream"), desperate to rejuvenate his planet's corrupted gene pool, lured unwary swinging-sixties chicks to an intergalactic fate worse than death by advertising for models to appear in *Bikini Girl* magazine.

By high school I was deep in thrall to horror movies, the dreamiest of celluloid dreams. I started an index card file of credits, synopses, and observations in a little metal box, with a one-to-five rating system of little bats. There were no VCRs or TiVo then: I had a standing date with *The 4:30 Movie*, a smorgasbord of (mostly) genre pictures that followed the Gothic soap opera *Dark Shadows* on ABC's New York-area affiliate, Channel 7. I kept a running list of movies I wanted to see in my head, and when one turned up in the TV listings for 3 a.m., I set the clock for 2:45 and got up. When you watch movies half asleep, they glide right through the barrier that separates received and invented images and become an indelible part of your mind's internal landscape. I can't count how many e-mails I've received in my Ask FlickChick mail box at TVGuide. com that began "I think this was a scene from a movie I saw, but I might have imagined it . . . "

The lurid allure of tiny newspaper ads for exploitation pictures playing in Times Square grind houses eventually overrode my trepidation, and I first braved Hell's Midway for a double bill of *The Beast Must Die* and Oliver Stone's *Seizure* (both 1974)—starring *Dark Shadows'* Jonathan Frid—at the decaying Lyric Theater. There's no rational reason to mourn the Times Square of the '70s, a pestilent swamp of junkies, hookers, and scabrous waste cases sleeping it off—whatever disgusting debauch *it* was—in rundown auditoriums where management never turned off the lights and pushers sold drugs from makeshift trays, prowling the aisles like living-dead cigarette girls. But I spent so much time there that its transformation into a vulgar, family friendly tourist attraction pains me: I can't look at the Ford Center for the Performing Arts without a piercing stab of longing for the Lyric and its neighbor, the Apollo, which were merged and remodeled beyond recognition to create it.

I escaped to movies on Christmas and Thanksgiving when the family drama was unbearable, and there will always be a place in my heart for James Glickenhaus's 1988 *Shakedown*, in which renegade cop Sam Elliot and crusading attorney Peter Weller take on corruption in the NYPD; I saw it at a now-demolished Upper West Side theater called the Olympia one particularly headache-inducing holiday. Movies can do the job of a stiff drink, but with no hangover.

In my first college film class I sat next to someone who claimed he'd discovered Jean-Luc Godard at age twelve. I realize now he was probably lying, but I was intimidated into mainlining world classics, from Yasujiro Ozu's exquisitely subtle family dramas and Wojciech Has's trippy *Saragossa Manuscript* (1965) to the films of Alfred Hitchcock—I can hardly believe that *Vertigo* (1958), *Rope* (1948), *Rear Window* (1954), *The Trouble with Harry* (1955), and *The Man Who Knew Too Much* (1956) had been out of circulation for decades when they were re-released to theaters in 1984, but they were and I was privileged to see them all with fresh eyes. I picked up prints at the United Nations for Hunter College's retrospective of Polish director Andrzej Wajda's extraordinary work, from *Kanal* (1957) to *Man of Marble* (1977), and took in new German films by Rainer Werner Fassbinder and Werner Herzog at the Cinema Studio near Lincoln Center. I saw classics of every stripe at the St. Mark's Cinema, the Regency, the Carnegie Hall Cinema, and the Thalia, all lost now to the relentless churn of urban development. I was well and truly hooked, driven by the restless urge to seek out the obscure, the forgotten, and the unknown, from Turkish exploitation movies to all-but-lost poverty-row thrillers like the amazing *Decoy* (see *Deadlier Than the Male*).

A professor suggested that I submit an intensely theoretical paper I had written for her about Michael Powell's *Peeping Tom* to an academic magazine called *Film/Psychology Review*; I did, and *The Ambiguities of Seeing and Knowing in Peeping Tom* became my first published article. Later—in the late 1980s, while I was working for the New York City Ballet—I met Powell at a backer's audition for what became the disastrous 1993 Broadway production of his much-loved *The Red Shoes* (see *Everything is Beautiful at the Ballet*). He was in his eighties, politeness personified. "You know," he said gently, "I never intended all those things. But you saw them, so they must be there." To this day I thank Powell for his extraordinary generosity of spirit and inherent understanding that no one owns the film that exists between the screen and a moviegoer's eyes. At their best, movies are an alternate reality that compresses, heightens, and makes sense of life's shabby chaos: to lose yourself in them a privilege, an out-of-body experience with a clear trail back. The titles in this book are a diverse lot: some serious, some silly, some famous, some obscure. I hope my recommendations lead to a movie you'll never forget, or reacquaint you with one that crept into your dreams when you weren't paying attention.

If critic Pauline Kael lost it at the movies, I found it. No matter how often individual films disappoint me, hope springs eternal: perhaps the next will be something extraordinary. And if not the next, then the one after that—there are enough to last me a lifetime.

ACKNOWLEDGMENTS

A ll my essays started with one movie. Some came together so fast I barely had time to write down the free-associative stream of titles that came tumbling out of memory. Others were the product of impromptu brainstorming sessions at home, over meals, at the office, and sitting in screening rooms waiting for the movie to start. I'd like to thank Frank Lovece, Ken Fox, Kerri Griffith, Angel Cohn, Sabrina Rojas Weiss, Jason Simos, Tom Phillips, and Michael Gingold for their suggestions. Some made it into the book and some didn't, but none went to waste.

ALL THE WORLD'S A STAGE

Williami Shakespeare famously wrote that "all the world's a stage and all the men and women merely players," and in the witty **Shakespeare in Love** (1998)—co-written by fiendishly clever playwright Tom Stoppard—struggling young Will S. (Joseph Fiennes) is himself a player in a behind-the-scenes "what if?" story told through some of his own favorite narrative tricks. While struggling to write *Romeo and Juliet*, Will falls in love with a feisty beauty (Gwyneth Paltrow) who wins the role of Romeo while dressed as a man because Elizabethan society forbids women to act.

Set almost entirely in a seedy boardinghouse ironically named the Footlights Club and packed to the rafters with unemployed actresses, the scathing **Stage Door** (1937) acknowledges the dirty little secret of actors' lives—they spend more time looking for work than working. The barbs fly fast and furious, and the cast includes Ginger Rogers, wisecracking Eve Arden, Lucille Ball, seventeen-year-old hoofer Ann Miller (who lied about her age to get the part), and Katharine Hepburn, whose lofty declaration that "the calla lilies are in bloom again" kept a generation of female impersonators in punch lines. **All About Eve** (1950) crucifies theater people, from stars to hangers-on, with ruthless style, and dished up Bette Davis's immortal warning: "Fasten your seat belts—it's going to be a bumpy night." As haughty, aging actress Margo Channing, she takes poor little starstruck Eve Harrington (Anne Baxter) under her wing and notices too late that this wolf in fan's clothing has designs on her fiancé, her friends, and her career. There isn't one false line or less-than-stellar performance, from professional cad George Sanders as a venomous critic to Thelma Ritter as Margo's seen-it-all dresser and a very young Marilyn Monroe as a no-talent starlet. Vivid, waspish, and gloriously synthetic from crown to toenail, West End diva Julia Lambert (Annette Bening) is the consummate star in **Being Julia** (2004), directed by Hungarian filmmaker Istvan Szabo with a script adapted from W. Somerset Maugham's sublimely melodramatic novel *Theatre*. Julia knows her years as queen of the boards are numbered but still has the wherewithal to squash *her* Eve Harrington—simpering, disingenuous ingenue Avice Crichton—like the annoying gnat she is; Juliet Stevenson's turn as Julia's sharp-tongued dresser is sublime. Szabo turned a less generous eye on the vanities and machinations of actors in the caustic **Mephisto** (1981), in which a German actor—played with seething intensity by Klaus Maria Brandauer—sells his soul to the Nazi party for fame.

The saying that no man is a hero to his valet goes double for actors and their dressers. Playwright Ronald Harwood's **The Dresser** (1983) examines the complex relationship between a once-legendary Shakespearean actor (Albert Finney) and his devoted dresser (Tom Courtenay), who struggles single-handedly to get "Sir," as he calls the great man, through a grueling WWII-era tour by prompting, flattering, cajoling, bullying, and nursing his supremely ungrateful employer through hangovers and emotional storms. A fourteenth-century troupe of traveling players (including Willem Dafoe, Paul Bettany, and Brian Cox) exposes a serial murderer in **The Reckoning** (2004), in which the mystery is rudimentary but the details of life as a touring player in medieval England are fascinating.

Dark and disillusioning, **An Awfully Big Adventure** (1995) chronicles the bleak coming of age of a bright-eyed Liverpool lass amid the "glamorous" environs of a shabby, post-WWII repertory troupe whose members include a manipulative, venomously embittered director (Hugh Grant) and an aging roue (Alan Rickman), the resident ham who provides the story's grimmest twist; the title alludes to a particularly gloomy line from *Peter Pan*. Set in the raffish theatrical world of 1820s Paris, **Children of Paradise** (1945) is a backstage story, a tribute to the intoxicating allure of illusion (the "children of paradise" are theater lovers who can only afford to sit in the highest balcony seats) and a poignant paean to the power of love—even when it's unreciprocated—wrapped into a three-hour package. It follows the fortunes of four men—a preening master thespian, a petty thief and self-styled poet, a wealthy count, and a soulful Pierrot—all of them in love with the same aloof, enigmatic beauty. And knee-jerk iconoclast Mel Brooks's **The Producers** (1968) blows a big, fat raspberry at the mystique of the theater, taking stinging potshots at actors, production designers, playwrights, and, of course, impresarios like Max Bialystock (Zero Mostel). With the reluctant assistance of his meek accountant Leo Bloom (Gene Wilder), Bialystock concocts a scheme to bilk investors by producing the biggest surefire flop of all time—a Nazi-glorifying musical called *Springtime for Hitler*—only to see it become a huge hit. How perfectly ironic that the movie's stage incarnation—a musical, no less—should have become the toast of Broadway . . . and that the 2005 movie of the musical should be exactly the sort of toothless, overproduced, pandering spectacle Brooks was lampooning!

DIRECTOR'S SPOTLIGHT:
PEDRO ALMODOVAR

On the evidence of **Women on the Verge of a Nervous Breakdown** (1988), an exhilarating, Feydeau-esque romp that revolves around a pregnant actress (Carmen Maura), her desirably located Madrid apartment, and the pitcher of barbiturate-laced gazpacho with which she intends to kill herself, Spanish director Pedro Almodovar emerged fully formed like a cross-dressing Athena from Zeus's forehead. The truth is slightly less dramatic.

Born in 1951, Almodovar escaped his impoverished small-town childhood at the movies, equally enraptured by the films of Marco Ferreri, Luis Bunuel, Alfred Hitchcock, and Douglas Sirk. He fled to Madrid as a teenager, formed a band, made super-8 shorts, and joined an avant-garde theater group where he met actors Maura, his muse until a falling out in the 1990s, and Antonio Banderas, who made five films with Almodovar before going Hollywood. His day job at Spain's national phone company paid the rent. *Women on the Verge* was Almodovar's seventh feature film in eight frenzied years, beginning with 1980's **Pepi, Luci, Bom and Other Girls on the Heap**, a rude, scruffy, amateurish sex comedy starring Maura and based on his own smutty fotonovela; its defiant vulgarity no doubt seemed funnier at the giddy height of *la movida*, the "anything goes" cultural movement that exploded in Madrid after the death of culturally conservative fascist dictator Francisco Franco in 1975.

Women on the Verge established Almodovar as a first-rate farceur who set his rollicking comedies of mistaken identities, intentions, and persuasions against a dazzling world of outrageous pop-art interiors and candy-colored costumes. But with **The Flower of My Secret** (1995), in which a middle-aged romance novelist struggles under the weight of her failing marriage, he segued into full-throated Sirkian melodrama and risked rejection by fair-weather fans like the whiners who haunt Woody Allen's sour *Stardust Memories* (1980), complaining that they liked his early, funny films better. But Almodovar's followers stayed and multiplied. Gender-bending liaisons, outrageous turns of fortune, and theatrical contrivances abound in **All About My Mother** (1999), which weaves an unsentimental celebration of friendship, family, and resilience from the tangled destinies of a nurse mourning the hit-and-run death of her son, a transgendered prostitute, an aging lesbian actress, and a pregnant activist nun (Penelope Cruz).

Simultaneously perverse, overwrought, deeply creepy, and truly moving, **Talk to Her** (2002) is an ode to the peculiar strength and flexibility of love that revolves around the deep, complicated friendship that develops between two men devoted to comatose women. **Bad Education** (2004), a bold, Hitchcockian thriller in the vein of *Vertigo* (1958), wraps its vivid colors and brittle cleverness around a dark, dark heart. A nesting box of interlocking stories that unfolds in three time periods—1964, 1977, and 1980—and refracts the same events through several levels of reality, it ties together the stories of an aspiring filmmaker, a transvestite junkie (Gael Garcia Bernal), and two ten-year-old schoolboys whose future paths were set by the actions of a pedophile priest.

Dark thematic underpinnings always lurk beneath layers of gleefully lewd slapstick in Almodovar's comedies, including **Labyrinth of Passion** (1982), **Dark Habits** (1983)—what the middle-of-the-road *Sister Act* (1992) would have been if Whoopi Goldberg's fugitive nightclub singer had landed in a convent full of oversexed junkie nuns—**What Have I Done to Deserve This?** (1984), **Law of Desire** (1986), and **Tie Me Up! Tie Me Down!** (1990), which created an especially fierce controversy by depicting a besotted mental patient's (Banderas) kidnapping and sexual enslavement of a junkie porn star (Victoria Abril) for queasy laughs. Almodovar's other films include the dark erotic thriller **Matador** (1986), **Live Flesh** (1997)—which reworked Ruth Rendell's psychological crime novel into a polished erotic melodrama—and **High Heels** (1991), a sort of comic dry run for *All About My Mother*.

In the '90s, Almodovar began extending a hand to younger Latin filmmakers, helping produce films by Guillermo del Toro (**The Devil's Backbone**, 2001), Lucrecia Martel (**The Holy Girl**, 2004), Isabel Coixet (**My Life Without Me**, 2003), and Alex de la Iglesia (**Mutant Action**, 1993).

ANIME FOR DUMMIES

A nime officially went mainstream in 2002, when Hayao Miyazaki's (see *Director's Spotlight: Hayao Miyazaki*) complex, magical children's tale **Spirited Away** (2001) won an Oscar. But Japanese feature-length animation runs the gamut from *Pokemon* to porno, and a bewildering number of titles crown video store shelves. This sampler offers a taste of what's out there.

Akira (1988): The violent postapocalyptic action-adventure that opened American eyes to the fact that there was more to Japanese animation than *Astro Boy* and *Speed Racer*.

Blood: The Last Vampire (2000): A schoolgirl vampire slayer who may not be what she seems investigates a Vietnam-era American military base in Japan plagued by bloodsuckers in this gory supernatural action story with political overtones.

Cowboy Bebop: The Movie (2001): A loose-knit team of perpetually cash-strapped futuristic bounty hunters—including a grizzled ex-cop, high-strung teenaged computer genius, and an unnaturally intelligent corgi—stumble onto a plot involving biological weapons in this spin-off from a series famous for its eclectic, ultracool pop soundtrack.

Escaflowne (2002): A depressed schoolgirl slips into an alternate world of warring clans and magical beings in this *Lord of the Rings*–meets–*The Wizard of Oz* fantasy, a darker spin-off from a popular TV series.

Ghost in the Shell (1995) and **Ghost in the Shell 2** (2004): Moody futuristic crime thrillers that unfold in a world where the line between man and machine is increasingly blurred.

Grave of the Fireflies (1988): A wrenching drama about a teenager trying to keep himself and his little sister alive in the countryside outside devastated Kobe during the last desperate days of WWII.

Jin-Roh: The Wolf Brigade (1999): Set in the early '60s, this thriller about rebels using young girls dubbed "Red Riding-Hoods" as suicide bombers and the "Wolf Brigade," a rogue force within the government's anti-terrorism unit, unfolds in an alternate Japan that lost the Second World War to Germany, instead of to the United States.

Legend of the Overfiend (1993): Warring demons use modern-day teenagers to fight their ancient, perpetual war; the high- (or low-) water mark of the sex-and-tentacles school of ultraviolent, erotic supernatural thrillers.

Millennium Actress (2003): Past and present, reality and fiction blend seamlessly in this dreamlike drama about a reclusive actress and the documentary filmmaker determined to find out why she abruptly abandoned her career thirty years earlier.

Perfect Blue (1997): A squeaky-clean teen pop star tries to reinvent herself as an adult actress in a lurid TV crime series, but is tormented by an obsessive fan . . . or is it her own conscience that's taunting her?

BACK TO THE BEACH

An offshoot of the low-budget monster, drag-racing, and rock 'n' roll movies aimed at the restless children of America's burgeoning post-WWII economy, beach-party movies—an endless summer fantasy of carefree young people enjoying upbeat music, chaste romance, and good, clean outdoor fun—were the feel-good alternative to angst-ridden pictures about delinquents and rebels.

The bright, sneakily charming **Gidget** (1959) was first into the water: All-American teen Sandra Dee plays the fifteen-year-old tomboy who loves sun, sand, and surfing. Four coeds—a brain, a good girl, a naif, and a "plain" hockey player who sings like a teen angel (pop sensation Connie Francis)—go to Fort Lauderdale for spring break because it's **Where the Boys Are** (1960); this sandy soap opera includes some darker elements, including date rape.

It's all sunshine and clear skies in the six beach movies starring prefab teen idols Frankie Avalon and Annette Funicello, breakout child star of Disney TV's squeaky-clean *Mickey Mouse Club*, as surfer Frankie and his girlfriend, beach-baby Dee Dee. Debating the relative merits of individual films is pointless. They're all pure retro fluff, as addictive as frozen drinks on a steamy day and packed with riffs on '60s youth-culture preoccupations (beatniks, the twist, body building, aliens, drag racing, bikers, go-go girls, monster movies, the British

Invasion), supporting turns by old-time stars like silent clown Buster Keaton and musical guests, notably "King of the Surf Guitars" Dick Dale (whose "Miserlou" jump-starts *Pulp Fiction*) and "Little" Stevie Wonder. In **Beach Party** (1963), a stuffy anthropologist investigates kicky teen culture. **Muscle Beach Party** (1964) pits the fun-loving surfers against beefy bodybuilders. **Bikini Beach** (1964) gives Avalon a dual role as Frankie and Brit-rocker "Potato Bug." In **Pajama Party** (1964), a Martian teen decides that Earth kids are too cool to conquer. Frankie and Dee Dee take skydiving lessons in **Beach Blanket Bingo** (1965), while one of the gang falls for a mermaid. In the fabulously titled **How to Stuff a Wild Bikini** (1965), Frankie is in the Navy and worried about Dee Dee's fidelity, so he gets a tropical witch doctor (Keaton) to conjure up a knockout in a "wild bikini" to distract the hound dogs back home. Two decades later, the affectionate homage/spoof **Back to the Beach** (1987) reunites Funicello and Avalon as middle-aged ex-surfers with their own wild kids.

An old-dark-house variation on the theme, **The Ghost in the Invisible Bikini** (1966) replaces Avalon and Funicello with former Disney child star Tommy Kirk and second-string Gidget Deborah Walley; it's not as racy as it would like to sound, but features Boris Karloff and swingin' Nancy Sinatra. Kirk and Walley reteamed for **It's a Bikini World** (1967), a battle-of-the-sexes comedy that straggled in at the tail end of the beach boom.

Hot Summer (1968) is a marvelous oddity, an Eastern Bloc–meets–West Coast romp starring married Iron Curtain pop singers Chris Doerk and Frank Schoebel as fun-loving socialist kids vacationing with their friends by the Baltic Sea. Drag-legend Charles Busch's broad parody **Psycho Beach Party** (2000) adds

Hitchcock-style thrills to its lampoon of the sand-and-surf formula. A hastily thrown-together showcase for first-generation American Idols Kelly Clarkson and Justin Guarini, **From Justin to Kelly** (2003) dares to play the cliches straight with modern-day flourishes; critics stomped it to the ground, but its modest charms hold out the hope that perhaps one day we can all go back to the beach.

BAD SANTAS

Stop reading if thoughts of Christmas and the benevolent, smiling face of Old Saint Nick wreathe you in joy. If, on the other hand, you regard the holiday season as an incrementally tightening vise of pressure, anxiety, and guilt, these dyspeptic pictures might be just the dose of satisfying bile you need.

Everyone knows department-store Santas are a dicey bunch. Even in the thoroughly pro-Santa **Miracle on 34th Street** (1947), Edmund Gwenn's saintly Kris Kringle enters on the heels of a reprobate who reports for North Pole float duty at the Macy's Thanksgiving Day parade so soused he can't stand. The sweetly nostalgic **A Christmas Story** (1983) includes a dreadful encounter with an impatient Santa. But Billy Bob Thornton's **Bad Santa** (2003) tops them all: In this very dark comedy, the alcoholic, foul-mouthed, child-hating Thornton and his sidekick, larcenous little person Tony Cox, hire themselves out as a Santa-and-elf duo to one unsuspecting department store each year and rob the place blind. Less scabrous but equally irreverent, **The Hebrew Hammer** (2003) pits a tough-talking Jewish detective against evil Santa

Damian (Andy Dick), who murdered his benevolent father and plans to destroy Hanukkah and Kwanzaa.

Among holiday-themed horror movies, there are none so gleefully transgressive as those featuring killer Santas. The most famous, 1984's **Silent Night, Deadly Night**, is standard-issue slasher stuff, but the poster, featuring Santa disappearing down a chimney with an ax, incited protests, picketing, and the sort of notoriety money can't buy. The story involves Billy, doubly traumatized as a child by the supposedly catatonic grandpa who hisses that "Christmas Eve is the scariest damn night of the year," and the stick-up man in a stolen Santa costume who murders his parents; he goes on a bloody rampage years later when fate forces him to don a Santa suit in a local toy store. The tables are turned in the sordid **Don't Open till Christmas** (1984), in which a London-based serial killer slays degenerates in Santa costumes. The lesson: Don't wear your Santa suit to the peep show. The best variation on the theme opens the multi-story **Tales from the Crypt** (1972). In "All through the House," Joan Collins, whose clueless husband imagines her "the best wife in the world" (as *if*), kills him with a fireplace poker on Christmas eve; unluckily for her, there's a homicidal maniac dressed as the jolly old elf on the loose, and her little daughter still believes in Santa. In **Christmas Evil/Terror in Toyland/You Better Watch Out** (1980), a toy company employee (played by singer Fiona Apple's dad, Brandon Maggart) dresses as Santa for a Yuletide rampage against the naughty; John Waters is a big fan. And remember—you'd better watch out and you'd better not cry, because Santa Claus *is* coming to town.

THE BEAUTY IN THE DARKNESS

Most horror pictures teach us to avoid the shadows, where monsters and murderers nursing dark intentions lurk. But a handful glory in the beauty within the gloom, achieving a rare and haunting poetry that lingers long after standard-issue shocks are forgotten.

No one ever forgets **Eyes Without a Face/Les yeux sans visage** (1959), a potboiler about a mad doctor peeling off girl's faces in hopes of restoring his own daughter's beauty, transformed into poetry by director Georges Franju's unerring eye for the haunting detail. A dead girl's dirty feet, a house full of blackened mirrors in ornate frames, and the unhappy wraith of a daughter (Edith Scob), her mutilated face hidden behind an impassive mask, gliding through her own home like a ghost. Italian director Mario Bava's **Black Sunday/I tre volti della paura** (1960) is a symphony of mist and shadow built around the English actress Barbara Steele's uniquely unsettling face, which shifts from radiant to menacing in the blink of a luminous eye. There's a story, too, about a resurrected witch seeking vengeance, but better to drown in Steele's gaze. **Night Tide** (1961) director Curtis Harrington, bewitched by the trance films of avant-garde filmmaker Maya Deren, gave sunny Southern California beaches a haunted ghostliness in his eerie tale about a sailor (Dennis Hopper) who falls in love with a free-spirited girl who claims she's a mermaid.

Cat People (1942), **The Leopard Man** (1943), **I Walked with a Zombie** (1943), **The Seventh Victim** (1943), and **The Curse of the Cat People** (1944), the high-water marks of producer Val

Lewton's experiment in classy horror on a budget, triumph over exploitative titles and hokey premises involving were-cats, voodoo hoodoo, and devil worshippers in Greenwich Village. Lewton's subtle sensibilities unified the work of multiple directors into a consistent vision favoring shivery suggestion over blatant shocks. In *Cat People*, artist Irina (the creepily kittenish Simone Simon) lives in modern-day Manhattan but believes the scary talk she heard in the old country about women doomed to become murderous cat creatures if they indulge their erotic natures. The haunting sort-of sequel revolves around a lonely, imaginative child retreating into fantasies of a marvelous best friend (Simone) who happens to be her father's late wife. *Zombie*, a clever variation on *Jane Eyre*, finds a no-nonsense nurse hired to attend a Haitian plantation owner's near-catatonic wife and coming to believe a voodoo curse caused her patient's languor, while a runaway leopard is blamed for a string of killings in *Leopard Man*, justly famous for the set piece in which a stern mother who's locked her daughter out of the house thinks the screaming girl is faking until blood begins to seep under the door. In the elegant *Seventh Victim*, an orphaned schoolgirl (Kim Hunter, in her first film) searching for her missing older sister in Greenwich Village tangles with eerily elegant cultists.

"Oh look! A lovely spider," chirps pretty, ten-year-old Flora. "And it's eating a butterfly." **The Innocents** (1961), based on Henry James's *The Turn of the Screw*, finds icy dread in the tinkling laughter of children and the gentle billows of gauzy curtains; a high-strung young governess (Deborah Kerr), caring for orphaned siblings Miles and Flora on their uncle's isolated country estate, becomes consumed by the conviction that the bright, curious, altogether enchanting children have been corrupted by the spirits of their late governess and her brutal lover. Be warned: **The Nightcomers** (1972), a vulgar prequel starring Marlon Brando and Stephanie Beacham as the perverted couple, delivers S&M-tinged sex but not a shred of atmosphere. A church organist survives a car accident but finds herself shadowed by raccoon-eyed ghouls in Herk Harvey's profoundly disquieting **Carnival of Souls** (1962). Should the desire to see the coarse, obvious 1998 remake come over you, lie down until it passes.

BEFORE THE CODE

Old movies aren't all separate beds and chaste kisses: In its untamed youth, Hollywood's pictures were so brazen that curators of the nation's collective virtue were up in arms. The notorious Motion Picture Production Code, a preemptive strike against government censorship, spelled out a bundle of taboo words, topics, and themes and was adopted by the Association of Motion Picture Producers in 1930. It was largely ignored until mid-1934, when crime stopped paying, good girls didn't, and nightclub "chantoosies" dropped songs like **42nd Street**'s (1933) "You're Getting to Be a Habit with Me" ("I used to think your love was something/That I could take or leave alone/But now I couldn't do without my supply . . . /I can't break away/I must have you every day") from their repetoires. Some of these pre-Code pictures are classics, others aren't. But they're full of sassy talk, bad behavior, and sexy shenanigans that suggest our grandparents' generation knew a thing or two about a thing or two.

In **Girls About Town** (1931), a pair of unrepentant gold diggers loll around in their scanties and make no bones about how their rent gets paid—they're not hookers, mind you, just savvy gals. Norma Shearer is **The Divorcee** (1930), who retaliates for her husband's one-night stand by seducing his best friend, divorcing him, and declaring, "From now on you're the only man in the world my door is closed to!" She doesn't make good on her bold threat, but *still*. Cecil B. DeMille's **The Sign of the Cross** (1932) delivers some pretty racy Roman decadence, including Claudette Colbert inviting a friend to get naked and join her in a milk bath, and the sultry "Dance of the Naked Moon," in which a hell-bound pagan trollop tries to fondle a good Christian out of her pious principles. Eddie Cantor's elaborate parody **Roman Scandals** (1933) includes some of Busby Berkeley's raciest production numbers.

Why exploitation giant Roger Corman never remade **Night Nurse** (1931) is a mystery: Private nurses Barbara Stanwyck and Joan Blondell are hired to tend to a wealthy lush's sickly children and uncover a plot to starve them and steal their trust fund. Bad chauffeur Clark Gable wallops Stanwyck in the jaw, Stanwyck's bootlegger boyfriend is a good guy, and the nurses spend an awful lot of time in their pretty underwear. Stanwyck's opportunistic **Baby Face** (1933) grows up in a steel-town speakeasy, being "friendly" to her father's customers; she escapes to New York City and uses what she has to get what she wants, sleeping her way up the ladder at a Manhattan bank, one department head at a time. Saucy Jean Harlow's **Red Headed Woman** (1932), a small-town stenographer with expensive tastes, takes the same route to self improvement:

"Can you see through this?" she asks a sales clerk while trying on a dress, and buys it when the answer is yes.

Bawdy, busty, good-time gal Mae West got away with slinging outrageously smutty double entendres in **Night after Night** (1932), **She Done Him Wrong** (1933), and **I'm No Angel** (1933), and make no mistake: She was never as good as when she was being bad, and her wings were clipped in later films. Marlene Dietrich was also at her peak in the pre-Code era, when her bold, ambiguous sensuality (she wears a tux, sleeps around, and kisses another woman on the lips) was celebrated by Josef von Sternberg in **Morocco** (1930), **Dishonored** (1931), **Blonde Venus** (1932), **Shanghai Express** (1932), and **The Scarlet Empress** (1934), the last exquisite release of the pre-Code era.

BEHIND THE CURTAIN

Hate it when people start hoofing and belting out tunes in the middle of an Oklahoma cornfield? Then backstage musicals might not be your ticket: People sing and dance because they're *show* people.

If the snappy **42nd Street** (1933) didn't mint the cliches, it polished them to a high shine, from lecherous producers and patrons to leggy chorus girls working their assets off, and the scrappy little understudy (Ruby Keeler) who goes out a "raw kid out of the chorus" and comes back a star. Highlights include "You're Getting to be a Habit with Me," which works its "love is the drug" metaphor with surprising frankness, and jaw-dropping choreography by

Busby Berkeley, who made chorines look like kaleidoscope chips. Berkeley's **Gold Diggers of 1935**, about the making of a charity show by guests and employees at a posh resort hotel, features the mind-blowing "Lullabye of Broadway" number, a dark mini-story about a doomed Broadway baby who gets shoved off a balcony by a mob of platinum blondes in black, midriff-baring evening dresses.

Royal Wedding (1951) includes two of Fred Astaire's most famous routines, his duet with a hat rack and the scene in which he dances on the ceiling; the plot revolves around a brother-and-sister dance team (any resemblance to Fred and Adele Astaire is not coincidental) who go to London to star in a new musical. In **Kiss Me Kate** (1953), a modern-day battle of the sexes erupts during rehearsals for a musical version of Shakespeare's *The Taming of the Shrew*; Cole Porter's score is a delight and the cast, including Howard Keel and brassy Ann Miller, sells it like troupers. The backstage shenanigans in **The Band Wagon** (1953) poke fun at a slew of Broadway stereotypes, from the pretentious director to the washed-up star (Fred Astaire) and the snotty ballerina (Cyd Charisse) who learns to let down her hair and hoof; built around the cream of the Howard Dietz/Arthur Schwartz songbook, it culminates in "Girl Hunt: A Murder Mystery in Jazz," a dazzling eleven-minute pastiche of Mickey Spillane–style pulp.

In the *Rashomon* of musicals, **Les Girls** (1957), a libel suit hinges on whose version of the demise of touring cabaret act "Les Girls" you believe; which of three gorgeous artistes had an affair with dashing dance master Barry (Gene Kelly) and tried to kill herself? Legendary director/choreographer Bob Fosse's dark, semiautobiographical **All That Jazz** (1979) chronicles the meltdown of legendary director/choreographer Joe Gideon (Roy Scheider) as he works on a new show and lets his life go to hell. Based on celebrity stripper Gypsy Rose Lee's life, **Gypsy** (1962) follows uber–stage mother Rose's (Rosalind Russell) efforts to make her daughters stars, even if it means pushing shy teen Louise (Natalie Wood) into a burlesque show; the music and lyrics by Jule Styne and Stephen Sondheim are legendary.

If you think the world of nineteenth-century operetta was all class and tea parties, think again: In **Topsy-Turvy** (1999) musical-theater sensations Gilbert and Sullivan rebound from a creative slump by beginning work on *The Mikado*, dogged by backstage sniping, spotlight hogging, and druggy star hijinks. A century later, sixteen hopefuls, from starry-eyed beginners to a washed-up headliner trying to get her foot back in the door, vie for a chance to dance in **A Chorus Line** (1985). The show, after all, must go on.

THE BEST OF BOND-AGE

My Bond bona fides are as follows: The first James Bond movie I saw in a theater was **Diamonds Are Forever** (1971), and Sean Connery defined 007 for me. I don't think much of **Never Say Never Again** (1983), but no matter how resolutely EON films and MGM pretend it's not part of the Bond series, it is. I liked **On Her Majesty's Secret Service** (1969) and thought George Lazenby might have settled into the role if it hadn't been unceremoniously yanked out from under him. I adored Roger Moore as playboy sleuth Simon Templar on TV's *The Saint*, but always found him too light to be a convincing Bond. I think Timothy Dalton got a raw deal—he brought real grit back to a character who does, after all, have a license to kill—and Pierce Brosnan struck a near-flawless balance of toughness and suave sophistication. I just wish he'd come into the series earlier, when the material was stronger. And for what it's worth, I think Daniel Craig could be just the shock to the system the franchise needs.

I'm not especially into gadgets, guns, or cars, but I think casting Judi Dench as M was a stroke of genius. I love Bond villains, even when they talk too much, and I love Bond girls, except when they're vapid twits like Tanya Roberts (1985's **A View to a Kill**). Names like

"Pussy Galore" make me laugh. Oh, and I blame the later Bond films for making cartoonishly preposterous action sequences *de rigueur* and for encouraging the trend toward too many endings. So now that you know where this list is coming from, here are my favorites.

Sean Connery

Dr. No (1962)
From Russia with Love (1963)
Goldfinger (1964)
Thunderball (1965)
You Only Live Twice (1967)

Roger Moore

Live and Let Die (1973)
For Your Eyes Only (1981)

Timothy Dalton

The Living Daylights (1987)
Licence to Kill (1989)

Pierce Brosnan

Goldeneye (1995)

BRUSH UP YOUR SHAKESPEARE

Moviemakers have always loved William Shakespeare. He could plot rings around the average screenwriter. He wrote vivid, psychologically rich roles for men *and* women. And he's long dead, so the whole package is free of charge, hence the bewildering pileup of adaptations ranging from great to pretty shabby.

All these films feature Shakespeare's rich and stylized language, though many rethink Shakespeare's settings, and I've spread the wealth around. You could create a terrific lineup of nothing but versions of *Hamlet, Macbeth,* and *Romeo and Juliet,* or from Laurence Olivier and Kenneth Branagh's Shakespeare films alone, but variety is the spice of life.

That said, both the Olivier and the Branagh versions of **Henry V** (1944 and 1989) are exemplary: rousing, complex depictions of men during wartime. Olivier's film, produced at the height of WWII, plays up the pomp and glory; Branagh emphasizes the mud and blood. Both were also brilliant playing **Hamlet**, though Olivier's 1948 film overall is a little stodgy and Branagh's four-hour 1996 epic is uneven. Campbell Scott's modest **Hamlet** (2000) is a small, overlooked gem.

Franco Zefferelli's **Romeo and Juliet** (1968) and Baz Luhrmann's **William Shakespeare's Romeo + Juliet** (1996) are wildly different and equally vivid; Zefferelli's went the traditional route but caused a stir by casting teenagers—Olivia Hussey and Leonard Whiting—as the star-crossed young lovers from warring families. Luhrmann ruffled some serious feathers by putting blank verse into the mouths of modern-day crime lords, TV commentators, messenger-service dispatchers, and trigger-happy drag queens; Claire Danes and Leonardo DiCaprio star.

Richard III (1995), starring Ian McKellen and based on his stage production, updates the story to an alternate 1930s Britain and makes Richard a homegrown Nazi who lets nothing stand between him and the throne.

Orson Welles's brooding **Chimes at Midnight** (1966) seamlessly combines the portions of *Richard II, Henry IV*, and *Henry V* that focus on Falstaff (Welles), Shakespeare's tragic, life-embracing buffoon. Welles's **Othello** (1952) is magnificently acted, though it's increasingly difficult to watch white actors in the role, especially on film.

Julius Caesar (1953) showcases a top-notch ensemble that includes Louis Calhern as the doomed tyrant, James Mason as Brutus, John Gielgud as the lean and hungry Cassius, and Marlon Brando—yes, method-man Marlon—as the opportunistic Marc Antony.

Paul Scofield is a powerhouse **King Lear** (1970), the aging monarch whose manipulations destroy his children and drive him mad.

Puppet-master Julie Taymor's **Titus** (1999) sets the rarely staged *Titus Andronicus* in decadent Rome by way of fascist Italy and/or some post-punk future; Anthony Hopkins and Jessica Lange are the victorious general and the conquered Goth queen whose hate-filled power struggle turns into a *Grand Guignol* spectacle few horror filmmakers could match.

BUCKLE ME SWASHES!

C ar chases and gun battles are all very well and good, but for sheer athleticism there's nothing quite like old-fashioned swordplay.

The Black Pirate (1926): First-generation swashbuckler Douglas Fairbanks, the sole survivor of a midsea raid by buccaneers, swears vengeance on all pirates; outstanding action, and it's in glorious color.

The Count of Monte Cristo (1934): Betrayed and imprisoned for years for smuggling a letter to the exiled Napoleon, Edmund Dantes (Robert Donat) escapes and reinvents himself as a mysterious count to stage an elaborate revenge; an outstanding version of a time-honored adventure.

Captain Blood (1935): Falsely accused of treason and sold into Jamaican slavery, compassionate doctor Peter Blood (Errol Flynn) transforms himself into the original pirate of the Caribbean. And now, a word about costar Basil Rathbone: The dapper English expat crossed swords with the best of Hollywood's swashbuckling stars and matched them move for move; Flynn and Tyrone Power were bigger stars, but if Rathbone's name is in the credits, expect great, graceful action.

The Prisoner of Zenda (1937): Ronald Colman plays both the King of Ruritania and the illegitimate, look-alike English cousin who helps him keep his throne; Douglas Fairbanks Jr. is the moustache-twirling villain.

The Adventures of Robin Hood (1938): Errol Flynn steals from the rich, gives to the poor, and goes *mano a mano* with, yes, Rathbone, as villainous Sir Guy.

The Mark of Zorro (1940): Tyrone Power plays fop-by-day/people's-crusader-by-night Zorro ("The Fox"); his duel with baddie Rathbone is among the best in movie history.

The Crimson Pirate (1952): Former circus acrobat Burt Lancaster cuts a swath through sixteenth-century Spain with a band of buccaneers and a mute but nimble sidekick (Nick Cravat, his old circus partner) in this comic adventure; look for a young Christopher Lee showing the form he displayed six decades later as Count Dooku in the second *Star Wars* trilogy.

Scaramouche (1952): Thirst for revenge drives dissipated aristocrat Stewart Granger to disguise himself as a masked player and to learn to wield the most elegant and lethal rapier in eighteenth-century France. Underrated.

The Three Musketeers (1973): A bawdy, grimy version of the much-adapted classic, chock-a-block with really brutal swordplay; Frank Finlay, Oliver Reed, and Richard Chamberlain are the musketeers, Michael York is wannabe D'Artagnan and Christopher Lee is their nemesis.

Rob Roy (1995): Wronged by English aristocrats, proud eighteenth-century highlander Liam Neeson (honing his Jedi-to-be skills) fights back; the sword fighting is exhausting, bloody, and bone-cracking, especially the climactic bout with sadistic Tim Roth.

On Guard!/Le bossu (1997): Family plots and counterplots, deceptions and swordplay in eighteenth-century France with Daniel Auteuil and smoldering Vincent Perez; old-fashioned (except for the casual sexual frankness) and rip-snorting.

The Mask of Zorro (1998): Aging Zorro Anthony Hopkins trains youngblood Antonio Banderas to take his place; even love interest Catherine Zeta-Jones gets to join in the spirited swordplay.

Pirates of the Caribbean (2004): Johnny Depp's woozy pirate-as-dissipated-rock-star performance got all the attention, but this tongue-in-cheek romp takes its swordplay seriously—he and Orlando Bloom also mastered moves that would have done Errol Flynn proud.

CABARET BALKAN

The brutal, six-year dissolution of the former Yugoslavia into a tangle of viciously warring republics produced an outpouring of films that grappled with the conflict from all sides and angles. For me, each of these films is a window into a conflict whose bitter roots stretch deep into blood-soaked Balkan history.

A newly married Serb/Croat couple is suddenly, viciously separated by war in **Vukovar** (1994), a hellish variation on *Romeo and Juliet* by Serbian filmmaker Boro Draskovic, himself the son of Croatian and Bosnian parents. Adapted from English television-journalist Michael Nicholson's memoir *Natasha's Story*, prolific English filmmaker Michael Winterbottom's **Welcome to Sarajevo** (1997) is a jagged, melancholy drama about war correspondents covering the chaos in 1992; Croatian actor Goran Visnjic (of TV's *E.R.*) has a small but affecting role. Bare-knuckle, cruelly comic, and almost unbearably tense, Bosnian writer-director Danis Tanovic's **No Man's Land** (2001)—which won a Best Foreign Language film Oscar—traps two soldiers, a Bosnian and a Serb, in a trench with a "corpse" who's actually very much alive and has an American-made "bouncing" mine buried beneath him; if he moves, he'll blow them all to pieces.

Anarchy reigns and ordinary people soldier on in Serbian director Goran Paskaljevic's **Cabaret Balkan** (1998), in which intersecting stories unfold over the course of one long, awful Belgrade night: a teenager smashes into an older man's car, a revolutionary hijacks a bus, a man tries to woo back the girlfriend he abandoned, a cabbie runs into a crippled ex-policemen who once beat him half to death, a confession between old friends leads to murder.

Macedonian expatriate Milcho Manchevski's glossy, mystical, and pessimistic **Before the Rain** (1994), billed as the first feature made in newly independent Macedonia, tells three stories of violence and chaos; grizzled Croatian actor Rade Serbedzija is now a familiar tough-guy face in U.S. movies. Manchevski puts the anarchic iconography of spaghetti Westerns to novel use in **Dust** (2003), a time-traveling, self-referential story of American-born brothers (David Wenham and Joseph Fiennes) who play out their bitter sibling rivalry in the wild, wild east of Macedonia at the dawn of the twentieth century; Manchevski twists and fractures his narrative, using jarringly disjunctive images to pull the past and present into a Moebius strip of cruelty, retribution, and hope of heaven.

In Serbian director Srdjan Dragojevic's **Pretty Village, Pretty Flame** (1996), Muslim troops trap a platoon of Serbian soldiers in a tunnel near the Bosnian-Serbian border for ten days, with a pair of boyhood friends on opposite sides. His surreal, jittery, mordantly funny **The Wounds** (1998) is a high-octane look at two juvenile delinquents coming of age in Belgrade during the turbulent years between 1991 and 1996. Macedonian filmmakers Aleksander Popovski and Darko Mitrevski's bizarre fairy tale **Goodbye, 20th**

Century! (1998) opens in year 2019 in postapocalyptic Macedonia, goes back to 1919 for a brief tale of incest and revenge, then hurtles forward to New Year's Eve, 1999; its stunning production design and cinematography, repetition of key images, and witty juggling of characters between the stories produce both a sense of cheerful anarchy and an obsessive, inchoate sense of loss.

Veteran Yugoslavian filmmaker Emir Kusturica rips through half a century of his homeland's history in the controversial, blackly comic **Underground** (1995), which charts the wildly different destinies of two friends who are both black marketers of WWII-era weapons. One tricks the other into taking refuge in his basement with a group of friends and family and never lets on that the war is over; while the cellar dwellers manufacture profitable munitions, he rises through the ranks of the post-war Communist Party. *Underground* was accused of being pro-Serbian propaganda, but sums up the tragic history of the Balkans in one resonant observation: "There is no war until a brother kills his brother."

CAMP FOLLOWERS

Surely the term *camp classic* is an oxymoron: The trashy, flashy, bad taste appeal of camp is the antithesis of such classical virtues as order, symmetry, and harmony. And you can't try to create a camp classic—that gets you **Flash Gordon** (1980), an expensive, willfully vulgar cartoon. Real camp takes conviction, however wrong-headed, ill-conceived, or misguided, and sometimes it's just what the doctor ordered.

In futuristic Faustian pop musical **The Apple** (1980), devilish agent-cum-guru Mr. Boogalow ruins a pair of idealistic balladeers from Moose Jaw, Canada, so his trashy prefab duo, Dandi and Pandi, can win the Eurovision song contest; highlights include a divinely hellish orgy, a dirty disco number, and an astonishing sequence in which every man, woman, and child drops what he or she is doing for the hour of aerobicizing mandated by fitness fascists of the future. Astronauts come face to face with the man-hating **Queen of Outer Space** (1958) and her all-girl utopia on Venus; slinky Zsa Zsa Gabor is a Venusian scientist who wants to depose the queen so she can get herself a hunky boyfriend. One-woman sexual revolution **Barbarella** (1968)—Jane Fonda in her Euro-pinup phase—sleeps her way around the galaxy in this live-action "adult" comic strip, crossing paths with alien sex fiends, killer dolls, a dominatrix queen (uber-groupie Anita Pallenberg), and a mad scientist named Duran Duran. **Cobra Woman** (1944) stars Dominican beauty Maria Montez as a virtuous sarong-clad South Sea princess and her evil twin, the wicked high priestess of a snake cult. It's a ludicrous Technicolor mishmash of demonic dancing, human sacrifice, riotously exotic costumes, and an ominously bubbling volcano.

Funded entirely by multimillionaire businessman Meshulam Riklis to showcase the talents of his thirty-years-younger wife, pouty-faced singer and starlet Pia Zadora, **Butterfly** (1982) turns James M. Cain's noir novel into a sweaty peep show about a ripe strumpet trying to seduce her daddy (except that he isn't—rest easy). Zadora, astonishingly, made her movie debut as a little green child in the equally jaw-dropping **Santa Claus Conquers the Martians** (1964), in which concerned Martian parents kidnap Santa so their kids can enjoy Christmas too. Zadora's spirit lives on in the sex-and-stardust saga **Glitter** (2000), starring chipmunk-cheeked Mariah Carey as a scantily clad little lost girl whose golden pipes take her to the lonely top of the music business heap.

Jacqueline Susann's overwrought expose of Hollywood's tawdry underbelly, **Valley of the Dolls** (1967), features more bitchery per minute than the average drag show, plus Patty Duke, the late Sharon Tate, and Barbara Parkins in an orgy of pill popping, cat fights, lecherous agents, debilitating diseases, and all-around bad behavior. Christina Crawford's tell-all memoir about life as Joan Crawford's adopted daughter is a straightforward account of a miserable childhood; **Mommie Dearest** (1981), built around Faye Dunaway's overwrought impersonation of the legendary Hollywood star, is a catalog of lunatic excesses. Based on the autobiography of George Jorgensen, who underwent the world's first sexual reassignment surgery in 1952, the painfully earnest **Christine Jorgensen Story** (1970) has the look of a second-rate 1950s melodrama and the tone of a very special *After School Special*. The words *road wreck* don't begin to do justice to its mesmerizing awfulness.

CHARLES IN CHARGE

He could plot like the devil—no-one delivered a cliffhanger like Charles Dickens, who knew how to hook readers in and keep them coming back for more of his serialized stories—and was a dab hand at creating colorful, unforgettable supporting characters, from chronic debtor Mr. Micawber and mad Miss Havesham, jilted at the altar and still wearing her tattered wedding dress decades later, to the despicable Uriah Heep and Jacob Marley's pitiful ghost. Born one hundred years later he'd have been the hottest screenwriter in town, but others have done right by him.

> **Great Expectations** (1946) by David Lean, with John Mills as upwardly mobile orphan Pip, and **Oliver Twist** (1948), with Alec Guinness as Fagin and little Anthony Newley as the Artful Dodger.

> **Oliver!** (1968), the musical that features an insanely catchy score and Oliver Reed's brutal performance as murderous Bill Sikes.

> **A Christmas Carol** (both the 1951 and 1984 versions), with, respectively, Alastair Sim and George C. Scott as the miserable, miserly Scrooge.

> **David Copperfield** (1935) by George Cukor, with W. C. Fields as Micawber.

> **A Tale of Two Cities** (1935), an epic with Ronald Colman as reprobate Sidney Carton, caught up the best and worst of times.

> **The Pickwick Papers** (1954), a cheerful distillation of Dickens's picaresque first novel about peripatetic clubmen getting in and out of trouble; a pleasant change of pace.

> **Little Dorrit** (1988), with Alec Guinness as a chronic debtor like Dickens's own father; really two intertwined films with an epic six-hour running time, but utterly engrossing from start to finish.

Nicholas Nickleby (2002), a stripped-down version of the adventures of teenaged Nickleby, forced to support his family after his father's death and horrified by the cruelty of strangers and relatives alike.

DIRECTOR'S SPOTLIGHT: HENRI-GEORGES CLOUZOT

Henri-Georges Clouzot (1907–1977) directed only eleven features. Admittedly, I've never seen five of them, though not for lack of trying. But he'd be an icon even if **Diabolique** (1954), **The Wages of Fear** (1953), and **Le corbeau/ The Raven** (1943)—three gripping thrillers rooted in the notion of fear as a disease that corrupts, degrades, and spreads "like smallpox"—were the sum total of his output. Clouzot grew up sickly and nearsighted; he spent four years in a tuberculosis sanitarium and gloomily claimed that was where he learned all he needed to know about human nature. He was notoriously cruel to actors and made few friends among other filmmakers, though Francois Truffaut remained his champion to the bitter end.

Arthur Miller's *The Crucible*, a classic story of a close-knit community shattered by rumors and hysteria, has nothing on *Le corbeau*.

Made during the Nazi occupation for a German-controlled studio but inspired by a notorious prewar scandal involving a five-year reign of terror by poison-pen letter in picturesque Tulle, it explored the same festering ugliness beneath the cherished pieties of small-town life. *Le corbeau*'s anonymous letter writer reveals personal and professional secrets, makes scandalous insinuations, and sews seeds of suspicion that systematically turn neighbor against neighbor in an unnamed hamlet ("here or elsewhere," says the prologue), revealing a fetid stew of hypocrisy, pettiness, duplicity, and willingness to turn on each other. *Le corbeau* was simultaneously reviled by the Nazis for making their bourgeois French informants look like weasels and denounced by the collaborationist Vichy government as an attack on the French national character. After the war, Clouzot was banned from the French film industry, though all was more or less forgiven by 1947, when he made *Quai des orfevres*, a raffish, pulpy little crime picture wreathed in cigarette smoke and tawdry atmosphere.

The suspenseful *Wages of Fear* opens in a destitute Latin-American town festering in the shadow of the Southern Oil Company, an American-owned corporation systematically plundering local resources and sending the profits overseas, where four broke, desperate, stateless European drifters languish with no way of earning passage out until a perilous opportunity arises. An oil rig is burning out of control, and the only way to douse the blaze involves nitroglycerine: Southern Oil needs four men to drive two trucks filled with the unstable explosive across three hundred treacherous miles of mountain roads. In *Diabolique*, the brutal headmaster of a boys' boarding school so abuses both his timid wife and his hard-boiled mistress (Vera Clouzot and Simone Signoret) that they band together to kill him. But the body vanishes: Is someone playing games or is their victim still alive? *Diabolique*'s international success lit a fire under "master of suspense" Alfred Hitchcock—then making the glossy entertainments he called "Technicolor baubles"—that brought forth the lean, mean *Psycho* (1960). But *Diabolique* is the bleaker, better film, its relentlessly dyspeptic vision steeped in base behavior and unmarred by hokey psychologizing. And yet Clouzot also made **The Mystery of Picasso** (1956), persuading the painter to sit behind sheets of porous white paper and work in magic marker, ink, and oil paint while he filmed from the other side. Picasso's trademark bathers, bulls, circus performers, goats, matadors, and flowers seem to appear magically in this mesmerizing document of the artistic process, which radiates a delight I simply can't reconcile with Clouzot's other work. Picasso is only one of its mysteries.

I'd like to revisit **La prisonnière** (1968), which I saw thirty years ago without subtitles at a revival house notorious for its bad projection and worse sound—all I remember of a film notorious for its psychedelic S&M excesses is the image of a man poking a rubber hula girl toy with the earpiece of his glasses. I look forward to one day tracking down the rest of his films, and I envy those who have yet to discover them.

COLOR ME BEAUTIFUL

I t's one thing to shoot a movie in color, it's another to make a color film—one that plunges wholeheartedly in the voluptuous possibilities of vivid hues and saturated shades, embracing their sensual richness and ignoring the petty demands of realism.

How did a petty government official (Jet Li) from an insignificant region kill three legendary martial artists who were planning to assassinate the emperor? Zhang Yimou's *Rashomon*-like **Hero** (2002), shot by Christopher Doyle, retells the story four times, each version putting a different coloration—literal and figurative—on the story.

Doyle also shot Wong Kar-Wai's mesmerizing **In the Mood for Love** (2000) and its sort-of sequel **2046** (2004). In *Mood*, set in 1964 Hong Kong, newspaper editor Tony Leung and shipping-firm secretary Maggie Cheung, whose spouses are having an affair, develop their own heart-stoppingly intimate relationship without actually becoming lovers. In the phantasmagoric *2046*, a sumptuous hall of mirrors thick with swoony visual poetry, an older and more dissolute Mr. Chow moves into the opulently rundown Orient Hotel, where he clings to the memory of his great, unconsummated love, dallies with stunning women, and writes a sci-fi fable about longing and loss.

Alfonso Cuaron reimagines Charles Dickens's **Great Expectations** (1998) as a tale of erotic obsession and shallow celebrity, starring Gwyneth Paltrow and Ethan Hawke and drenched in vibrant greens (courtesy of cinematographer Emmanuel Lubezki) and images of water. William Cameron Menzies's sci-fi horror classic **Invaders from Mars** (1953), in which a small boy is the only witness to the landing of Martians who possess his parents and all the other adults in town, captures the haunted quality of a child's nightmares through strangely canted angles, near-Expressionist sets, and the deep saturated colors of John F. Seitz's photography. In visual sensualist Michael Powell's **Black Narcissus** (1946), shot by Jack Cardiff, five starchy Anglican nuns find their pious asceticism undermined by the relentless barrage of seductive sights, scents, and sensations of a remote Himalayan mountain village. The son of Impressionist painter Pierre-Auguste Renoir, Jean Renoir made his first first color film with **The River** (1951), a languid, richly hued coming-of-age drama set in India, based on a novel by Rumer Godden and shot by Renoir's nephew Claude; two English girls fall in love with a wounded WWII veteran who is in turn intoxicated by a Eurasian beauty, as the implacable Ganges River rolls on, oblivious to their petty problems. In **Amélie** (2001), French director Jean-Pierre Jeunet's valentine to oddballs everywhere, a lanky gamine (Audrey Tautou)—imagine Olive Oyl with a Louise Brooks bob—anonymously brightens her neighbors' lives with random (and eccentric) acts of kindness; Bruno Delbonnel's sunny photography was extensively manipulated in post-production to create a fantasy version of Paris's bohemian Montmartre district.

Based on Virginia Woolf's 1928 novel about an ageless youth (androgynous Tilda Swinton) who begins life as a seventeenth-century man and later becomes a woman, Sally Potter's **Orlando** (1993), shot by Alexei Rodionov, is pretentious but swooningly gorgeous. Stanley Kubrick's painterly **Barry Lyndon** (1975), shot by John Alcott and based on William Makepeace Thackeray's biting novel about a seventeenth-century Irish rake's (Ryan O'Neal) progress, was filmed entirely without artificial light, including scenes lit only by flickering candles. Teinosuke Kinugasa's **Gate of Hell** (1953), only the second Japanese film shot in color, tells the story of a samurai obsessed with a married noblewoman in twelfth-century Japan and contrasts cinematographer Kohei Sugiyama's dazzlingly beautiful images with the characters' ugly emotions. Yoshio Miyajima's ravishing cinematography makes **Kwaidan** (1964), a quartet of ghost stories, as exquisitely beautiful as it is haunting.

Some films turn the color up; others turn it down to mesmerizing effect. Twins Mark and Michael Polish's willfully obtuse fable **Northfork** (2003) takes place on an about-to-be flooded Montana plain where black-clad government evacuators try to get the last holdouts to higher ground and a sick child imagines himself a lost cherub and tries to convince four artfully bedraggled angels he's one of them; M. David Mullen's cinematography leaches the color from the film's startling images, producing an artfully bleached vision in gray, sepia, and sickly flesh tones.

CONSIDER THE SOURCE: TRICKY NARRATIVES AND UNRELIABLE NARRATORS

Sometimes you just want to sit back and enjoy a nice, soothing comfort meal for the mind, a simple story with a beginning, a middle, and an end—in that order. Other times you crave something more adventurous, full of surprising textures and unexpected bursts of flavor. Such occasions were made for the joys of puzzle movies and unreliable narrators. Entertaining though they are, I'm not thinking of pictures that pack a last-minute Big Surprise that changes everything, such as **Angel Heart** (1987), **Jacob's Ladder** (1990), **The Sixth Sense** (1999), **The Others** (2001), **High Tension** (2003), **The Machinist** (2004), or the crowd-pleasing **The Usual Suspects** (1995), a shaggy-dog story about an elaborate heist that goes terribly wrong, told by a guy named Verbal—*verbal*, for heaven's sake! I'm thinking *Who Killed Roger Ackroyd?*–style tales in which no one and nothing can be taken at face value.

Or movies such as Quentin Tarantino's **Pulp Fiction** (1994), whose narrative somersaults elevate four cleverly overlapping stories of lowlifes and high times into an exhilarating celebration of pop-culture chit-chat and B-movie cliches. Or Christopher Nolan's **Memento** (2001), a revenge tale reflected in the shattered mirror of a mind trapped in an eternal present: Bit by bit, a man whose ability to form new memories was beaten out of his brain the night his wife was murdered pieces together the story of his search for her killer. But the information flows through his mind like water, and changes every time he goes to the well. Nolan's lean debut, **Following** (1998), uses elliptical flash-forwards and flashbacks to twist a noir-ish modern-day crime story into a chilling puzzler.

The pulpy **21 Grams** (2001) darts back and forth in time, fragmenting the stories of three strangers—an academic with a fatal heart condition, a reformed ex-con, and a one-time party girl who's just lost her whole family to a hit-and-run driver—on a collision course with disaster. In the extraordinary **Fight Club** (1999), charismatic rebel Tyler Durden (Brad Pitt) lures an unhappy cubicle slave Edward Norton into an underground world of redemption through bare-knuckle brawling. But there's more to Durden's Fight Club than meets the eye. In the Spanish thriller **Open Your Eyes** (1998), a horribly disfigured man hiding behind an eerie mask tells his psychiatrist how a vengeful ex-girlfriend ruined his golden life. But the doctor swears there's nothing wrong with his face. The U.S. remake, **Vanilla Sky** (2001), can't keep up with the original's hairpin turns, but Penelope Cruz plays the dream girl in both versions.

Some movies warn you upfront not to believe everything you see: The grand-daddy of them all is, of course, Akira Kurosawa's **Rashomon** (1950), in which four witnesses (including a ghost) tell the story of the same rape-murder in entirely different ways. Zhang Yimou's intoxicating **Hero** (2002) reworks a much-adapted story about a second-century B.C. Chinese emperor and the assassins who conspire to dethrone him into a series of color-coded variations on a theme, featuring Jet Li, Maggie Cheung, and Zhang Ziyi. The fact-based **Wonderland** (2003) examines porn star John Holmes's (Val Kilmer) involvement in a gruesome 1981 multiple murder. Francis Ford Coppola's paranoid **The Conversation** (1974) and David Cronenberg's icy 2002 **Spider**, based on the tricky Patrick McGrath novel, entangle you in the distorted worldviews of desperately damaged men—paranoid wiretap expert Gene Hackman in the former, recently released mental patient Ralph Fiennes in the latter. So do Lodge Kerrigan's dizzying **Clean, Shaven** (1995) and **Keane** (2005), each of which revolves around an unstable father in search of a missing child; excruciating performances by Peter Greene and Damian Lewis, respectively, are the unreliable but sympathetic anchors that keep the pyrotechnics from sweeping the stories out to sea.

CRY ME A RIVER

S ometimes the best thing for what ails you is a little hair of the dog. So when life gives you lemons, forget that nonsense about making lemonade—reach for one of these three-hankie sobfests.

Let's start by making something clear: Tearjerkers are not just a girlie thing. Stone-cold bruisers have been reduced to puddles by **Brian's Song** (1971), about the deep friendship between real-life Chicago Bears running backs Gale Sayers (Billy Dee Williams) and Brian Piccolo (James Caan), who died of cancer at age twenty-six. In **Bang the Drum Slowly** (1973), star pitcher Michael Moriarty learns that teammate Robert De Niro, a none-too-bright hayseed with a knack for rubbing people the wrong way, has Hodgkin's disease and vows to keep him on the team until the bitter end. **I Never Sang for My Father** (1970) cuts to the quick with its depiction of a dutiful son (Gene Hackman) torn between his own problems and responsibility to the overbearing, aging father (Melvyn Douglas) who's spent his life manipulating his children.

Imitation of Life (1934 and 1959), **Stella Dallas** (1937), and **Terms of Endearment** (1983) entangle themselves in the thorny relationship between mothers and daughters. Rebellious, down-to-earth Debra Winger defies her materialistic, possessive, status-conscious

mother (Shirley MacLaine) to marry an English teacher in *Terms*, but tragedy trumps estrangement. In *Imitation of Life*, two single mothers—one black, one white—become lifelong friends and share the heartbreak of difficult children: One daughter falls for her mother's suitor and the other severs contact so she can pass for white. The 1934 version stars Claudette Colbert and Louise Beavers, with Rochelle Hudson and Fredi Washington, star of early all-black films, as their teenaged daughters. The remake showcases Lana Turner, Juanita Moore, Sandra Dee, and Susan Kohner, and the Technicolor gloss doesn't diminish its emotional wallop—the climactic funeral scene gets me *every time*.

Tough cookies crumble at the spectacle of doomed romance, and in these films the combination of subtly nuanced performances and the very-British tension between propriety and passion is almost unbearable. Celia Johnson and Trevor Howard, both happily married, strike up a friendship on the afternoon train in **Brief Encounter** (1945); when they unexpectedly fall in love, they're forced to choose between hurting themselves and hurting their spouses. **The Heart of Me** (2002) parses a romantic triangle that begins in the 1940s and devastates a businessman (Paul Bettany), his willfully oblivious, socially connected wife (Olivia Williams), and her impulsive, bohemian sister (Helena Bonham Carter). Graham Greene's novel **The End of the Affair** has been filmed twice and overall I prefer the 1999 version, with Julianne Moore as a WWII-era housewife whose affair with her long-suffering husband's (Stephen Rea) friend (Ralph Fiennes) precipitates a spiritual crisis. The 1955 version is talky and American Van Johnson is miscast as the lover, but Peter Cushing's fiercely restrained portrayal of the betrayed husband is superior to Rea's and Deborah Kerr every bit as good as Moore.

Heartbreakingly poignant without degenerating into sloppy sentiment, **Finding Neverland** (2004) evokes the odd, creatively fertile relationship between playwright J. M. Barrie (Johnny Depp) and the four young small sons of a tubercular widow (Kate Winslet) for whom he wrote *Peter Pan*. It's hard to imagine another actor so gracefully evoking Barrie's childlike qualities without seeming creepy or emotionally malformed, and only the hard of heart will come away dry-eyed.

DEADLIER THAN THE MALE

Femme fatales, like the poor, are always with us—as long as there's a poor sap waiting to be lead around by his libido, a black widow will be ready and willing to oblige. German starlet Marlene Dietrich's transformation into a razor-cheekboned icon began with her performance as **The Blue Angel**'s (1930) opportunistic cafe singer Lola Lola, who destroys a middle-aged schoolteacher; a year later she was in Hollywood. Louise Brooks, who played heedless heartbreaker Lulu in **Pandora's Box** (1929), got a one-way ticket to obscurity for her trouble, but her portrayal of a siren who steams through life without a thought for the ruined wrecks bobbing in her wake is stunningly modern.

Demure-looking Mary Astor uses a sob story about her missing sister to entangle detective Sam Spade (Humphrey Bogart) in a no-holds-barred scramble for **The Maltese Falcon** (1941). Cunning, chillingly self-centered Jane Greer double- and triple-crosses both her gangster boyfriend (Kirk Douglas) and the flunky (sleepy-eyed Robert Mitchum) who falls for her in **Out of the Past** (1947). Gimlet-eyed Barbara Stanwyck buys an insurance policy with a **Double Indemnity** (1944) clause in her husband's name from salesman Fred MacMurray, then plots with him to collect. Hotter-than-a-pistol sideshow sharpshooter Peggy Cummins wraps a weak-willed gun-lover around her trigger finger in **Gun Crazy** (1949). Money-hungry Jean Gillie suckers a gangster, corrupts a slum doc-tor, and hauls a man back from the dead (really!) in the obscure, poverty-row thriller **Decoy** (1946). **The Postman Always Rings Twice** was made twice, with Lana Turner (in the 1946 version) and Jessica Lange (in the 1981 remake) as ruthless waitress Cora, who seduces a drifter (John Garfield and Jack Nicholson, respectively) into helping her kill her husband. Lange epitomizes rawboned, slat-ternly desperation; Turner is a scheming creamsicle.

Credulous lawyer William Hurt gets fair warning in **Body Heat** (1981) when another Turner, husky-voiced Kathleen, purrs, "You're not too bright—I like that in a man," but helps her murder her inconvenient husband anyway. Straying spouse Michael Douglas gets more than he bargained for after a steamy one-night stand with medusa-haired Glenn Close in **Fatal Attraction** (1987), who exacts her revenge when he tries to ignore her. (The original ending, reshot after negative pre-release test screenings, is the real killer.) Douglas gets put through the ringer again in **Basic Instinct** (1992), courtesy of Sharon Stone's ice-cold, bisexual, and very possibly homicidal seductress; the scene in which she undoes a roomful of macho morons by giving them a glimpse of her delta of Venus may be vulgar, but it gets to the core of the femme fatale's power. *Basic* director Paul Verhoeven cast Dutch actress Renee Soutendijk in a strikingly similar role a decade earlier; in the twisty, "is it real or isn't it" thriller **The Fourth Man** (1983), she's an icy, enigmatic blond who seduces alcoholic, bisexual writer Jeroen Krabbe and may have murdered three husbands.

When **The Last Seduction**'s (1994) sinewy, hot-eyed Linda Fiorentino finishes fleecing a sap he's both broke and unmanned. But even by these high standards of viciousness, the most blood-chilling femme of them all may be **Detour**'s (1945) Ann Savage, a dead-eyed chippie so bitter she never even bothers to hide her claws; she hitches a ride from hard-luck musician Tom Neal, and by the time she's done with him he's a haunted, hunted husk who's lost everything—even his name—and is just waiting for fate to put him out of his misery.

THE DEVIL, YOU SAY

You have to hand it to the Prince of Darkness: He always snares the best lines and brings out the best—or is it the worst?—in actors. Here are some things movies taught me about the devil.

The legal profession is his playground. Exhibit A: **The Devil's Advocate** (1997), starring a prancing Al Pacino as the Prince of Evil, Esq.—need I say that his offices are in New York?—who tempts eager young defender Keanu Reeves with a taste of the Big Apple. Of course, the devil's devious disciples occasionally turn the tables on him: Legendary legal eagle Daniel Webster (a *principled* lawyer, if you please) comes to the aid of the down-on-his-luck farmer who made the usual deal in **The Devil and Daniel Webster** (1941); Mr. Scratch (Walter Huston) is not pleased.

The devil loves a bad pun: Why else would he dub himself "Lewis Cypher" (Robert De Niro in **Angel Heart**, 1987), Daryl Van Horn (Jack Nicholson, to whom devilishness is second nature, in **The Witches of Eastwick**, 1987), or Mr. Chapell (Peter Weller in **Shadow Hours**, 2000). Oh, that infernal wit!

And the devil loves, loves, *loves* a stacked deal: That there's anyone who doesn't know better than to sign in blood on the dotted line is a tribute to the Evil One's mysterious ways. Brit-wits Peter Cook and Dudley Moore bring a brittle, witty, oh-so-English sense of humor to swinging sixties romp **Bedazzled** (1967), in which lovelorn sad sack Moore sells his soul to mod, bitterly self-important Cook, for a chance at winning his dream girl; the Mendacious One gives him *seven* but there's always a catch—the devil is in the details. The 2000 remake is an exercise in pointlessness, but Elizabeth Hurley's hip-swinging Madame Satan, a bossy, frightfully upbeat saleswoman peddling perdition through self-indulgence, is a bit of fizzy brilliance—she even has hellhounds named Peter and Dudley.

A baseball fanatic sells his soul to "Mr. Applegate" (Ray Walston) for the opportunity to lead his beloved Washington Senators to victory against those **Damn Yankees** (1958); it's hard to resist a musical that gives off a faint whiff of fire and brimstone, and Gwen Verdon's slinky turn as temptress Lola is the closer. **South Park: Bigger, Longer & Uncut** (1999) serves up a reminder that dealing with the Prince of Lies is dangerous business: You can bet Saddam Hussein didn't know he'd be working off his sins as Satan's sex slave.

Sometimes casting makes all the difference: Rosalinda Celentano's spookily androgynous Lucifer is the one surprise in Mel Gibson's pious gorefest **The Passion of the Christ** (2004). Jeff Goldblum's sublimely malicious **Mr. Frost** (1990) claims he's the devil in the flesh and toys maliciously with the shrink who thinks he's just another sadistic serial murderer. Even bad movies can be redeemed by a fabulously devilish performance. Peter Stormare stops the gloomy **Constantine** (2005) dead with his eleventh-hour entrance in an ice-cream suit and filthy bare feet. **Deconstructing Harry** (1997) is the usual sour latter-day Woody Allen: Thank God for Billy Crystal's hipster Beelzebub, whose air-conditioned hell comes complete with hot tub and jazz band—it really *is* the devil's music! Was any actor ever better cast as the silver-tongued, scene-stealing Lord of the Lake of Fire than Vincent Price in the bloated, all-star **The Story of Mankind** (1957)? Pity poor Ronald Coleman, who has to argue on behalf of the human race in front of an outer-space tribunal (don't ask—too complicated) while Price makes the case for wiping us off the face of the Earth. It's a wonder we're still here.

THE DIRT ON PORN

Serious or superficial, movies dealing with the adult-film industry all come with built-in voyeuristic appeal coupled with the assurance that you're not a pervert for watching—they aren't porn, they're *about* porn.

"Oh my God, it's my daughter!" wails George C. Scott in Paul Schrader's overwrought but often-affecting **Hardcore** (1979); as a devoutly religious Midwesterner in search of his runaway teenager, Scott takes a hellish trip through the L.A. underworld of peep shows, massage parlors, and X-rated movie sets. Schrader took up the subject again in the stylish **Auto Focus** (2002), about professional nice guy Bob Crane (Greg Kinnear), amiable star of TV's *Hogan's Heroes*, whose secret addiction to amateur smut ended with his unsolved 1978 murder; he was beaten to death with a tripod. David Cronenberg's visionary **Videodrome** (1983) follows ambitious cable programmer James Woods into a hallucinatory thicket of greed, politics, and mind control by television as he tries to uncover the truth about a *sub rosa* snuff show hosted by Blondie's seductive Deborah Harry. French director Olivier Assayas's **Demonlover** (2002), a glossy meditation on alluring surfaces and hidden ugliness, starts out a straightforward tale of industrial espionage, veers into the shadow world of extreme online pornography, and twists itself into an icy knot of existential angst so tight it makes your head hurt. Its flip side: Joel Schumacher's addictively sleazy **8mm** (1999), in which minor-league private eye Nicolas Cage tumbles down the rabbit hole of unthinkable human degradation while investigating what may be a bona fide snuff film...

let's watch! Peter Stormare's swaggering portrayal of wicked film-maker Dino Velvet is mesmerizing.

Title to the contrary, Milos Forman's **The People vs. Larry Flynt** (1996) is no lesson in First Amendment ethics. It's an epic romance between soul mates Flynt, who founded the scabrous *Hustler* and fought his way to the Supreme Court for the right to mock the Reverend Jerry Falwell, and underage, bisexual stripper-turned-junkie Althea Leasure. Rock 'n' roll road wreck Courtney Love is a revelation and Woody Harrelson (*Cheers'* dimwitted bartender) nails Flynt's cornpone showmanship—his impassioned avowal that since God created women's genitals, glorifying them in girlie pictures is a holy calling is a meretricious marvel. The made-for-cable **Rated X** (2000) stars brothers Charlie Sheen and Emilio Estevez (who also directed) as porn pioneers Artie and Jim Mitchell, who made the porno-chic blockbuster **Behind the Green Door** (1972), which launched Marilyn Chambers's career, and wound up locked in a poisonous Cain-and-Abel rivalry that culminated in one brother's death at the other's hand.

Straight smut's first male superstar, Mr. Big Stuff John Holmes, was a scrawny farm boy with a 13½ inch "pot of gold at the end of his zipper" (as colleague Bill Margold aptly put it). The rise and fall of Dirk Diggler (Mark Wahlberg), the Holmes-inspired protagonist in **Boogie Nights** (1997), unfolds against a backdrop of the golden age of adult movies (1977–1984), which ended when home video quashed the industry's pretensions to being more than an aid to self gratification; supporting players Burt Reynolds and Julianne Moore snared Oscar nominations for playing an arty smut-meister and a sex star who pays steep personal price for the liberation and sense of family she finds in the business.The *Rashomon*-like **Wonderland** (2003) offers three conflicting versions of Holmes's involvement in 1981's sordid "four on the floor" killings, which left four people hammered to death at 8763 Wonderland Avenue, a modest house in Los Angeles's Laurel Canyon;Val Kilmer's woozily paranoid performance as Holmes is riveting and Eric Bogosian's turn as thug Eddie Nash is hypnotically repellent (Alfred Molina's variation on the same character in *Boogie Nights* is equally riveting). Veteran dirty movie director Wesley Emerson called *Boogie Nights* "a fantasy"; it inspired him to set the record straight (under the pseudonym Cass Paley) in the exhaustively researched documentary **Wadd:The Life and Times of John C. Holmes** (2001), named for the oversexed private dick Holmes played in a series of hardcore detective pictures.

Other documentaries that shed light on the business include Fenton Bailey and Randy Barbato's engrossing **Inside Deep Throat** (2005), which dissects the history, legend, and social context of perhaps the best-known and most profitable pornographic movie in history, and **Porn Star: The Legend of Ron Jeremy** (2001), which tries to answer the question, "How did a short, fat, hairy, not-very-attractive guy nicknamed 'the hedgehog' become the clown prince of porn?" **The Girl Next Door** (2000) profiles Stacy Valentine, whose perky enthusiasm gives way to a darker cynicism as the film progresses; the footage of Valentine undergoing breast implant surgery, collagen injections, and liposuction in pursuit of Barbie-doll perfection is more obscene than any hardcore hijinks.

The disturbing **Sex:The Annabel Chong Story** (2000) chron-icles Chong's transformation from convent-schooled aspiring lawyer to gonzo star of 1991's **World's Biggest Gang-Bang**. Chong has a good line of academic patter about reclaiming the female sexual experience from male-generated stereotypes and deconstructing sexual discourse that's undermined by her self-destructive behavior and juvenile need to shock. A breezy, shallow, and raunchily entertaining look at the gay adult-film industry, **Shooting Porn** (1997) features directors and stars discussing the tricks of their trade. Is there any aspect of the business too intimate to discuss? You bet: money.

DIRTY COPS

L awmen look long into the abyss and the abyss looks right back at them in these good movies about bad cops. Harvey Keitel's hair-raisingly naked (in all ways) performance drives **Bad Lieutenant** (1992); he's a drugging, gambling, sexually abusive cop who pins his slim hope of salvation on finding the thugs who raped a nun. A police officer (Gary Oldman) with a lucrative sideline in betraying witnesses to the mob meets his match in a demonic Russian hit woman (Lena Olin) in **Romeo Is Bleeding** (1994). Set on the Mexican side of a corrupt border town, **Touch of Evil** (1958) stars Orson Welles as a thoroughly rotten detective undone by his attempt to pin a fatal car bombing on an innocent man; Welles's sinuous, lengthy opening tracking shot, which follows the doomed Cadillac as it inches along crowded streets, finally exploding at the border checkpoint, is a tour de force.

Hard-boiled novelists William McGivern and James Ellroy are both on intimate terms with the dirty secrets and rotten deeds lurking under the sun-washed glamour of Los Angeles. In **Rogue Cop** (1954), based on McGivern's book, everyone knows a dapper police sergeant is in cahoots with gangsters, but no one does anything until his brother, a good cop, is killed for not playing ball. A brutal officer robs and murders a bookie so he can buy a house away from the mean streets in **Shield for Murder** (also '54), while in **The Big Heat** (1953), an ex-cop (Glenn Ford) out to avenge his wife's murder becomes as brutally degraded as the mobsters and shady cops who killed her. Unforgettable scene: thug Lee Marvin throwing a pot of scalding coffee in moll Gloria Grahame's face.

Ellroy's *Blood on the Moon* became **Cop** (1988), with James Woods as a burnt-out sleaze pursuing a serial killer. Don't fast-forward the opening credits; the phone conversation in which a tipster tries to get around admitting that he discovered a corpse while burgling the victim's apartment is a masterpiece of black humor. **L.A. Confidential** (1997) and **Dark Blue** (2003) unfold against a backdrop of institutionalized corruption. *Confidential* engulfs three cops—straight arrow Guy Pearce, starstruck sellout Kevin Spacey, and nut case Russell Crowe—in a sleazy tidal wave of drugs, smut, blackmail, scandal magazines, and prostitution. Same dirty town, forty years later in *Dark Blue*: A crooked detective (Kurt Russell) unravels in the days leading up to the Rodney King riots.

Internal Affairs (1990) and **Training Day** (2001) pair young officers with charismatic but bad-to-the-bone mentors Richard Gere and Denzel Washington. In **Narc** (2002), a disgraced undercover cop gets the chance to redeem himself by cracking the murder of another undercover officer, only to run afoul of the dead man's unrepentantly dirty partner (a seethingly intense Ray Liotta).

A Swedish police inspector (Stellan Skarsgard) accidentally kills his partner while investigating a small-town Norwegian murder in the icy **Insomnia** (1998); he tries to blame the still-at-large killer, but loses his grip in the twenty-four-hour glare of the Nordic summer midnight. The 2002 remake with Al Pacino is fine, but the original is chilling. The deeply dark comedy **Gang Related** (1997) puts the screws to partners in crime Tupac Shakur and Jim Belushi, who've been supplementing their paychecks by shaking down and killing drug dealers and need a plausible fall guy for their murder of an undercover DEA agent. "What's the worst possible case scenario?" asks Belushi after another bombshell shatters their plans. "We get arrested, go to jail, get sent to the electric chair, die, and go to hell!" sputters Shakur. On the bright side, hell is full of guys like them.

DON'T BOX ME IN

The sweet science was made for movies and while the details change, boxing movies hew closely to time-honored themes. They're about strength of mind and weakness of flesh, maintaining the balance between aggression and calculation, the battle between integrity and a fat-but-dirty payoff, the promise of a way out of poverty, the pursuit of the one break that could start a new career or salvage a flagging one. These films understand the formula and work it till it works.

> **The Set-Up** (1949), with Robert Ryan (a college boxing champ who made his movie debut as a dirty fighter in 1940's *Golden Gloves*) as an over-the-hill fighter who doesn't know his manager has sold him out.
>
> **Raging Bull** (1980), with Robert De Niro as the brutal, tormented real-life "Bronx Bull," Jake La Motta—by most estimates, the best boxing movie of all time.
>
> **Golden Boy** (1939), with William Holden as a violinist who supports his family in the ring but risks his musical career with every blow.

Body and Soul (1947), with John Garfield as an amoral fighter who'll do anything to get to the top.

Million Dollar Baby (2004), with Hilary Swank as a white-trash scrapper who finally gets her shot—be warned: There's an abrupt detour into tearjerking tragedy.

Rocky (1976), with Sylvester Stallone as a "bum" who becomes a contender—the most-loved boxing movie.

The Mouse (1997), with John Savage as real-life professional loser Bruce "the Mouse" Strauss, who parlayed his willingness to get knocked out into a novelty career.

Girlfight (2000), with Michelle Rodriguez as a seething teenager slugging her way out of Brooklyn's violent Red Hook housing projects.

Requiem for a Heavyweight (1962), with Anthony Quinn as a veteran who loses his last bout (to a young Cassius Clay) but still has to save his manager's sorry hide.

Fat City (1972), with Jeff Bridges and Stacy Keach as, respectively, a none-too-promising newcomer and a down-and-out veteran chasing a pipe dream of getting back in the ring.

Somebody Up There Likes Me (1956), with a very young Paul Newman as real-life fighter Rocky Graziano, who trained him for the role.

The Great White Hope (1970), with James Earl Jones playing a thinly veiled version of Jack Johnson, the first African American heavyweight champion (he took the title in 1908) and a victim of racist persecution.

Gentleman Jim (1942), with Errol Flynn as nineteenth-century brawler Jim Corbett, who crusaded to bring "scientific methods" to the then bare-knuckle sport.

EASY DOES IT

C rescent City detective Dennis Quaid purrs "just relax, darlin'," in **The Big Easy** (1987). "Folks have a certain way of doin' things down here." Sultry, seamy, hopped up, and laid back, faded to genteel perfection and vibrating with raunchy rhythm, fueled by a twenty-four-hour appetite for hot food and ice-cold drinks: Beautiful, battered New Orleans may never be the same, but its dreamy, timeless essence colors these films.

Paul Schrader relocated **Cat People** (1982) from Manhattan to New Orleans, whose aura of lush degeneracy better suited his erotic take on the story of women whose desires turn them into murderous cat creatures. Alan Parker did the same with William Hjortsberg's novel *Falling Angel*, about hell-bound, hard-boiled detective Harry Angel; the book stayed in New York City, but Parker's **Angel Heart** (1987) sends Angel (Mickey Rourke) to sweltering New Orleans for the final leg of his date with destiny. Playwright Tennessee Williams was born in Mississippi but blossomed in the hothouse ambiance of New Orleans. Neither **A Streetcar Named Desire** (1951), which traps Marlon Brando, Vivien Leigh, and Kim Hunter in a sexually charged power struggle, nor **Suddenly, Last Summer** (1959), a perverse gumbo of rape, madness, incest, pedophilia, and cannibalism starring Katharine Hepburn and Elizabeth Taylor, was shot on location, but both drip with steamy Southern sensuality.

The French Quarter shimmers in luminous black and white in Elvis Presley's **King Creole** (1958) and Depression-era melodrama **Walk on the Wild Side** (1962). Cautionary showbiz tale *Creole*, about an ambitious teen trying to claw his way out of poverty, ranks with The King's best films; the deliciously tawdry *Wild Side* follows naive Texas farm boy Lawrence Harvey as he searches for his lost love (elegant French model-turned-actress Capucine), who works at lesbian madam Barbara Stanwyck's Chartres Street bordello; a very young Jane Fonda plays saucy, underage tramp Kitty Twist. The Depression drives vagrant Charles Bronson into the world of bare-knuckle boxing in the gritty **Hard Times** (1975). Public Health Service investigator Richard Widmark has forty-eight hours to find the small-time thug (veteran tough guy Jack Palance, in his movie debut) spreading pneumonic plague in Elia Kazan's documentary-style thriller **Panic in the Streets** (1950); portly comedian Zero Mostel's turn as Palance's surprisingly nimble sidekick is an eye-opener.

Louis Malle's controversial **Pretty Baby** (1978) weaves together the story of real-life photographer E. J. Bellocq (Keith Carradine), who shot portraits of prostitutes in turn-of-the-century Storyville, New Orlean's red-light district, and the fictional tale of "pretty baby" Violet (twelve-year-old Brooke Shields), groomed by her mother (Susan Sarandon) to conquer the world's oldest profession. New Orleans is only a stopover in **Easy Rider** (1969), but what a stopover: Hookers (future "Hey, Mickey!" singer Toni Basil and Karen Black), Mardi Gras, and an acid-fueled trip in the historic above ground St. Louis Cemetery No.1. Clint Eastwood tracks a serial killer through Bourbon Street's sleaziest dives in **Tightrope** (1984).

"There's always a kid, isn't there," says world-weary poker champ Edward G. Robinson in **The Cincinnati Kid** (1965); Steve McQueen is the lean and hungry up-and-comer looking to take Robinson's place at the top of the deck. Sweet Tuesday Weld, naughty Ann-Margret, and corrupt old-money gambler Rip Torn sweeten the pot, which comes with a guided tour of smoky, sweaty blues bars, pool halls, back alleys, cockfight pits, and backroom poker games. *The Big Easy*'s charmingly corrupt Quaid sexes up prissy district attorney Ellen Barkin in an atmospheric thriller that never lets work get in the way of a sizzling good time or a smoking soundtrack that mixes and matches jazz, zydeco, R&B, and Cajun music. *Laissez les bon temps roulez!*

EDGE OF NIGHT

N*oir* this, neo-*noir* that, post-*noir* the other thing: You hear quite a lot about *film noir*—a loose-knit collection of alienated, fatalistic thrillers made in the 1940s and '50s—but with so many darkly promising titles crowding the shelves, it's hard to know where to start. With this list as your guide to lost highways, cruel twists of fate, tough dames, and hard-boiled chumps, the only wrong turns you'll take are the ones you choose.

Insurance salesman Fred MacMurray and high-maintenance hussy Barbara Stanwyck conspire to murder her husband and collect the insurance in **Double Indemnity** (1944), based on the novel by pulp pioneer James M. Cain. Tough-guy detective Dana Andrews falls for the faceless corpse whose shotgun murder he's investigating in the sleekly perverse **Laura** (1944), and things only get more complicated when Laura (Gene Tierney), the protege of waspish newspaper critic Waldo Lydecker (Clifton Webb), turns out to be alive. Meek, middle-aged cashier and thwarted artist Edward

G. Robinson falls for the tawdry charms of hard-eyed Greenwich Village opportunist Joan Bennett in **Scarlet Street** (1945).

Edgar G. Ulmer's poverty-row **Detour** (1945) is stripped down to the bleached bones of noir fatalism: Hard-luck pianist Tom Neal thumbs a ride to California to be with his girl, but gets tangled up with hitchhiker Ann Savage, a pitiless chippie whose scheming lands him in a purgatorial diner stripped of everything he ever held dear, even his name. Small-time thug Robert Mitchum double-crosses his gangster boss (Kirk Douglas) for femme fatale Jane Greer in **Out of the Past** (1947); when she plays him for a chump he tries to build a new life, but the past won't let him go. Glenn Ford plays a brutal croupier in thrall to his boss's sultry wife (Rita Hayworth) in **Gilda** (1946), which contains Hayworth's devastatingly sexy "Put the Blame on Mame" striptease, in which she sheds nothing but a pair of gloves.

If there's a more perfect noir opening than that of **D.O.A.** (1950), in which Edmond O'Brien staggers into a Los Angeles police station and says, "I want to report a murder—mine," I've never seen it; a restless small-town accountant, O'Brien goes for a weekend getaway in San Francisco and gets dosed with a luminous, poison that will kill him in a week—who gave it to him and why? Jules Dassin's London-set **Night and the City** (1950) follows hustler Richard Widmark's increasingly desperate efforts to weasel his way into the one big score he thinks is coming to him. Widmark, whose gaunt, hungry face made him a natural for noir's fatalistic tales of doomed fringe dwellers, plays a New York pickpocket who inadvertently gets himself involved with espionage in two-fisted auteur Samuel Fuller's **Pickup on South Street** (1953).

Adapted from Mickey Spillane's novel, **Kiss Me Deadly** (1955) came at the tail end of the noir cycle and follows brutal private investigator Mike Hammer (Ralph Meeker) down a rabbit hole of corruption and murder prompted by "the great whatsit," a box whose glowing contents (later alluded to by Quentin Tarantino in *Pulp Fiction*) pack an apocalyptic punch. By most reckoning, *Kiss Me Deadly* marked the end of the noir cycle—it's hard to top a detective film that ends in atomic fire—but noir's gloomy legacy lives on.

EVERYTHING IS BEAUTIFUL
AT THE BALLET

Scratch a glittering ballerina and odds are you'll find a little girl who swooned over Michael Powell's **The Red Shoes** (1948), in which dancer Victoria Page (flame-haired Sadler's Wells star Moira Shearer) must choose between love and art. It's the yardstick by which all ballet movies are measured and they all come up short because *The Red Shoes* is *sui generis*, a hothouse wallow in romantic suffering distilled into something utterly unreal and incredibly potent. But there's room on the shelf for a few more items, starting with **Shall We Dance** (1937), a musical romp starring Fred Astaire as a faux-Russian ballet star who can't resist the siren call of tap and Edward Everett Horton as a Sergei Diaghilev–like impresario.

An old-fashioned backstage melodrama tarted up with some feminist pirouettes, **The Turning Point** (1977)—directed and produced by American Ballet Theatre alumni Herbert Ross and Nora Kaye—culminates in a doozy of a hair-pulling, evening-dress-rumpling catfight between fading ballerina Anne Bancroft and former rival Shirley MacLaine, who sacrificed dance for love and marriage. The bonus: great rehearsal and performance footage featuring Leslie Browne—an extraordinary dancer and a terrible actress—and a young Mikhail Baryshnikov, playing the heartbreakingly talented roue who drags her heart around.

A poor, working-class youngster (Jamie Bell), **Billy Elliot** (2000) skips out of boxing lessons and finds he likes ballet class; both tough-minded and heartwarming, it ends with a snippet of bad-boy British choreographer Matthew Bourne's all-male *Swan Lake*. A labor of love for star Neve Campbell, who studied at the National Ballet of Canada's school until injuries forced her to rethink her dreams, **The Company** (2003) is a Robert Altman–directed ensemble piece about a troupe very like the Joffrey Ballet of Chicago, whose repertory and participation lend authenticity to the backstage drama. Eccentric filmmaker Guy Maddin's **Dracula: Pages from a Virgin's Diary** (2002) reimagines a Royal Winnipeg Ballet production of *Dracula* (choreographed by Mark Godden to excerpts from Mahler's Symphonies No. 1 and No. 2) as a feverish, mesmerizing silent-film-style fantasy (with sound effects and music), complete with missing frames, tinted sequences, damaged stock, and intertitles. But for lethal terpsichorean thrills, Italian horror stylist

Dario Argento's **Suspiria** (1976), a candy-colored fairy tale set in a haunted German ballet academy, is the ticket. A nightmarish spook show in which the red shoes are bloody and the ballerina's partner is Death, it sets the *barre* high at the start and keeps topping itself.

Balletomanes and newcomers alike can enjoy these documentaries. Narrated by Grace Kelly, **The Children of Theatre Street** (1977) is a Soviet-era portrait of the Vaganova Choreographic Institute, training ground for Kirov Ballet dancers. The sober, precise **Tout près de les étoiles** (2001) parses the rigorous process by which the four-hundred-year-old Paris Opera Ballet school and company mold adorable youngsters into world-class dancers; ballerina Ghislaine Thesmar briskly sums it up as "a machine that crushes the weak." **Ballets Russes** (2005) touches briefly on Diaghilev's pioneering company but focuses on its successors, which helped bring classical dance—including some daringly modern ballets—to the masses; it's rich with amazing archival footage and interviews with aging but still-elegant ballerinas possessed of excellent memories and sharp tongues. Though veteran documentarian Frederick Wiseman is famous for brutally revealing portraits of institutions ranging from mental hospitals to high schools, his **Ballet** (1995)—a fly's eye look at dancers and staff of the American Ballet Theatre as they prepare for and then undertake a 1992 European tour—is surprisingly short on diva-tude and bloody toes; it is, however, an absorbing chronicle of a great company getting down to the day-to-day work of making dance.

F FOR FAKE (AND FEROCIOUS)

Contrary to popular belief, **The Blair Witch Project** (1999) didn't invent the scare-your-pants off mockumentary. That honor, if we can call it that, belongs to Italian exploitation guru Ruggero Deodato's unrelentingly nasty **Cannibal Holocaust** (1979), in which the fate of four filmmakers who vanished in the Brazilian jungle while making a documentary about cannibals is revealed when their grisly footage is found. Only part of its running time is truly mockumentary, but the words "The Amazon Cannibal Project" are hard to get out of your head. Beware the real scenes of animal slaughter.

Inspired by Orson Welles's *War of the Worlds* hoax, **Special Bulletin** (1983) flawlessly duplicates the look of local news coverage of a developing story involving disgruntled American scientists and a clandestinely built nuclear device; if anything, it's more alarming now than it was two decades ago. The Belgian **Man Bites Dog/ C'est arrivé près de chez vous** (1992) is a one-joke film, but the joke is pitch black and flawlessly delivered. A film crew—played by the real filmmakers, using their own names—is making a low-budget documentary about a smug, self-absorbed serial killer with a windy, pseudo-intellectual opinion about everything, from race relations to the best way to cook shellfish; they treat his psychotic crime spree as though it were just a somewhat unpleasant but interesting line of work, like being a kosher butcher or an undertaker. It is genuinely funny, but you don't feel good about laughing, which is a recommendation rather than a criticism.

And then came *Blair Witch*, a litmus test that divided the horror cognoscenti into sneering naysayers who saw it as an overhyped rip-off that didn't deliver the goods and shuddering fans who thought it the creepiest piece of fright-by-suggestion since *The Haunting* (1963). The setup is simplicity itself: Footage shot by three student filmmakers who disappeared into the woods near Burkittsville, Maryland, in 1994 while making an anthropology-class documentary about a local campfire story is unearthed. It shows their journey into nerve-scraping terror courtesy of some unseen something in the dark. The movie's Web site, viral marketing, and tie-ins were brilliant, but with the hoopla now history, I still find it as chilling as Algernon Blackwood's elegantly unnerving short story "The Willows," which it resembles in many respects.

You can't talk about *Blair Witch Project* without mentioning Stefan Avalos and Lance Weiler's **The Last Broadcast** (1998), the movie in-the-know types swore *Blair Witch* filmmakers Eduardo Sanchez and Dan Myrick ripped off. *Last Broadcast* is styled as a documentary by one David Leigh about the murders of Steven Avkast (Avalos), Locus Wheeler (Weiler), and Rein Clackin, respectively the hosts and soundman of hokey cable show *Fact or Fiction*, by a self-proclaimed psychic while deep in New Jersey's desolate Pine Barrens taping a segment about the legendary Jersey Devil. Actually, *Broadcast* looks less like *Blair Witch* than Myrick and Sanchez's promotional companion piece, *In Search Of . . .* –style **Curse of the Blair Witch** (1999), which expands effectively on the movie's backstory and looks even more like the real thing than *The Blair Witch Project* itself. But give credit where it's due: *Broadcast* delivers some creepy moments until it shoots itself in the footage with a ridiculous ending.

My Little Eye (2002) puts a reality-TV twist on one of the oldest setups in the horror repertory: a small group of people trapped in a scary house. Five contestants sign on for a *Big Brother*–style show: If they all stick out six months of living in an isolated house with cameras broadcasting their every move online, they share one million dollars. If anyone leaves, everyone loses. Until it tips its hand about three-quarters of the way through, this reality spook show is truly creepy and cracks the toughest nut of old-dark-house thriller conventions, providing a plausibly compelling reason why the victims-to-be don't leave the *minute* scary things start happening.

F FOR FAKE (AND FUNNY)

This Is Spinal Tap (1984) didn't invent mockumentary; earlier examples include **Citizen Kane**'s (1941) fake "News on the March" newsreel and Monty Python alumnus Eric Idle's spot-on Beatles spoof **The Rutles: All You Need Is Cash** (1978). But the keenly hilarious *Spinal Tap* is the fake that launched a thousand imitations; Rob Reiner's "rockumentary" brilliantly nails the cliches of VH1's *Behind the Music* before there was such a program to mock and, like *The Blair Witch Project* fifteen years later, fooled quite a few people into believing it was real. The criminally underrated **Fear of a Black Hat** (1994) uses the *Tap* template to skewer the worlds of rap, hip-hop, and trip-hop, and it's so funny it hurts. **Best in Show** (2000) and **A Mighty Wind** (2003) feature combinations of *Spinal Tap* cocreators Christopher Guest, Michael McKean, Harry Shearer, and

Second City TV alumnus Eugene Levy, and apply the *Spinal Tap* method to dog shows and folk music.

Lord of the Rings director Peter Jackson's dazzling **Forgotten Silver** (1995, co-directed with Costa Botes) purports to examine the brilliant career of forgotten New Zealand filmmaker Colin MacKenzie, whom cruel fate robbed of credit for inventing the tracking shot, the close-up, color photography, the handheld camera, synchronized sound, and feature-length filmmaking. In **The Big Tease** (2000), a starry-eyed Scottish hair stylist (Craig Ferguson) heads for the L.A.-based World Freestyle Hairdressing Competition with a blow-dryer, a dream, and a BBC film crew in tow; that he was only invited to be in the audience, not the competition, isn't going to stop him from coming home a winner.

Woody Allen's ingenious **Zelig** (1983) sneaks some serious thoughts about assimilation and cultural identity into the story of "human chameleon" Leonard Zelig (Allen), whose ability to change his appearance to suit his surroundings is mirrored in the way Allen blends himself into faux-historical footage of everything from a chichi party with press baron William Randolph Hearst to a Nazi rally. At the other end of the technical spectrum, writer-director-star Cheryl Dunye's scrappy, low-tech **The Watermelon Woman** (1996) skewers pious pretensions about racial, sexual, and cultural identity; it follows young, black, lesbian aspiring filmmaker "Cheryl" as she tries to document a forgotten black actress of the 1930s billed only as "The Watermelon Woman," straining her relationships with her family, friends, and new girlfriend (*Go Fish* co-writer/star Guinevere Turner). And screenwriter-turned-director Zak Penn's **Incident at Loch Ness** (2004) has a blast tweaking the

Hollywood house of mirrors: A documentary crew follows notoriously intense German director Werner Herzog as he makes a documentary about the myth of the Loch Ness monster for duplicitous screenwriter-turned-producer Zak Penn. Who'd have guessed that Herzog, who notoriously came to blows with Klaus Kinski, and who hypnotized the cast of one film and hauled his crew up the side of an about-to-explode volcano for another, had such a gift for sly, self-deprecating comedy?

FAIRY TALES FOR GROWN-UPS

D isney's child-friendly fairy-tale movies are fine for the small fry, but these clever variations on classic tales tease out their creepier themes and more disturbing implications.

Jacques Demy's weird musical fantasy **Donkey Skin** (1971) weaves variations on "The Goose that Laid the Golden Egg" (transformed into a donkey that defecates precious jewels), "Cinderella" and "Little Red Riding Hood" into the tale of a widowed king determined to marry his daughter (Catherine Deneuve)—who isn't entirely opposed to the idea, since she loves her father dearly—and the fey efforts of her fairy godmother (the mysterious Delphine Seyrig) to avert this unwholesome turn of events; the fairy's coquettish song about why "girls do not marry their daddies" sums up the film's archly dark sense of whimsy.

Sigourney Weaver's complex performance as the "wicked" stepmother is only one of the surprises in the criminally underrated **Snow White: A Tale of Terror** (1997); this sinister version of the classic fairy tale pits a resentful stepdaughter on the verge of womanhood against her widowed father's vain second wife, who only retaliates when her own much-anticipated child is stillborn. "A wolf may not be what he seems," counsels gray-haired granny Angela Lansbury, a font of salacious advice about randy priests and big bad wolves who look like men—by their unibrows you shall know them. The worst wolves of all, she warns her blossoming granddaughter, Little Red Riding Hood, "are hairy on the inside." Granny's perversely cautionary stories drive Neil Jordan's feverish **The Company of Wolves** (1984), a collection of fairy tales filtered through the sexed-up imagination of bad-girl writer Angela Carter, who knew a thing or two about women who run with wolves.

Matthew Bright's audacious **Freeway** (1996) spins "Little Red Riding Hood" into the modern-day story of fifteen-year-old white-trash runaway Reese Witherspoon, who runs afoul of a modern-day big bad wolf—razor-wielding serial killer Kiefer Sutherland—while thumbing a ride. He followed it with a scabrous spin on "Hansel and Gretel," **Freeway 2: Confessions of a Trickbaby** (1999), in which bulimic lost "child" White Girl (Natasha Lyonne) breaks out of a harsh detention facility with her sexually traumatized, serial-killer cell mate and winds up in the Tijuana lair of witchy Sister Gomez (Vincent Gallo), who seems inordinately interested in feeding her young charges. Writer-director Wayne Kramer takes a bold trip into Bright country with the incredibly violent and scorchingly foulmouthed **Running Scared** (2006). It may *look* like a crime story, thick with second-tier Russian and Italian mobsters, gang bangers, pimps, whores, corrupt cops, and junkies. But Kramer's tale of an abused boy with a grown-up gun traveling through the deepest, darkest heart of the woods is an abject lesson in the truth of Carter's warning that the worst wolves are hairy on the inside—the Stepford couple who love children in the worst possible way put the gingerbread-house witch to shame.

"Hansel and Gretel" gets another reworking in the odd **Who Slew Auntie Roo?** (1971), part of the 1960s/'70s cycle of fright films starring aging movie stars as deranged harridans. Set in 1920s England, it's powered by Shelley Winters's go-for-broke perfor- mance as rich widow Auntie Roo, who kidnaps a pair of orphaned siblings because the girl looks like her dead daughter; the brother (Mark Lester) becomes convinced that, like the fairy witch, Auntie Roo intends to fatten them up and eat them.

Edgar G. Ulmer's **Bluebeard** (1944) recasts the fairy-tale wife killer as a nineteenth-century Parisian puppeteer (John Carradine) driven by the compulsion to strangle women; Carradine's marvelously sub- tle performance and Ulmer's ingenuity transform what could have been a low-budget throwaway into a small marvel. Wickedly funny and deeply disquieting, animator Jan Svankmajer's live-action **Little Otik** (2000) is based on a Czech fairy tale with nightmare echoes of *Pinocchio*; a man gives his barren wife a gnarled tree stump that resembles a baby, which she names Otik and treats like the real thing until it actually comes to life. And Little Otik is *hungry*. The disturbing and nearly dialogue-free **Secret Adventures of Tom Thumb** (1993) mixes live action and spooky, Quay Brothers–like stop-motion animation; it unfolds in a medieval-looking dystopia where science and alchemy are all but indistinguishable and babies are produced by the Super Seed Insemination factory, where an assembly-line mishap produces malformed, six-inch-tall Tom. His nightmarish misadventures begin with imprisonment in a scientific compound filled with mutant oddities and end with ascension to heaven in a cloud of flies.

French poet Jean Cocteau's **Beauty and the Beast** (1946), a symphony of elegantly eerie images—human arms clutching candelabras sprouting from walls, moving statues, and living faces gazing out from ornamented fireplaces—has been sampled by the best. Disney's animated version turned the same talking household objects into cute asides to a light romance, but Cocteau preserved the fairy tale's dark heart and prompted Greta Garbo, on viewing the film, to cry, "Where is my beautiful beast?" when Beauty's love transforms him into handsome but all-too-ordinary Jean Marais. Garbo and Cocteau shared a secret: Real life pales beside the vivid seductiveness of dreams, even dark ones.

FATHERS AND SONS

The diverse films that follow examine the powerful bonds that unite fathers and sons, as well as the conflicts that divide them.

Peevish, estranged son Billy Crudup tries to have a heart-to-heart talk with his dying dad (Albert Finney in the present-day scenes, Ewan McGregor in flashbacks), a lifelong fabulist in **Big Fish** (2003), a deft blend of fantastic noodling and astute psychological drama; but the old man has an inexhaustible supply of amusing anecdotes, shimmering fables, and cleverly spun tall tales. Impoverished Swedish widower Max von Sydow emigrates to Denmark with his ten-year-old **Pelle the Conqueror/Pelle erobreren** (1987), but instead of a better life they find punishing poverty and hard truths, including the growing boy's inevitable realization that his devoted, hardworking father is a flawed man, not an idol. Unprincipled Texas heel **Hud** (1963)—played by Paul Newman—butts horns with his father, Melvyn Douglas, whose fundamental honesty may cost him his ranch.

Spare and evocative, **The Return/Vozvrashcheniye** (2003) revolves around the reappearance of a prodigal father, who takes his wary, emotionally conflicted adolescent sons—strangers to him, as he is to them—on an arduous fishing trip that may have some darker purpose. A poor Italian poster hanger searches devastated post-WWII Rome with his small son in **The Bicycle Thief/Ladri di biciclette**(1948), trying to recover the bicycle he desperately needs to keep his new job. Neurotic James Dean vies with his twin brother for the affection of their stern, judgmental patriarch (Raymond Massey) in **East of Eden** (1955), directed by Elia Kazan and based on the John Steinbeck novel.

In the grimly compelling psychological thriller **Flesh and Bone** (1993), vicious career criminal Roy (James Caan) and his grown son, Arliss (Dennis Quaid), are bound by the memory of a twenty-year-old crime: Burglar Roy used Arliss as a decoy to gain access to a house, but wound up slaughtering the whole family—all except a wailing infant. Now cruel fate has led Arliss to fall in love with the fragile, damaged woman (Meg Ryan) that baby grew up to be, and Roy sees a loose end that needs tying up. Hard-drinking, quick-fisted Vermont cop Nick Nolte is trapped by the lessons he learned from his snarling, junkyard dog of a father (James Coburn) in the icy, lacerating **Affliction** (1999), a meditation on family legacies of violence adapted from Russell Banks's novel.

A ten-year-old discovers a kidnapped boy his own age hidden in a pit in **I'm Not Scared/Io non ho paura** (2003), a coming-of-age thriller set in parched, poverty-stricken southern Italy in the 1970s, and comes to realize that his beloved father is a kidnapper. A creepy slice of gothic rural Americana marred only by a gimmicky ending, **Frailty** (2002) is about a widowed mechanic (Bill Paxton) who receives a revelation from God and enlists his twelve- and nine-year-old sons—one a willing participant, the other increasingly convinced that his father has gone mad—in his holy mission to kill the demons who walk among us disguised as ordinary people.

DIRECTOR'S SPOTLIGHT: ABEL FERRARA

The short list of quintessential New York filmmakers is short
indeed: Martin Scorsese, Woody Allen, Spike Lee, Sidney
Lumet, and black sheep Abel Ferrara, who's revered in
Europe but strictly a cult item at home. And unfortunately, his U.S.
cult is a cult of personality, fueled more by gossip about drugs, on-
set lunacy, and foul-mouthed public freak-outs than Ferrara's body
of work: The "Oh, man, *The Driller Killer* is *so messed up!*" school of
critical appreciation doesn't do him justice.

Born in the Bronx and raised largely in Peekskill, Ferrara came
back to New York City in the dark days of the '70s and never left.
Leaving aside the weirdly arty hardcore film **9 Lives of a Wet
Pussy** (1976), which did nothing for Ferrara's career but added
another layer to his bad reputation, his output began with **The
Driller Killer** (1979), which promised grind-house audiences
standard-issue slasher movie thrills and delivered a grungy, Euro-
art-film-influenced portrait of a high-strung painter (Ferrara, cred-
ited as "Jimmy Laine") living in a rundown Manhattan loft—back
when broke artists, not celebrities and obscenely wealthy Wall Street
wolves, lived in lofts—and losing his mind to the relentless racket
of a no-talent new-wave band. He takes his portable power drill to
pathetic bums and winos—*so* not fun or sexy. Ditto the notorious
rape-revenge thriller **Ms. 45** (1981), in which a mute seamstress

(Zoe Tamerlis) is assaulted twice in one day and makes the entire male sex pay.

Ferrara flirted with Hollywood, butting heads with the producers of the compromised **Fear City** (1984) and **Cat Chaser** (1991), directing the vivid pilot for the series **Crime Story** (1986) and a tidy remake of *Invasion of the Body Snatchers*—**Body Snatchers** (1994)—that made brilliant use of star Meg Tilly's spookily empty eyes. But he always came home, prowling New York's subways, parks, court houses, and bars from the Bronx to Battery Park, with practiced ease. **China Girl** (1987), a lush spin on *Romeo and Juliet*, exploits the tension between residents of Little Italy and Chinatown, adjacent ethnic enclaves in lower Manhattan. The hypnotically lurid **King of New York** (1990) explores New York's uneasy intersection of race, class, and money through the eyes of drug lord Christopher Walken, who moves freely between the old-line luxury of the Plaza Hotel, chichi downtown scene-makers, and the still-rundown streets of Times Square. **'R Xmas** (2001), lesser but still interesting, returns to the same ground: Married drug dealers Lillo Brancato and Drea DeMatteo scramble to hold it together when the wall between their dirty business and apparently respectable lives is suddenly breached. And the excoriating **Bad Lieutenant** (1992), a gritty parable of degradation, despair, and the slim hope of redemption, bubbles with Harvey Keitel's brutally exposed (literally and figuratively) performance as a nameless corrupt cop on a downward spiral so squalid it verges on poetry.

Opinion on Ferrara's more outre films is fiercely divided, but one thing is certain: No one ever leaves in a comfy cocoon of complacency. Ferrara lays into the pretensions of Hollywood hustlers in meta-fictions **Snake Eyes** (1993) and **The Blackout** (1997); the former stars Madonna as a Madonna-like celebrity making a psychodrama called *Mother of Mirrors* for viciously manipulative director Keitel; the latter features Matthew Modine as a newly clean-and-sober actor undone by his determination to find out how his girlfriend (Beatrice Dalle) died—Dennis Hopper capers in for a cameo as a gleefully debased director. The black-and-white vampire fable **The Addiction** (1995) is one long metaphor punctuated with pitiless jabs at academics and hipsters, while cyberpunk puzzler **New Rose Hotel** (1998), with Willem Dafoe, superstar Japanese artist Yoshitaka Amano, and Asia Argento—whose semi-autobiographical **Scarlet Diva** (2000) includes a dissolute director clearly modeled on Ferrara—ties itself into a suffocating knot of lies-within-lies obfuscation. So all hail Abel, the once and future King of motherf@#*%& New York!

A FLUTTER OF WINGS

L et us now praise angels, too often overshadowed by the showboating Mr. Scratch (see *The Devil, You Say*).

If you just *think* you've seen **It's a Wonderful Life** (1946) because you've absorbed so many heartwarming commercials over the course of umpteen holiday seasons, sit down and prepare to be surprised; this fantasy in which an angel shows suicidal small-town banker James Stewart how much poorer the world would have been without him has a real dark edge. In the sublime **Wings of Desire** (1987), melancholy angels Bruno Ganz and Otto Sander hover around the monochromatic edges of earthly life until Ganz falls in love with a trapeze artist and experiences life in all its colors. A panel of angels judge newly disembodied souls in the bittersweet comedy **Defending Your Life** (1991); utterly decent Meryl Streep is a shoe-in for promotion to a higher plane of existence, but shallow, obnoxious adman Albert Brooks has a tougher row to hoe. Streep and Emma Thompson both play multiple roles, including honest-to-God angels, in the phantasmagoric **Angels in America** (2003), adapted from playwright Tony Kushner's epic examination of the American character in a "greed is good" age of intolerance and pious hypocrisy. Sax-playing boxer Robert Montgomery is taken before his time by overzealous angel Edward Everett Horton in **Here Comes Mr. Jordan** (1941); heavenly higher-up Jordan (Claude Rains) must find him a new body in which to live out his life. Skip the remakes—the musical *Down to Earth* (1947), the flabby Warren Beatty vehicle *Heaven Can Wait* (1978), and the vulgar Chris Rock version of *Down to Earth* (2001).

Dapper heavenly messenger Cary Grant discretely helps an Episcopalian clergyman and his wife (David Niven, Loretta Young) through a rough patch in the gently comic **The Bishop's Wife** (1947); Denzel Washington does the same for Courtney P. Vance and Whitney Houston in **The Preacher's Wife** (1997). Just how important is baseball? Important enough to merit diabolical intercession in **Damn Yankees** (1958) and divine assistance in **Angels in the Outfield** (1951), a charmer in which angels answer a little girl's prayers on behalf of the beleaguered Pittsburgh Pirates. Of the 1994 remake, let's just say it *wasn't* touched by an angel. Cynical tabloid reporters don't know what to make of **Michael** (1996), the "angel" (John Travolta) parked in a small-town reader's spare room: He's fat, unshaven, petulant, lustful, and crude, but those *wings* are a puzzler. For a picture about warm and gooey things, it's got some bite.

Dogma (1999), Kevin Smith's foul-mouthed, affectionately blasphemous, and pretty damned funny comedy of cosmic errors revolves around banished angels Ben Affleck and Matt Damon and their quest to get back to heaven. In the odd screwball comedy **The Horn Blows at Midnight** (1945), archangel Jack Benny is sent to Earth to signal the arrival of Judgment Day and a pair of fallen angels try to stop him; it's all a dream—Benny is really a third-rate big-band trumpeter—but comedies about the apocalypse are few and far between. In the overlooked and underrated **The Prophecy** (1995), the war in heaven—good angels vs. bad—plays out on Earth; Christopher Walken is one scary Gabriel. And a special mention to naughty outer-space romp **Barbarella** (1968), which features the divinely handsome John Phillip Law as a blind "ornithothrope"— that's angel to you—who regains his ability to fly after succumbing to the charms of interstellar good-time girl Barbarella (Jane Fonda). Hey, it was the '60s.

DIRECTOR'S SPOTLIGHT: JOHN FRANKENHEIMER

A curious case, John Frankenheimer: When he was good, he was very, very good and when he was bad he was awful. When Frankenheimer died in 2002 of complications following spinal surgery, many obituary writers waffled, as though afraid to get solidly behind a director whose filmography included such flat-out dreck as eco-scare picture **Prophecy** (1979) and the 1996 remake of **The Island of Dr. Moreau**—to be fair, a project he took over midstream, but still a mind-blowing train wreck chronicling the adventures of a grotesquely obese Marlon Brando and his own personal Mini-Me on freak island.

But Frankenheimer's best was as good as it gets: **The Manchurian Candidate** (1962), **Birdman of Alcatraz** (1962), **Seven Days in May** (1964), **The Train** (1964), the bizarre and undervalued **Seconds** (1966), **The Fixer** (1968), **Black Sunday** (1977)—based on the novel by writer Thomas Harris (*Red Dragon/Silence of the Lambs*) about Palestinian terrorists hijacking and plowing a Goodyear blimp into a packed stadium during the Super Bowl, which today carries a chilling post-9/11 resonance—the unrepentantly sleazy **52 Pick-Up** (1986), and **Ronin** (1998). Born in 1930 and raised in Queens, Frankenheimer flirted with the idea of being a tennis pro or an actor. Credible rumor has it that he was asked to screen-test for the role of James Bond back in the early 1960s, and he made a late-life cameo in trashy thriller **The General's Daughter** (1999). But making documentaries for the Air Force motion-picture squadron, where Frankenheimer did his Korean War–era military service, revealed a knack for directing. Frankenheimer flourished in New York–based live television during the 1950s and turned to movies when it dried up, clinging to the grit, low-key realism, and social consciousness that distinguished the golden age of TV drama.

His first two films were small-scale, above-average problem pictures about troubled teenagers; **The Young Stranger** (1957) was adapted from a teleplay he directed in 1955 and **The Young Savages** (1961), which dealt with gang violence, marked his first (of five) collaborations with actor Burt Lancaster. And then came *The Manchurian Candidate*, whose brilliantly paranoid story of a brainwashed sniper directed by foreign handlers to gun down a major political figure was widely dismissed as preposterous to the core, even as Frankenheimer's moody direction and handling of actors, notably Frank Sinatra and the handsome but often-wooden Lawrence Harvey, was praised. Thirteen months after its October 1962 release, the assassination of President John F. Kennedy cast *The Manchurian Candidate* in a different light. Longtime Kennedy associate Sinatra purchased all rights to the film and then removed it and the unjustly obscure *Suddenly* (1954, directed by Lewis Allen)—in which *he* played a would-be presidential assassin—from circulation. I didn't see the by-then legendary *Manchurian Candidate* until its 1987 theatrical re-release.

Though Frankenheimer made a string of excellent post–*Manchurian Candidate* films, his career took a nosedive after Robert Kennedy's death; a Kennedy insider, Frankenheimer drove the presidential candidate to the Ambassador Hotel the night he was assassinated. He never entirely lost his chops, but for the next twenty-five years his films became so wildly uneven that a lot of us just gave up. He began rehabilitating his reputation in the 1990s by going back to his roots, directing a series of solid historical and issue-oriented films for HBO. His sudden death cruelly quashed *Ronin*'s promise of a full-fledged theatrical comeback. I'll mention the explosive contention of Michael Bay, director of *Bad Boys* (1995) and *Pearl Harbor* (2001), that Frankenheimer may have been his biological father only because if true it's conclusive proof that talent is more than the luck of the genetic draw (Frankenheimer admitted a relationship with Bay's mother but a paternity test was negative in the 1980s, which predated sophisticated DNA testing).

DIRECTOR'S SPOTLIGHT:
WILLIAM FRIEDKIN

William Friedkin's reputation is in tatters, dragged down by a steady stream of mediocre works for hire. But attention must be paid to the filmmaker who made **The French Connection** (1971), **The Exorcist** (1973), **Cruising** (1980), **To Live and Die in L.A.** (1985), and the unfairly maligned **Sorcerer** (1977), a formidable remake of Henri-Georges Clouzot's 1953 film *The Wages of Fear* (see *Director's Spotlight: Henri-Georges Clouzot*).

Born in Chicago in 1935, Friedkin came up through documentary television and began attracting attention with his one-hour documentary **The People vs. Paul Crump** (1962), which made brash use of reenactments, staged interviews, and other traditional documentary no-no's to make the impassioned case that Crump, a black man on death row for his part in a 1953 robbery, had been railroaded. It never aired (private screenings may have helped get Crump's sentence commuted) and Crump may have been guilty, but it put Friedkin on the industry radar. He stumbled through a series of trendy experiments (the 1967 counterculture comedy

Good Times, with Sonny and Cher; 1970's self-hating bitchfest **The Boys in the Band**) before finding his footing: Legendary director Howard Hawks, whose daughter Friedkin was dating, advised him to forget the social-problem stuff and do an action picture. Friedkin made *The French Connection*, a social-problem picture that set the standard for car chases for years to come, showcased star-making performances by Gene Hackman and Roy Scheider as complex, compromised N.Y.C. cops, and attracted hordes of moviegoers despite its muddy morality and downbeat ending. Movies like *The French Connection* are why we look back on the 1970s as the grimy golden age that preceded Hollywood's descent into blockbuster-and-merchandising-driven mediocrity.

After more than thirty years worth of rip-offs, sequels, and parodies, *The Exorcist* still packs a gut punch. Its 2000 theatrical re-release didn't play like gangbusters just because of eleven minutes of additional footage and digitally tweaked special effects: It packed them in because the sheer horror of utter helplessness in the face of forces that defy rational, constructive, scientific solution is as potent today as it was in the social, economic, and spiritual chaos of the 1970s. *Sorcerer* tanked, alienating in one fell swoop *Exorcist* fans (the sorcerer in the title is a truck!), critics hostile to any Hollywood remake of *The Wages of Fear*, and industry moneymen, who watched its ballooning budget with impotent horror. But it's a first-rate suspense film and its much-maligned electronic Tangerine Dream soundtrack—the insinuating accompaniment to a descent into hell on Earth—sounds better than ever. The elegant, ice-cold *To Live and Die in L.A.* is a gripping story of dead souls in constant motion and its chic, limpid look isn't a cynical rip-off of then-popular *Miami*

Vice aesthetics—it's an indictment. *Cruising*'s controversial depiction of gay leather bars and S&M excesses (which I remember vividly as key scenes that were shot on my block) is a provocatively nightmarish vision of identity as a frighteningly unstable set of conventions. The flawed but disturbing **Rampage** (1992), inspired by the 1985 crime spree of "Vampire of Sacramento" Richard Chase and driven by questions about the insanity defense, got lost in the collapse of the DeLaurentiis Entertainment Group; made in 1988, it was shelved for five years and remains virtually unknown.

FROM BAD TO WORSE

Usually a false step means nothing more than a small detour. But sometimes one thing leads to another and before you know it everything has gone to blazes. You can play the scenario for light laughs and come up with **Risky Business** (1983), in which a night with kittenish hooker Rebecca De Mornay nearly derails college-bound suburbanite Tom Cruise's shiny future plans. But more often things play out like **Very Bad Things** (1998), a vicious black comedy that starts in Las Vegas and ends in some circle of hell; along the way, the lives of five friends unravel after they accidentally kill a stripper at groom-to-be Jon Favreau's bachelor party and bad-influence Christian Slater persuades them to hide the body. The low-budget **Stag** (1997), released a year earlier, plays the premise straight; it's the lesser movie but features a great performance by former brat-packer Andrew McCarthy as a sleazy drug dealer. Mild-mannered computer programmer Griffin Dunne ventures into the wilds of Soho in Martin Scorsese's **After Hours** (1985), loses his money, and can't get back to the safe Upper East Side no matter how hard he tries. In Spanish director Alex de la Iglesia's blacker-than-black comedy **Perfect Crime** (2002), a vain, womanizing salesman accidentally kills his rival for the coveted position of floor manager and is blackmailed into near insanity by the homely but unexpectedly shrewd salesgirl who saw him dump the body.

In **The Big Clock** (1948), married true-crime magazine editor Ray Milland, who specializes in finding fugitives before the police, spends an ill-advised night bar crawling with the embittered mistress of his boss, media magnate Charles Laughton; Laughton later kills her in a jealous rage and decides to pin it on her drinking companion, whom he assigns Milland to find. A humiliated job applicant curses corporate suck-up Rick O'Lette (Bill Pullman) in **Rick** (2003), a loose reimagining of *Rigoletto* (scripted by Daniel Handler before he became children's book phenomenon Lemony Snicket), and his life slaloms into the abyss in the days leading up to the company Christmas party, a holly-jolly orgy of insincere corporate cheerleading, forced merriment, and drunken despair. Brothers Bill Paxton and Billy Bob Thornton find a downed plane and a gym bag stuffed with $4.4 million in clearly dirty cash in **A Simple Plan** (1998); their plot to keep the pennies from heaven precipitates a downward spiral that's like a slow-motion highway pileup: You think you don't want to watch, but you can't tear your eyes away.

Wall Street lawyer Ben Affleck and insurance salesman Samuel L. Jackson, a recovering alcoholic enmeshed in a contentious custody battle with his estranged wife, are both rushing to court appearances in Brooklyn when their cars collide in **Changing Lanes** (2002), triggering a calamitous chain of bad decisions, rash acts, and dangerous overreactions.

A deaf, orphaned aspiring artist desperate to pay for his dying sister's kidney transplant kidnaps the child of the man who fired him in Korean director Park Chan-wook's **Sympathy for Mr. Vengeance/Boksuneun naui geot** (2002), and it's hard to say whether what happens next is a comedy punctuated by spasms of calamity or a tragedy studded with grim laughs. Park's even more audacious **Oldboy** (2003) begins with the kidnapping and fifteen-year imprisonment of a thoroughly ordinary man; the brutal, bizarre calamities that follow his inexplicable release culminate in a stroke of hauntingly outrageous misfortune. An angel-faced nineteen-year-old takes the rap for kidnapping and murdering a small boy in **Sympathy for Lady Vengeance/Chinjeolhan geumjassi** (2005), then spends fourteen years in a casually abusive women's prison cultivating a reputation for kindhearted good works while secretly hardening her heart and plotting the payback her duplicitous accomplice richly deserves. Alternately bleakly funny and brutally resonant, it's the perfect conclusion to Park's grimly exhilarating trilogy.

GLITTERING OBJECTS

Some films are so ravishingly beautiful you could drown in them. Kerry Conran's **Sky Captain and the World of Tomorrow** (2004) is a rapturous homage to golden-age pulp magazine fantasies that pits a girl reporter (Gwyneth Paltrow) and an airborne adventurer (Jude Law) against sundry evildoers in a world of flying bat-bots, glittering skyscrapers, gleaming rocket ships, and metal-tentacled robot monsters. It's a mesmerizing fantasia on the theme of yesterday's tomorrows, rendered in a slightly soft, silvery palette that's more than black and white and less than living color. The intersecting stories about bad men and fatal femmes are a bundle of recycled pulp cliches, but **Frank Miller's Sin City** (2005), directed by Robert Rodriguez and Miller, has a look to die for, a mix of live actors and CGI cityscapes rendered in the stark black and white of Miller's graphic novels and film noir's visual vocabulary of glistening shades of gray, all spattered with gouts of primary color.

Francis Ford Coppola calls **One from the Heart** (1982) a fable—about a couple who fight, indulge in brief flings with suave waiter Raul Julia and wide-eyed, lush-lipped, bespangled circus performer Nastassja Kinski, and afterward realize there's no place like home. I'd say it's a "hackneyed breakup/makeup story," but the luscious, color-saturated cinematography and fantasy re-creation of Las Vegas—built entirely on Coppola's newly acquired Zoetrope lot—are intoxicating, and the exquisitely stylized fantasy sequences are the stuff dreams are made of. Jean-Jacques Beineix's **The Moon in the Gutter** (1983) takes tough-guy romantic David Goodis's lurid story about a dockworker (Gérard Depardieu) obsessed with finding the rapist who drove his sister to suicide and sets it in a sweaty, sleazy, surreal fever dream of a Marseille slum. Squalor and despair never looked so dreamy. In Gregg Araki's postmodern road movie **The Doom Generation** (1995), Gen-X guttersnipes Amy Blue (Rose McGowan), Jordan White (James Duval), and Xavier

Red (Johnathon Schaech) go looking for America and find a surreal nightmare of sex and violence op art directed within an inch of its life.

Criminal masterminds aflame for spectacular jewels slink through Mario Bava's **Danger: Diabolik** (1964) and Kenji Fukasawa's **Black Lizard** (1968), wild exercises in 1960s pop-art direction. The glamorous Black Lizard (Kabuki-theater transvestite Akihiro Miwa) worships beauty and has a room full of taxidermied "human dolls" (including novelist/bodybuilder Yukio Mishima) to prove it. Black-masked Diabolik (John Philip Law) and his gorgeous girlfriend (Euro-stunner Marisa Mell) loll on stolen bills in their super-groovy underground hideaway and rob the rich for kicks. You won't remember what happened five minutes later, but the sexadelic ambiance lingers like exotic perfume. James Bidgood's **Pink Narcissus** (1970) is a dazzling succession of arty gay pinup images imagined by a daydreaming hustler (physique model Bobby Kendall); it was shot in bits and pieces between 1964 and 1970, and its lush sets were painstakingly created in photographer/costume designer Bidgood's tiny apartment and look as lavish as an MGM musical's—but be warned: It's porn.

The self-absorbed artist Matthew Barney's Cremaster cycle—**Cremaster 1 & 4** (1996), **Cremaster 2** (1999), **Cremaster 3** (2002), and **Cremaster 5** (1997)—is an epic, mind-bending celebration of freaky images, elusive fragments of narrative, layers of mythic and conspiracy-culture allusions, and Barney's willingness to torture himself and others (from aging *Dr. No* pinup Ursula Andress to legless model Aimee Mullins) into grotesquely surreal forms. You've never seen anything like it. Ever. Bill Morrison's unclassifiable **Decasia**

(2002) finds mesmerizing beauty in pieces of decaying nitrate film, wildly disparate snippets from early silent movies transformed by the bubbles, streaks, and warping of chemical erosion into haunting, dreamlike images.

GO WEST, YOUNG MAN

The Western is America's great, homegrown metaphor for its own fractious, contradictory "man's gotta do what a man's gotta do" history. Dime novels and Wild West shows reworked the morally compromised, hopelessly untidy, and often brutally ugly truth of how the West was won into reassuring fiction as it was still unfolding; legendary lawman Wyatt Earp not only survived the gunfight at the O.K. Corral but lived to befriend silent cowboy stars Tom Mix and William S. Hart and cross paths with both an aspiring director named John Ford and strapping prop boy Marion Morrison, later reborn as John Wayne. Every time it seems as though there isn't *one more word* to be said about the West, someone finds one. So don't consider this list definitive: Just call it a start.

Many fine actors made fine Westerns, but John Wayne and Clint Eastwood helped define them. If John Ford's **Stagecoach** (1939) looks cliched, it's because everybody's stolen from it: He packs a cross-section of frontier society, including principled fugitive the Ringo Kid (Wayne), into a stagecoach and lets their stories unfold against the soon-to-be-iconic backdrop of Utah's Monument Valley. Cynics who dismiss Wayne and Ford as cheerleaders for a simplistic, morally unambiguous view of the West haven't seen **The Searchers** (1956), a dark, complex meditation on violence, racism and self-loathing wrapped around former Confederate soldier Wayne's search for a niece kidnapped by Comanche raiders, while the rueful **Man Who Shot Liberty Valance** (1962) pairs James Stewart and Wayne as tenderfoot and a quiet tough guy, one of whom liberated rough-and-tumble Shinbone from bad man Liberty Valance (Lee Marvin); years later, when the frontier is well and truly tamed, legend trumps fact.

Lanky Eastwood graduated from the '50s TV series *Rawhide* to the spaghetti Westerns (proof positive that America has no monopoly on its own myths) that made him a star: In Sergio Leone's **A Fistful of Dollars** (1964), **For a Few Dollars More** (1965), and **The Good, the Bad and the Ugly** (1966), Eastwood's nameless gunslinger negotiates an absurd, nihilistic, amoral West where men live and die by blind chance. Eastwood brought the spaghetti Western's bitter lessons home in **High Plains Drifter** (1973), a tart fable in which a mysterious stranger forces a desert town to reckon with its ugliest secret, and **Unforgiven** (1992), the melancholy story of a reformed gunfighter forced to acknowledge that killing is what he does best; the stellar supporting cast includes Gene Hackman, Richard Harris, and Morgan Freeman.

Among the classic Westerns, principled gunslinger Alan Ladd defends a family of homesteaders from ruthless cattle barons and their malevolent enforcer (Jack Palance) in **Shane** (1953). The **Ox-Bow Incident** (1942) poses the question "when does a posse become a lynch mob?"; Henry Fonda is outstanding as the voice of reason. Abandoned by cowardly townspeople and at odds with his Quaker bride (Grace Kelly) who abhors violence, newly retired lawman Gary Cooper awaits the arrival of a vengeful outlaw in **High Noon** (1952). Terrorized Mexican villagers hire **The Magnificent Seven** (1960)—gunslingers-for-hire Yul Brynner, Steve McQueen, Charles Bronson, Robert Vaughn, Brad Dexter, James Coburn, and Horst Buchholz—to protect them from a ruthless bandit (Eli Wallach) and his gang in this Americanization of Akira Kurosawa's **Seven Samurai** (1954).

As America grew more cynical, Westerns became more bitter. In Sam Peckinpah's bittersweet **Ride the High Country** (1962), aging lawmen Joel McCrae and Randolph Scott, both painfully aware they've outlived their era, escort a gold shipment through the Sierra Nevada. Set in 1913 Texas, Peckinpah's brutal **The Wild Bunch** (1968) sends William Holden's gang of aging outlaws running smack into the brick wall of modern times, where there's no room for them. The real-life Wild Bunch was a loose-knit gang of outlaws led by Butch Cassidy in the 1890s; **Butch Cassidy and the Sundance Kid**, released the same year as *The Wild Bunch*, bucked the cynical trend; it's a sunny, terrifically entertaining whitewash starring Paul Newman and Robert Redford as dapper rogues who rob trains but don't have a mean bone in their bodies. In the bitter **Ulzana's Raid** (1972), veteran Indian fighter Burt Lancaster and naive cavalry officer Bruce Davison try to stop an Apache raiding party on a rape-and-murder spree. Robert Altman's pipe dream, **McCabe & Mrs. Miller** (1971), weaves a haunting vision of a West built on murder and lies around entrepreneurial gambler Warren Beatty and opium-addicted madam Julie Christie. Even John Wayne lent his gravitas to revisionist Westerns: In **The Cowboys** (1972) he's a veteran cattleman forced to undertake an arduous cattle drive with a crew of schoolboys. In the elegiac **The Shootist** (1976)—his last film—he plays a dying gunslinger who "never killed a man who didn't deserve it" and hopes to go gently into that good night. But what kind of legend dies in his sleep? It's not the American way.

GOOD ENOUGH FOR SECONDS

Conventional wisdom says that remakes are always trash, but there are signficant exceptions, as the following films prove.

The Manchurian Candidate (1962/2004): In John Frankenheimer's adaptation of Richard Condon's cynical Cold War thriller about a plot to rig an American presidential election, the strings are being pulled by Chinese communists; Jonathan Demme's new version updates the power behind the scenes—it's a multinational corporation called Manchurian Global. Both feature phenomenal performances: Angela Lansbury and Meryl Streep as monstrously ambitious mothers, Lawrence Harvey and Liev Schreiber as their sons (veterans of the Korean and Gulf Wars, respectively), and Frank Sinatra and Denzel Washington as the fellow vets who tease out the awful truth.

What Price Hollywood? (1932)/**A Star Is Born** (1937/1954/1976): A grand slam! George Cukor's *What Price* is the template for gimlet-eyed stories about the high cost of dreams, loosely based (by journalist/screenwriter Adela Rogers St. John) on the real-life story of silent star Colleen Moore and her husband, an alcoholic producer; Constance Bennett is the Hollywood up-and-comer who marries a hard-drinking director on the way down. The 1937 *Star* is a tough little number starring Janet Gaynor as the ingenue and Fredric March as her husband, now an actor; the eight screenwriters included Dorothy Parker, Ring Lardner Jr., and Budd Schulberg. Cukor came back for 1954 *Star*, a musical starring the fragile Judy Garland and English matinee idol James Mason; it's the best of the four and one of the definitive behind-the-scenes Hollywood stories. As for the bloated 1976 Barbra Streisand/Kris Kristofferson version, it's not as bad as its reputation suggests and Kristofferson is thoroughly convincing as an arena rocker on the skids. But the only time Streisand stops her brassy, bossy braying is when she lets that magnificent voice rip—there's no vulnerability to her screeching caricature of an ascendant star, and her performance isn't a patch on Garland's vulnerable, heartbreaking portrait of a woman whose love can't save her husband from the demons that nearly take her down as well.

Cat People (1942/1982): In Jacques Tourneur's original, kittenish Simone Simon was tormented by a legend about women whose sexual natures unleash killer panthers; in Paul Schrader's take, alley cat Nastassja Kinski follows in her doomed tracks. Tourneur's Manhattan-set film is a cool, black-and-white nightmare filled with shadows; Schrader's New Orleans variation is a fever dream dripping with sweaty sensuality. Very different, equally haunting.

The Maltese Falcon (1931/1941): Here's a case where the remake is the definitive version. John Huston's pitch-perfect casting included Humphrey Bogart as hard-boiled detective Sam Spade, Mary Astor as the femme fatale, and Peter Lorre, Sidney Greenstreet and Elisha Cook Jr. as the unforgettable gallery of rogues who'll do anything to get their hands on a certain statue of a black bird. But the earlier version of Dashiell Hammett's seminal noir story—later retitled *Dangerous Female*—is more risque (it was made before Hollywood's censorious Production Code took hold in 1934); Ricardo Cortez, a silent-era Latin lover in the Valentino mold (though he was actually Austrian and Jewish) plays Spade as relentless womanizer and Bebe Daniels is a frisky femme. A comic version called **Satan Was a Lady** (1936) came in between (obviously inspired by the success of 1934's *The Thin Man*, based on Hammett's lightest book), but it's a curiosity, noted primarily for the presence of a young Bette Davis as the duplicitous dame.

Scarface (1932/1983): Howard Hawks's crime drama about the rise and fall of an insanely violent gangster (based on real-life hood Al Capone) stars Paul Muni as Chicago-based, Prohibition-era bootlegger Tony Camonte; Brian De Palma's remake turns him into Cuban-born drug lord Tony Montana (Al Pacino) and relocates to Miami. De Palma's film is more graphic but they're both brutal and the new version's incest-tinged subplot comes straight from the original.

Fingers (1978)/**The Beat That My Heart Skipped** (2005): Weird, but it works—French filmmaker Jacques Audiard transplanted James Toback's psychological crime film about a young man (Harvey Keitel, in peak form) torn between becoming a pianist like his late mother or following in the footsteps of his low-level thug father to Paris. Romain Duris put a completely different but totally legitimate spin on Keitel's role: Even Toback liked the result.

King Kong (1933/1976/2005) Tampering with Merian C. Cooper and Ernest B. Schoedsack's original beauty-and-the-beast fable *King Kong* is risky business, and the 1976 man-in-a-gorilla-suit version was a dud of massive proportions (though in retrospect the sight of the brand-spanking-new World Trade Towers might bring a tear to the eye). But Peter Jackson's 2005 remake, in which animal essence meets human hubris with tragic results, is three solid hours of breathless, enchanting entertainment, equal parts razzle-dazzle and pulp poetry. Jackson, such a fan of the original that he painstakingly recreated its legendary lost "spider pit" sequence in glorious black and white just for the thrill of it (the scene is included on the special edition DVD), then did it *again* for his own film, remains true to Kong's fairy-tale heart while using every trick of modern technology to resurrect not one but *two* lost worlds—the neverland of Kong's Skull Island as well as 1930s Manhattan.

GROWING UP IS HARD TO DO

There are children's movies, and then there are movies *about* children. U.K. director Danny Boyle, best known for vicious thrillers like *Shallow Grave* (1994), gives a sharp edge to the fairy-tale-like **Millions** (2005), in which two motherless brothers, a dreamy seven-year-old fascinated by the gory lives of the saints and a pragmatic nine-year-old with a head for finance, find a bag full of stolen money and decide to keep it. French filmmakers Jean-Pierre Jeunet and Marc Caro's **The City of Lost Children** (1995) is a far gloomier fantasy in which an evil genius unable to dream kidnaps the youngsters of a dismal port city so he can plunder their sweet nighttime reveries; but something goes wrong with his dream-catching machine and it extracts nothing but nightmares.

The Bad Seed's (1956) camp reputation belies its fundamentally chilling premise: A quintessential middle-class '50s housewife, who never knew she was adopted and that her biological mother was a murderess, gradually realizes her angelic-looking eight-year-old (Patty McCormack), apparently the sweetest, politest, most mature little moppet in the world, is a spiteful congenital sociopath who blithely murders anyone who thwarts her. The disturbing **Mean Creek** (2004) revolves around three sixth graders whose plan to humiliate the class bully goes horribly wrong, thanks to a volatile teenager who's along for the ride. Luis Bunuel's ferocious **Los olvidados** (1950) is a brutally clear-eyed account of "The Forgotten Ones," Mexican street children trapped in a dismal, marginal existence ruled by neglect and violence. Fernando Meirelles's blistering, exhilarating **City of God** (2002) follows the intertwined destinies of three boys growing up in one of Brazil's lawless, squalid *favelas*—mass-produced slums on the outer fringes of Rio de Janeiro— during the 1970s.

Seven-year-old Brooklynite Joey, convinced that he's accidentally killed his older brother, runs away to Coney Island in the groundbreaking **The Little Fugitive** (1953), an unsentimental slice of New York childhood shot on the fly by former journalists Ray Ashly, Morris Engel, and Engel's wife, photographer Ruth Orkin. Set on Manhattan's pregentrified Upper West Side, Engel and Orkin's **Lovers and Lollipops** (1956) follows a young widow's tentative new relationship through the eyes of her small daughter, who has mixed feelings about her mother's new boyfriend. In Rene Clement's devastating WWII-era **Forbidden Games** (1952), an eleven-year-old country boy and the orphaned five-year-old girl his parents take in cope with the harsh realities of wartime life by building their own secret world that revolves around a hidden animal cemetery where they conduct elaborate memorial services. Carol Reed's **The Fallen Idol** (1948), based on Graham Greene's novel, views the baffling complexities of adult life from the perspective of the neglected eight-year-old son of an often-absent diplomat, who finds a substitute father in the embassy's butler (Ralph Richardson); when the butler's shrewish wife has a fatal accident, the boy's childish efforts to "protect" his idol backfire.

The Rocking Horse Winner (1949) revolves around a sensitive twelve-year-old boy named Paul who discovers that by riding his new rocking horse—a spooky looking thing with a wicked face—so ferociously that his younger sisters cower, he can pick winners at the track and sate his spendthrift parents' endless thirst for money. But the windfalls come at a terrible price. Where Anthony Pelissier's adaptation of D. H. Lawrence's story is a lucid nightmare, Michael Almerayda's 1997 short version, shot in smudgy "pixelvision" using a toy camera—the PXL-2000—manufactured by Fisher-Price in the '80s, pares the story to its bare essentials and has the bleary intensity of a fever dream. In Francois Truffaut's **The 400 Blows** (1959), the first of what eventually became a five-film series about his fictional alter ego Antoine Doinel (Jean-Pierre Leaud), twelve-year-old Antoine is unloved, under-supervised, and on a collision course with juvenile authorities; its poignant concluding freeze-frame has become the international symbol of frustrated youth.

HANGING ON THE TELEPHONE

How did we ever live without the telephone—a whole genre of glossy Italian melodramas were dubbed "white telephone movies" because every swanky suite had one. A witty, vivacious answering-service operator (the gloriously ditzy Judy Holliday), who's secretly in love with "Mr. PLaza0-4433" (velvet-voiced Dean Martin), charms customers with her chatter in **Bells Are Ringing** (1960), but gets so tongue-tied in person that no gentleman caller ever calls twice. It's a delightful musical comedy featuring lyrics by the incomparable Betty Comden and Adolph Green, and music by Jule Styne. A flashback to a time when alcoholism was comical and well-to-do New Yorkers shared phone lines, **Pillow Talk** (1959) is a Technicolor riot of Freudian jokes, white-bread hepcats, swanky populuxe decor, and thinking in voice-over, the epitome of the "risque" romantic comedies that paired professional virgin Doris Day and closeted Rock Hudson. Brittle career gal Day shares a party line with womanizer Hudson and can't get a call in edgewise for his chattering chippies. Its claim to fame is the split-screen phone conversations between Day and Hudson—especially the one from their respective tubs—but the best part is Hudson coyly warning Day about men who are "very devoted to their mothers" and "like to collect cooking recipes and exchange bits of gossip."

In **Sorry, Wrong Number** (1948), wealthy, demanding invalid Leona Stevenson (Barbara Stanwyck) is home alone, trying to call her husband, Henry (Burt Lancaster), when crossed wires let her eavesdrop on two killers plotting to murder a woman later that night. But what woman, and why isn't Henry home? The movie was based on a famous radio play, which veteran exploitation writer-director Larry Cohen heard as a young man and never forgot. Years later, he turned an idea that had been buzzing around in his head since the 1970s into a script called **Phone Booth** (2002), in which philanderer Colin Farrell impulsively picks up a ringing phone in the last booth in Manhattan and finds himself trapped in a high-stakes cat and mouse game with an anonymous psycho (the silky voice of Kiefer Sutherland) with a high-powered rifle and an unobstructed view of his squirming victim. In **I Saw What You Did** (1965), two teenage girls making random prank calls giggle "I saw what you did and I know who you are" to the wrong person: A man who's just murdered his wife. Fourteen-year-old **Lisa** (1990), kept on a frustratingly short leash by her overprotective mom, compensates by cultivating secret telephone relationships with strangers, one of whom turns out to be the notorious "Candlelight Killer"; unjustly condemned to obscurity by a truncated and under-publicized theatrical release, writer-director Gary Sherman's sharply plotted thriller is a small gem that's ripe for rediscovery.

"Have you checked on the children?" In **When a Stranger Calls** (1979), a babysitter—tremulous, doe-eyed Carol Kane—is plunged into a white-knuckle nightmare. The middle is slow and everyone's heard the punch line, but the first twenty minutes is unbeatable. In the suspenseful **Black Christmas** (1974), three sorority sisters—'70s beauties Margot Kidder and Olivia Hussey, plus *Second City TV*'s Andrea Martin—remain on their near-deserted campus over the holidays and are terrorized by an obscene caller. Ringing, chirping, and buzzing phones haunt several recent Asian horror films, starting with the groundbreaking **Ringu** (1998)—a chilling phone call goes hand-in-hand with the skin-crawling videotape. And there's bad mojo on the line in both the bluntly named, Korean-made **Phone** (2002), in which a series of scary cellphone calls turn a sweet little girl into a mini-monster, and gonzo Japanese director Takashi Miike's **One Missed Call** (2003), about a group of friends who start receiving calls from their future selves that predict their imminent deaths. Are you *sure* you wouldn't rather let the answering machine pick up?

DIRECTOR'S SPOTLIGHT:
ALFRED HITCHCOCK

Every time someone makes a halfway decent suspense thriller, someone calls it Hitchcockian—that's how good British-born Alfred Hitchcock, the master of suspense, was. Though he started directing silents and made his last movie at the height of the New Hollywood era of the 1970s, chances are you've only seen **Psycho** (1960), much imitated by lesser filmmakers who learned all the wrong things from this stark tale of a boyish serial killer (Anthony Perkins), his suffocating mother, and the bad things that happen in isolated motel showers. Other delights await.

In **Strangers on a Train** (1951), an ambitious tennis pro with an inconvenient wife meets a spoiled mama's boy whose father stands between him and his inheritance, and the talk turns to reciprocal murder as a solution to their problems. Only one of them is joking. In the underrated **Rope** (1948), a pair of self-proclaimed ubermenschen commit a thrill murder and hide the corpse in a trunk just before the arrival of their dinner guests, including the victim's family and friends; designed to look as though it's shot in one continuous take (impossible with the technology of the time),

Rope is enthrallingly perverse. **Rear Window**'s (1954) peeping protagonist, macho photographer James Stewart, is laid up with a broken leg and gets hooked on watching the soap opera lives of his Greenwich Village neighbors. Then the quarrelsome, bedridden wife of a hulking salesman disappears—did he murder her and smuggle the body parts out in his sample cases?

In the glossy **Dial M for Murder** (1954), a trophy husband blackmails a man into murdering his rich, straying wife (Grace Kelly), but the plan unravels spectacularly when she turns the tables and kills her attacker. Sparks, romantic and larcenous, fly between debonair reformed jewel thief Cary Grant—who may have gone back to his old ways—and American heiress Grace Kelly in the light-as-air French Riviera caper **To Catch a Thief** (1955). There's a spy story hidden somewhere in what may be the greatest of Hitchcock's "Technicolor baubles," **North by Northwest** (1959), but the fun is in the set pieces—Cary Grant chased by a crop-dusting plane, the fight on the face of Mount Rushmore—and bizarre complications.

Detractors call Hitchcock cold, but **Notorious** (1946) seethes with creepy, conflicted desire: Government agent Cary Grant seduces desperately unhappy party-girl Ingrid Bergman, the disgraced daughter of a convicted traitor, then pressures her to serve her country by marrying a mother-fixated Nazi hiding out in Brazil. **Shadow of a Doubt** (1943), which Hitchcock often called his own favorite, is a nail-biting ode to lost innocence, the tale of two Charlies, a small-town girl with big dreams, and the worldly visiting uncle (Joseph Cotten) she idolizes. Dread and regret intertwine as young Charlie's illusions are poisoned by the growing suspicion that debonair Uncle Charlie is the "Merry Widow" strangler wanted by the FBI. And **Vertigo** (1958) may be the most perverse story of obsessive love ever made. Private investigator James Stewart, who has a crippling fear of heights, falls for the troubled rich man's wife (Kim Novak) he's hired to follow, fails to prevent her suicide, then makes over another girl in the dead woman's image, uncovering a wicked crime in the process. The older you get, the more devastating its ending becomes.

HORSE SENSE

D ogs may be man's best friends, but horses carry a hint of the divine. That's no doubt why they figure into so many stories of lost souls who find their way with the help of a handsome steed.

> **The Red Pony** (1949): A poignant adaptation of John Steinbeck's story about a farm boy who escapes his troubled home life by raising a cinnamon-colored colt.

> **National Velvet** (1944): Butcher's daughter Elizabeth Taylor turns a headstrong hunter into a disciplined jumper and rides him all the way to England's Grand National Steeplechase.

> **Smoky** (1946): Utah cowboy Fred MacMurray captures and trains a wild horse, loses him in a cattle raid, and finds him again years later.

> **My Friend Flicka** (1943): Rancher's son Roddy McDowall proves that an unpromising colt is a diamond in the rough.

Run Wild, Run Free (1969): A mute boy's (*Oliver!* star Mark Lester) intense relationship with a white colt helps him re-establish a connection with the world.

Seabiscuit (2003): Based on a true story, enigmatic trainer Chris Cooper and damaged jockey Tobey Maguire turn a runty, headstrong, crook-legged horse into a winner who captures the imagination of Depression-era America.

The Black Stallion (1979): Shipwrecked on a deserted island, a boy and an Arabian stallion form a bond that holds even after they return to civilization.

Black Beauty (1971): Based on Anna Sewell's classic children's novel (which reduced me to tears when I first read it), this picaresque tale follows a handsome black horse through a string of owners, some cruel and some kind.

Into the West (1993): An enchanting story about motherless Irish brothers who rediscover their gypsy heritage through a mysterious white horse.

Phar Lap (1984): A trainer and a stable boy turn a New Zealand–born horse with no pedigree into the toast of the Australian racing world; based on a true story.

HOW LONG HAS THIS
BEEN GOING ON?

With some movies—any Pauly Shore comedy, say—eighty-five minutes feels like a lifetime. With others, you check your watch when the credits roll and can't believe more than two hours have gone by. Some movies are so engrossing that that the butt-numbing factor ceases to matter; every film on this list runs more than two hours, and every one is worth every minute. And no, *Titanic* (1997) didn't make the cut—it's insipid—but *Heaven's Gate* (1980) does: I stood in line to see the first and longest theatrical version of *Heaven's Gate* and all the studio infighting and gossipy "the movie that sank venerable United Artists" press aside, it's a damned good movie. Bear in mind that some of these movies exist in multiple versions with different running times.

> Francis Ford Coppola's **Apocalypse Now** (1979): 156 minutes (the 2001 **Apocalypse Now Redux** runs 202 minutes, and while some great scenes are restored, I think it plays better at the shorter length)
>
> Brian De Palma's **Scarface** (1983): 170 minutes

D. W. Griffith's **Intolerance** (1916): 178 minutes

Michael Cimino's **The Deer Hunter** (1978): 183 minutes

Steven Spielberg's **Schindler's List** (1993): 185 minutes

Stanley Kubrick's **Spartacus** (1960): 196 minutes

Akira Kurosawa's **Seven Samurai** (1954): 200 minutes

George Stevens's **Giant** (1956): 201 minutes

Spike Lee's **Malcolm X** (1992): 202 minutes

William Wyler's **Ben-Hur** (1959): 212 minutes

Michael Cimino's **Heaven's Gate** (1980): 216 minutes

David Lean's **Lawrence of Arabia** (1962): 216 minutes

Victor Fleming (and George Cukor and Sam Wood)'s **Gone with the Wind** (1939): 220 minutes

Abel Gance's **Napoleon** (1927): 234 minutes

Erich von Stroheim's **Greed** (1925): 240 minutes (this length refers to the 1999 reconstruction in which production stills stand in for some of the missing sequences; at its longest, *Greed* ran close to nine hours long)

Ronald F. Maxwell's **Gettysburg** (1993): 261 minutes

Wolfgang Petersen's **Das Boot** (1981): 293 minutes

Hans-Jurgen Syberberg's **Our Hitler: A Film from Germany** (1977): 450 minutes

Peter Jackson's *Lord of the Rings* trilogy:

The Lord of the Rings: The Fellowship of the Ring (2001): 208 minutes

The Lord of the Rings: The Two Towers (2002): 222 minutes

The Lord of the Rings: The Return of the King (2003): 251 minutes

HUSH!

Sound came to the movies in 1927, and early cineastes wailed that the art of visual storytelling would be lost in the incessant chatter while regular moviegoers fell instantly in love with the talkies. The naysayers weren't completely wrong: You can follow the average movie with your eyes shut, while with the sound off you're lost. The fun of the movies listed below is seeing filmmakers come up with creative ways to pare down the dialogue without giving the story short shrift.

One of the best-loved and least sentimental children's films, **The Red Balloon** (1956) chronicles the friendship of a lonely French schoolboy and the large red balloon that follows him like a dog; its images tell the story so skillfully that many people don't realize there's no dialogue until it's pointed out. The sweetly sinister, animated **Triplets of Belleville** (2003), also French, plunges a tiny, determined, club-footed granny into an intricately imagined, virtually wordless big-city underworld where her kidnapped grandson is being held by gangsters. French comedian Jacques Tati's alter ego, the lanky, unfailingly polite one-man disaster area Mr. Hulot, is as iconic in France as Charlie Chaplin's little tramp; he debuted in **Mr. Hulot's Holiday** (1953), taking a seaside vacation and leaving everwidening ripples of chaos in his wake; though there's almost no dialogue, Tati employs a rich repertory of sound effects and music.

French action filmmaker Luc Besson's first feature, the stylish, black-and-white **Le dernier combat** (1983), takes place in a speechless postapocalyptic world where it rains fish, everyone is mute, and a young Jean Reno plays "The Brute." A unique Cold

War thriller, **The Thief** (1952) stars Ray Milland as an American nuclear-physicist-turned-spy haunted by having betrayed his country: not one word from beginning to end. Shot in black and white and colorized in jewel-toned washes of red, gold, and blue, the whimsical, near-wordless fable **Tuvalu** (2001) is set in an ornate but sadly dilapidated Bulgarian bathhouse; love triumphs over greed and bad plumbing. The oddball **Dementia** (1953) uses sound effects but no speech and unfolds at the intersection of avant-garde and exploitation, following a beatnik chick as she wanders through run-down Venice, California, kills a man, and is haunted by his mutilated ghost, all to the discordant strains of George Antheil's experimental score. A slightly re-edited version called **Daughter of Horror** features voice-over narration by Johnny Carson's future *Tonight Show* sidekick Ed McMahon. The sly Hungarian **Hukkle** (2001) is a chilling murder mystery wrapped in an experimental portrait of life in a rural town; it unfolds in striking images—a mole eating an earthworm in an underground tunnel, lilies of the valley exploding through the soil, bones visible like an x-ray—and a symphony of sounds.

David Lynch's **Eraserhead** (1978) and **Tetsuo: The Iron Man** (1988) favor nightmarish images over words. *Eraserhead*, an anxiety attack on film, revolves around an alienated loner with a *Bride of Frankenstein* coif and his mutated, perpetually crying baby; little is said, but the soundtrack is full of ominous sighs, rumbles, clangs, clatters, squeals, plus a freaky little ditty called "In Heaven." In the cyberpunk *Tetsuo*, an office worker accidentally runs down a self-mutilating metal fetishist and somehow "catches" his disease, which triggers his slow, bizarre transformation into a tortured man-machine. The minimal dialogue is repetitive and muffled. The polarizing **Begotten** (1991) is a hellish, completely wordless creation myth told in painstakingly distressed images of disembowelment, torture, and seriously creepy sex accompanied by a disturbingly squishy soundtrack; love it or hate it, it's unforgettable—believe me, I've tried.

I GOT THE MUSIC IN ME

There are all kinds of terrible movies about all kinds of musicians, but these movies pull off the biopic trifecta: interesting lives, strong acting, and showstopping musical performances. No wonder the word *Oscar* recurs with such frequency.

Sissy Spacek won a well-deserved Academy Award for her portrayal of legendary country singer Loretta Lynn, the **Coal Miner's Daughter** (1980), and earned a Grammy nomination for her versions of Lynn's songs about the poverty, heartache, and cruel turns of fate she knew all too well. So did Joaquin Phoenix and Reese Witherspoon for their "hotter than a pepper sprout" portrayals of Johnny Cash and June Carter—later June Carter Cash—in **Walk the Line** (2005), which focuses on their long, complicated courtship and his battle against addiction and despair; both also performed all their own songs and captured Cash and Carter's body language with eerie precision. Surprisingly, David Carradine was overlooked for what should have been his star-making performance as activist folk singer Woody Guthrie in **Bound for Glory** (1976), which racked up six other nominations and won two.

The cast of Robert Altman's breathtaking **Nashville** (1975), a razor-sharp dissection of American self-mythologizing through the prism of the country-music industry, went one step farther: They not only sang their own numbers, but wrote them as well. The singer-songwriters include Karen Black, Barbara Harris (try to get her bluesy "It Don't Worry Me" out of your head), Ronee Blakely— her performance as emotionally fragile, Loretta Lynn–like Nashville royalty Barbara Jean sends chills down my spine, and her signature song, "My Idaho Home," brings me to tears—and Keith Carradine (David's half brother), whose smug country-rock crossover composition "I'm Easy" won a Best Original Song Oscar and became a hit.

The crowd-pleasing **Shine** (1996) recounts the stranger-than-fiction travails of Australian piano virtuoso David Helfgott, a child prodigy who spiraled into madness; then unknown Australian actor Geoffrey Rush, who played the adult Helfgott, not only won an Academy Award but saw his career skyrocket.

Both Kirk Douglas and granite-faced *Dragnet* creator and star Jack Webb both played thinly veiled versions of jazz cornet Bix Beiderbecke, who drank himself to death at age twenty-eight. Douglas's unsparing **Young Man with a Horn** (1959) features performances by Hoagy Carmichael—whom Biederbecke encouraged to write music—Lauren Bacall as a twisted rich girl, and former band singer Doris Day as a torchy chanteuse (rumor has it that her turbulent early life inspired Liza Minnelli's character in Martin Scorsese's 1977 **New York, New York**). Big-band-era trumpeter and bandleader Harry James dubbed Douglas's playing. Webb's **Pete**

Kelly's Blues (1955) boasts convincing down-and-dirty atmosphere and an impressive roster of world-class jazz performers, including Matty Matlock, Moe Schneider, George Van Eps, Ella Fitzgerald, and Peggy Lee; Webb's playing was dubbed by trumpeter Dick Cathcart. A tribute to the life and genius of Charlie "Yardbird" Parker, **Bird** (1988) was a labor of love for lifelong jazz fan Clint Eastwood, who as a teenager played jazz piano in local clubs; it's anchored by Forest Whitaker's portrayal of the tormented saxophonist and featuring previously unreleased Parker solos painstakingly restored by Eastwood and musical director Lennie Niehaus.

The wrenching **Hilary and Jackie** (1998) tells the story of world-renowned classical cellist Jacqueline du Pre (Emily Watson), whose brilliant career was cut cruelly short by multiple sclerosis, through her relationship with her loyal, less incandescently talented sister, flutist Hilary (Rachel Griffiths). The hugely entertaining **Amadeus** (1984) depicts musical prodigy Wolfgang Amadeus Mozart as a sort of amiable eighteenth-century punk who lived fast, died young, and gave rein to the anarchic impulses of a child, while forging a genuinely provocative philosophical debate from the fanciful rumor that Mozart was poisoned by jealous rival Antonio Salieri (F. Murray Abraham). Both Hulce and Abraham were Oscar nominees, and in the sort of irony you wouldn't dare make up it was Abraham who won.

IT CAME FROM THE TV

I've tackled a wide range of movie-related topics in my online column Ask FlickChick, but the most popular kind of question starts "I once saw this movie and all I remember is a scene where . . ." and ends "my friends think I made it up—can you help me with a title?" And it wasn't long before I realized how many of the indelible images haunting my readers—a woman terrorized by a spear-wielding doll, a disturbed boy living behind the walls, a young wife tormented by wizened gremlins—came from made-for-TV horror/sci-fi/thrillers that first aired in the 1970s and early '80s. These are the all-time champs, most of which I saw when they were new and am pleased to report hold up surprisingly well, despite downscale production values and the choppy pacing that comes with building in regularly spaced commercial breaks.

There are three stories in **Trilogy of Terror** (1975), but only one matters: Timid Karen Black buys a toothy little African fetish figure called He-Who-Kills that comes to chattering, malevolent life and terrorizes her—the last shot is sheer, creepy genius. Gay filmmaker David Briggs's smart-alecky short **Karen Black Like Me** (1997) reimagines it with Black and He-Who-Kills replaced by a prissy sissy and a humongous animated dildo; it's a one-joke movie, but the joke is great. Easily intimidated young wife Kim Darby inherits a ramshackle house from her grandmother in **Don't Be Afraid of the Dark** (1973), only to find after she and her ambitious, status-conscious husband have moved in that it comes complete with scary little creatures that drive her half mad with fear; the downbeat ending is bracingly cruel. Another young wife (Hope Lange) inherits property—the rambling **Crowhaven Farm** (1970)—and convinces herself that moving will shore up her shaky marriage until the vivid nightmares about witches start; the scene everyone remembers involves a Pilgrim woman being pressed to death under a board piled high with stones. In **Bad Ronald** (1974), an outcast teenager accidentally kills a girl and his overprotective mother constructs a secret room behind the walls of their house where he can hide; she dies unexpectedly and the house is sold to a family that has no idea there's someone watching their every move. A bright, inexplicably angry teenager learns that she's a clone in **Anna to the Infinite Power** (1983), whose banal direction, flat cinematography, and wooden acting actually make the conspiracy more disturbing.

Divers find the long-lost wreck of a WWII-era luxury liner in **Goliath Awaits** (1981) and discover an amazing secret: 240 survivors and descendents are still aboard, and their ingenious, tightly run underwater society isn't as idyllic as it first seems. In **The Bermuda Depths** (1978), an orphaned college student still haunted by his father's long-ago death returns to Bermuda and finds the mysterious childhood love whose portentous name—Jennie Haniver—he once carved into the shell of a giant sea turtle. The effects are rudimentary by today's standards, but I get more mail about this one than most of the others combined. Rumpled reporter Karl Kolchak (Darrin McGavin) got his own series after tracking down a Las Vegas vampire in **The Night Stalker** (1972) and a one-hundred-year-old killer cutting a bloody swath through Seattle in **The Night Strangler** (1973). Finally, after years of trying to match a title to a scene in which a girl dies in a burning car, unable to escape because a sibling tied her shoelaces together as a prank, I figured out I was looking for **Don't Go to Sleep** (1982) and tracked down a copy. Is a vengeful little-girl ghost really maneuvering members of her family into fatal "accidents," or are they punishing themselves for their complicity in her death? This seriously spooky psychological thriller is a real gem.

IT'S A MIXED-UP, MUDDLED-UP, SHOOK-UP WORLD

So you think gender confusion is a modern muddle? Consider William Shakespeare's four-hundred-year-old **Twelfth Night** (1996): Shipwrecked Viola (Imogen Stubbs) assesses her prospects as a penniless foreign woman and decides she's better off presenting herself as a beardless lad named Cesario. She falls for the lovesick Duke who hires her as his page, reluctantly agrees to help him woo an aloof countess (Helena Bonham Carter), and finds herself fending off the smitten lady's advances. In the delightfully clever **Shakespeare in Love** (1998), the struggling Will (Joseph Fiennes) falls victim to his own narrative tricks; while writing *Romeo and Juliet*, he falls in love with a lady of the court (Gwyneth Paltrow) who, unable to audition for Juliet because Elizabethan society forbids women to act, wins the part of Romeo while dressed as a man.

Romantic entanglements get very tangled in **Sylvia Scarlett** (1935), as a woman on the lam (the coltish Katharine Hepburn) disguises herself as a gangly young man. In the sparkling **Some Like It Hot** (1959), regularly voted the best comedy ever, musicians Tony Curtis and Jack Lemmon hide out from gangsters by joining an all-girl band and find their love lives getting very problematic; Marilyn Monroe is at her breathy best as singer Sugar Kane. In **Tootsie** (1982), vain, egomaniacal, and unemployable actor Dustin Hoffman wins a soap opera role by pretending to be an actress named Dorothy Michaels, which complicates his personal life while opening his eyes to what a jerk he is. A small gem set in 1950s Brooklyn, **Mob Queen** (1999) revolves around two small-time flunkies trying to impress their boss with the gift of a classy hooker, not realizing she's a girl with something extra.

Gender confusion isn't always a laughing matter. Twenty years after James Dean's death, members of a small-town Texas fan club—including Cher, Sandy Dennis, and Kathy Bates—hold a reunion in **Come Back to the Five and Dime, Jimmy Dean, Jimmy Dean** (1982). But why doesn't anyone remember Joanne (Karen Black), who seems to know everything about them? Oddball cult item **Liquid Sky** (1983) is a layer cake of sex, drugs, murder, performance art, and UFOs; androgynous actress Anne Carlisle's dual performance as perpetual victim Margaret and male model Larry is the icing.

Stage Beauty (2004), the flip side of *Shakespeare in Love*, spins a story about celebrity and fickle fans around real-life seventeenth-century actor Edward Kynaston (Billy Crudup), whose success in women's roles attracts fans of both sexes. Simultaneously epic and intimate, **Farewell My Concubine** (1993) folds fifty tumultuous years of Chinese history into the relationship between two stars of the all-male Peking Opera whose lives echo their signature roles in the tragic romance *Farewell my Concubine*. **M. Butterfly** (1993) tells the fascinating true story of a French diplomat (Jeremy Irons) who never realized that his longtime lover, a glamorous opera star spying for the Chinese government, was a man.

In **The Crying Game** (1992), a low-level IRA member promises to look after the girlfriend of a doomed prisoner, only discovering the most talked-about plot twist of the early '90s after he's fallen in love with the bewitching Dil (Jaye Davidson). Finally, Hilary Swank's wrenching performance in **Boys Don't Cry** (1999) brings the real-life tragedy of Teena Brandon into vivid focus; a small-town dreamer who reversed her name to Brandon Teena, she enjoyed the life of a charismatic young man until the masquerade was discovered and triggered a brutal backlash.

IT'S ALL TRUE

Gone are the days when the word *documentary* inevitably meant dull: These stylish, engaging films are good and good for you.

Vintage promotional, classroom, and industrial films, with their mix of naive optimism, ham-fisted scare tactics, and blatant propaganda, vividly reflect changing mores. **The Atomic Cafe** (1982) uses them to examine Cold War paranoia and the military-industrial complex's love affair with atom bombs. **Hell's Highway: The True Story of Highway Safety Films** (2003) incorporates them into the weird story of highway safety crusader Rick Wayman, who invented "scared safe" driver's ed films. **The Last Cigarette** (1999) weaves together a crazy quilt of American cultural attitudes about smoking, while **Grass** (2000) offers a hipster's eye view of the war against marijuana.

DVD extras have made the phrases *behind the scenes* and *promotional puff piece* interchangeable, but these films take a bracingly clear-eyed look at moviemaking. **Lost in La Mancha** (2003) bears witness to the collapse of veteran fantasist Terry Gilliam's *The Man Who Killed Quixote*, buffeted by a perfect storm of mistakes, unforeseeable calamities, and nervous financiers. "Every gray hair on my head I call Kinski," sighs German director Werner Herzog in **My Best Fiend: Klaus Kinski** (1999), which examines the dynamics of collaboration in light of the five films he made with the volatile actor. **Overnight** (2004) chronicles the sudden success of brash Troy Duffy, who rode a screenplay called **The Boondock Saints** (1999) into the kind of sweet deal aspiring filmmakers dream about and torpedoed it through sheer, overweening arrogance.

Love him or hate him, gadfly Michael Moore gets the blood up and the conversation going. His debut, **Roger & Me** (1989), probes the protracted decline of his hometown of Flint, Michigan, a one-industry town whose fortunes rise and fall at the whim of auto giant General Motors; **Bowling for Columbine** (2002) takes on America's gun culture. Morgan Spurlock's **Super Size Me** (2004) charts the frightening results of a thirty-day, all-McDonald's diet on his health and appearance. Errol Morris's **The Thin Blue**

Line (1988) investigates the murder of a Texas cop and its aftermath, which sent an innocent man to death row; it's as gripping as any thriller. Morris's quirky follow-ups include **Fast, Cheap & Out of Control** (1997), about four passionate eccentrics, and **The Fog of War: Eleven Lessons from the Life of Robert S. McNamara** (2003).

In the Realms of the Unreal (2004) immerses itself in the imagination of reclusive janitor Henry Darger, whose unremarkable existence hid a bizarrely elaborate fantasy life recorded in a seventy-thousand-page sci-fi epic illustrated with hundreds of bizarre collage/paintings of monsters and naked little girls with horns, butterfly wings, and penises. The uniquely weird **Hybrid** (2000) chronicles an Iowa farmer's life-long obsession with corn hybridization and uses Quay Brothers–like animation to bring ears of corn to creepy, skittering life.

For armchair nature lovers, **Winged Migration** (2001) offers close-up footage of birds in flight so freakishly intimate that the film opens with an assurance that no special effects were used. **Microcosmos** (1996) uses microphotography to spy on bug life, while **Deep Blue** (2004) not only plumbs the deep sea's wonders—freakish hammerhead sharks, stinging coral polyps, and the pale, phosphorescent things lurking in the blackness of the ocean floor—but includes sights like shearwater birds diving beneath the water's surface and using their wings as fins to compete with seals and marlin for food. **March of the Penguins** (2005) follows comically dignified emperor penguins on their grueling annual trek across miles of bitterly cold ice to mate, brood their eggs, and raise their chicks. Their trevails earned a best documentary Oscar.

THE JOY OF GIALLO

N ever again need you stand in embarrassed silence while smug eurotrashiastes debate the relative merits of obscure *gialli* when you don't even know what they're talking about. *Giallo* (plural *gialli*) just means "yellow" in Italian, but it describes a loose-knit group of flamboyantly violent thrillers, mostly Italian and made in the 1960s and '70s. (The term arose from the distinctive yellow book covers slapped on translations of American and English mystery novels and, later, original Italian-language thrillers by Milan's Mondadori Publishing.) Strictly speaking, they're just convoluted mysteries like Agatha Christie's *Ten Little Indians*, but connoisseurs treasure the genre's perversely elaborate murder scenes, ornate titles, riotous psychedelic fashions and decor, wild jazz-pop scores, nude and near-nude starlets (Edwige Fenech, Barbara Bouchet, Florinda Bolkan, et al.), and the overall aura of sleaziness.

The great-granddaddy of all *gialli* is sublimely stylish director Mario Bava's **Blood and Black Lace** (1964), in which a black-gloved sadist murders the models of Christian Haute Couture. Bava's disciple, Dario Argento, helped perfect the formula. His **Deep Red/Profondo rosso** (1976) revolves around Rome-based Englishman David Hemmings, who saw something that could solve a murder and needs to figure out what it was before the murderer gets to him; the score by prog-rockers Goblin is mind-blowing. Argento's **Tenebrae** (1982) and **Opera** (1987) are worthy successors, lushly photographed and baroquely cruel.

Aldo Lado's **Short Night of the Glass Dolls** (1971) and **Who Saw Her Die?** (1972) are high-water marks of sheer bizarreness.

Glass Dolls opens with the discovery of a foreign reporter's corpse in a Prague park ... except that he's not dead, only drugged into catatonia while his mind remains frantically active; utterly weird, from the tortured tomatoes (you read that right: tomatoes subjected to horrid experiments) to the cruel climax. In *Who Saw Her Die?*, bereaved American artist George Lazenby hunts the child murderer who killed his daughter in Venice; Ennio Morricone's crazed, children's choir-heavy score is simply delirious. Another freaky child killer stalks a small Italian town in cannibal-zombie specialist Lucio Fulci's **Don't Torture a Duckling** (1972), featuring Bouchet as a nymphomanical rich girl; the murderer's disturbing phone calls, delivered in a Donald Duck voice, are unforgettable. Fulci's **Lizard in a Woman's Skin** (1971) whips together decadent jet-setters, English aristocrats, and drugged-out hippies into a freaky frappe of false leads and bizarre dream sequences connected to the murder of a depraved beauty.

A missing schoolgirl is the key to a series of vicious killings in **What Have You Done to Solange?** (1972), but her debauched classmates have their own sordid secrets. Trampy models are the victims in trashy treat **What Are Those Strange Drops of Blood on Jennifer's Body?** (1972)—also called **Night of the Bloody Iris**—but the sleaziest of them all is **Strip Nude for Your Killer** (1975), which starts with a model dying during a back-alley abortion. The doctor and an accomplice try to make it look as though she had a heart attack in her bathtub, but someone knows otherwise. Soon the lying, backstabbing, money-grubbing, frequently naked sexual predators of Milanese fashion photo house Studio Albatross, where the dead model worked, are being murdered, and they're all so unrepentantly awful you're almost rooting for the killer.

JUST BECAUSE YOU'RE PARANOID . . .

Behind the official story, there's always another story. The assassination of President John F. Kennedy was God's gift to suspicious minds, but it's only the tip of the iceberg.

Executive Action (1973): As somber and melancholy as Oliver Stone's better-known *JFK* (1991) is smoking, stuttering mad, this unfairly forgotten thriller is just as convinced that Lee Harvey Oswald was a patsy for a cabal of disgruntled fat cats.

Winter Kills (1979): A wealthy political family, a ruthless patriarch (John Huston), and an assassinated president whose younger brother (Jeff Bridges) gets wind of a convoluted plot are played for pitch-black comedy.

The Parallax View (1974): Three years after a senator is killed by a waiter at the Space Needle restaurant (shades of Robert F. Kennedy's assassination in the kitchen of the Ambassador Hotel), all the witnesses are dead and newspaper reporter Warren Beatty uncovers a sinister connection to the mysterious Parallax Corporation.

These films explore other plots and plotters.

Seven Days in May (1964): General Kirk Douglas suspects that his boss, hard-line Chairman of the Joint Chiefs of Staff Burt Lancaster, is plotting a military coup against "soft on Soviets" president Fredric March; director John Frankenheimer also made 1962's deeply paranoid *The Manchurian Candidate* (see *Good Enough for Seconds*).

The Day of the Jackal (1973): A riveting adaptation of
Frederick Forsyth's novel, which details the meticulous
preparations of professional assassin "The Jackal" (Edward
Fox) for his murder of French president Charles de Gaulle
at the behest of a secret French military cabal, and the
law's efforts to stop him; the 1997 remake, *The Jackal*, jetti-
sons most of the story for generic bang-bang posturing by
Bruce Willis, Richard Gere, Sidney Poitier, et al.

Three Days of the Condor (1975): Bookish, bottom-rung
CIA employee Robert Redford (code name: Condor)
comes back from lunch to find his co-workers dead and
his days numbered.

Capricorn One (1978): Slack execution, but a great premise—what if the naysayers who claim man never walked
on the moon were right?

Cutter and Bone (1981): Beach bum Jeff Bridges thinks
he sees a local bigwig disposing of a corpse and his old
friend, crippled Vietnam veteran John Heard, sets off a
brutal chain of events by trying to blackmail him.

Chinatown (1974): Hired to follow a cheating husband, low-
rent detective Jack Nicholson uncovers a tangle of murder
and institutionalized corruption.

THE KILLER MUST KILL AGAIN

I confess that I have a serious weakness for movies about multiple
murderers, but if I had a dollar for every formulaic slash-'em-
up I've sat through, I could retire to my dream house—which

would, of course, come equipped with excellent locks. These pictures all got under my jaded skin.

Roly-poly Peter Lorre, not yet slimmed down by Hollywood, is a tormented child killer hunted by cops and criminals alike in Fritz Lang's chilling **M** (1931), inspired by "Vampire of Dusseldorf" Peter Kurten, who terrorized post-WWI Germany. Kurten's contemporary, "Butcher of Hanover" Fritz Haarman, inspired Ulli Lommel's **Tenderness of the Wolves** (1971), produced by Rainer Werner Fassbinder and starring hulking Fassbinder regular Kurt Raab as a black marketeer who preys on runaway boys. The real-life murders in 1949 (by "Lonely Hearts" killers Ray Fernandez and Martha Beck) of lonely women who answered personal ads are dramatized in the stark **The Honeymoon Killers** (1969), starring Tony Musante and Shirley Stoller; original director Martin Scorsese was replaced by one-shot-wonder Leonard Kastle, who delivered a seriously creepy film. Mexican director Arturo Ripstein transplanted the story to northern Mexico and gave it a darkly comic spin in **Deep Crimson** (1997).

Director John McNaughton took his cue from the lengthy killing spree of drifters Henry Lee Lucas and Otis Toole for his **Henry: Portrait of a Serial Killer** (1986), a documentary-like chronicle of the day-to-day grind of day in/day out murder, anchored by Michael Rooker and Tom Towles's unsparing performances; the result was so bone-chilling that it sat on the shelf for three years and earned an X rating. Chuck Parello's **Henry: Portrait of a Serial Killer 2** (1998) gets a bum rap; it suffers from Rooker's absence, but it's still a chilling exploration of miserable malaise that unfolds at the intersection of blue-collar despair and stone psychosis.

Peeping Tom (1960), a sympathetic portrait of a multiple murderer (Carl Boehm) who films his victims just before he kills them, was critically lambasted and ruined the career of veteran U.K. director Michael Powell (*The Red Shoes*), but was rediscovered in the '80s after director Martin Scorsese championed it. I prefer Michael Mann's limpid **Manhunter** (1986) to Jonathan Demme's **Silence of the Lambs** (1990) largely because I find actor Brian Cox's smoothly insinuating interpretation of Dr. Lecter far more disturbing than Anthony Hopkins's hammy posturing. David Fincher's rhapsodically gloomy **Se7en** (1995) is a brilliant variation on the "killer with a system" formula, in which a fiendish psychopath is committing killings based on the seven deadly sins, but I have a soft spot for the low-rent **Resurrection** (1999), which features Christopher Lambert as a traumatized cop on the trail of a religious fanatic who's murdering victims with biblical names and absconding with various body parts. What could he be doing with them?

The really nasty, Hong Kong–made **Dr. Lamb** (1992) stars Simon Yam as a taxi driver on a mission to slaughter "dirty" women; the movie's contrast between grisly horror and slapstick humor is truly bizarre. And that brings us full circle to Germany and the sleazily enthralling **Tattoo** (2002), a procedural that pits mismatched cops against a sadistic uber-killer who targets alienated hipsters and skins the elaborate tattoos right off their bodies. All together now: Ewwwwwwwwww!!!!!

LANDMARK THEATRE

There are two kinds of fans in the world: those who make lists and those who don't. For those who don't and would like to understand those who do, I recommend **High Fidelity** (2000), based on Nick Hornby's novel and starring John Cusack as a die-hard music lover trying to make sense of life through compulsive, eccentric list making. Every cinemaniac has a highly personal list of movie landmarks, and this is mine; yours may be entirely different, but if you haven't seen these pictures, your bona fides are in danger.

Quo vadis? (1912). Back when the average movie was less than half an hour long, this Italian historical epic delivered a whopping two hours of pagan Roman debauchery, martyred Christians, chariot races, and the spectacle of Rome in flames. Its U.S. distributor cut it in half, ignored savvy showmen who sneered it was still twice the length audiences would tolerate, and made a bundle. The days of one-reelers were numbered.

The Cabinet of Dr. Caligari (1919) and **Battleship Potemkin** (1925). These groundbreakers in the use of film language put the world on notice: Just because film captures the image of real things, creating the seamless illusion of reality isn't the only way to tell a story. Influenced by German Expressionist art—which depicts inner reality, not surface appearances—*Caligari*'s insanely distorted sets cast the story of the three friends who run afoul of sinister carnie Caligari and his fortune-telling somnambulist in a uniquely nightmarish light. Russian filmmaker Sergei Eisenstein gave a fact-based story of sailors rebelling against Czarist troops poetic and metaphorical depth through highly stylized editing, using repetition, contrast, and creative juxtaposition to make the building blocks of realistic images add up to more than the simple sum of their parts. Contrary to naysayers' predictions, moviegoers got it.

The Jazz Singer (1927). Popular jazz singer Al Jolson declared "You ain't heard nothing yet!" and everyone listened. Its story of American-born children clashing with their old-world parents was already old hat (and still rehashed regularly, witness 2005's **The Gospel**), it wasn't technically the *very* first sound film, and Jolson's blackface routine is painfully out of sync with modern sensibilities. But after it opened, silent movies were yesterday's news.

Snow White and the Seven Dwarfs (1937). Three years in the making and wildly overbudget, this gorgeous, richly imagined fairy tale was derided as "Disney's Folly"—who would sit through a feature-length cartoon?—until its triumphant opening night. *Hello*, feature-length animation.

Citizen Kane (1941). *Wunderkind* Orson Welles reset the bar for mainstream filmmaking, combining a gripping story about corrosive power, media manipulation, and the dark side of the American dream with an artfully fractured narrative, a dazzling synthesis of innovative editing, cinematography, and set design, and flawless performances.

Rome: Open City (1945), Roberto Rossellini's innovative fusion of documentary and melodrama, was shot before, during, and immediately after the Allied liberation of Italy during WWII, cast with non-professionals—the exception, earthy sex symbol Anna Magnani, was a dance-hall girl—and shot on location without sync sound and using scavenged stock. Its story of wartime resistance and betrayal verges on the cliched, but its raw immediacy lit a fire under filmmakers weaned on the polished control of studio filmmaking.

Breathless/À bout de souffle (1959). One of the first commercial movies made by serious film buffs, *Breathless* was the creation of critics Francois Truffaut and Jean-Luc Godard, whose intellectual hipster spin on Hollywood gangster movies ushered in a new world of homage and self-referentiality. Can you say "Quentin Tarantino"?

Sweet Sweetback's Baadasssss Song (1971). It stars "The Black Community," opens with a dedication "to all the Brothers and Sisters who had enough of the Man," and ends with the promise that "A Baad Asssss Nigger is coming back to collect some dues." One angry, defiantly DIY, kick in the groin of a movie, wholly financed by writer-director-star Melvin Van Peebles. The ur-Blaxploitation movie, an inspiration to African American actors and filmmakers and proof to outsiders of every ethnicity, class, race, and persuasion that the system can be beaten.

Deep Throat (1972). The blue movie that brought porn out of the gutter and onto the talk-show circuit. Not great smut by today's standards—too much story, too little silicone— but it ran a carnally candid banner up the flagpole and America saluted.

Jaws (1975) and **Star Wars** (1977). Good movies, bad lessons. The one-two punch that made merchandising king and infected studio executives with blockbuster fever, leading them to abandon the old-fashioned strategy of spreading money around a diversified slate of prestige projects, mid-budget pictures, and inexpensive genre fare in favor of gambling the farm on big-budget versions of the monster movies and space operas that used to squat at the bottom half of double features.

LESBIAN MOVIES FOR GUYS

L esbian movies for guys are, of course, by definition not lesbian movies at all. First, if there's a man interested in **Desert Hearts** (1985) or **Go Fish** (1994), I have yet to meet him—the appeal is scenes, not themes. And while *actresses* (I use the term loosely) like Misty Mundae have built their careers delivering on the promise of girl-girl action, that hint of the unexpected is what really gets guys interested: A big name in a real movie with an hon-est-to-God story dramatically increases the value of even a fleeting thrill—it's the difference between an unexpected glimpse of a naked neighbor and a Jenna Jameson movie. A "practice" kiss between Sarah Michelle Gellar and Selma Blair in **Cruel Intentions** (1999)—let alone French ice-goddess Catherine Deneuve and Oscar-winner Susan Sarandon in **The Hunger** (1983)—trumps all manner of anonymous soft-core hijinks.

By my informal and thoroughly unscientific reckoning, all-time favorite Sapphic pairings include Gina Gershon and Jennifer Tilly in **Bound** (1996); Lynn Lowry and Mary Woronov in **Sugar Cookies** (1973); Laura Harring and Naomi Watts in **Mulholland Dr.** (2001); Denise Richards and Neve Campbell in **Wild Things** (1998); Marianne Morris and Anulka in **Vampyres** (1974); Mia Kirshner and Dominique Swain in **New Best Friend** (2002); Jane March and Lesley Ann Warren in **Color of Night** (1994); Anne Heche and Joan Chen in **Wild Side** (1996); and Peta Wilson and Ellen Barkin in **Mercy** (2000). I can also heartily recommend the "documentary" **Girls Who Like Girls** (2001), a compendium of lesbian-themed scenes culled primarily from sexadelic 1960s/'70s Euro-thrillers and exploitation pictures.

LET'S GET SMALL

The world is tough enough when you're not in danger of drowning in a margarita glass. In these movies—even the comedies—the phrase *it's a small world after all* is chilling rather than cloyingly cute.

In Tod Browning's perverse **The Devil-Doll** (1936), a dying scientist hopes to alleviate world hunger by shrinking everyone to one-sixth normal size. But the disgraced banker who helps him escape from prison uses the doctor's miniaturized people to punish the men who framed him; cool and creepy, from the fugitive's masquerade as a sweet old lady to a wee couple's S&M-tinged *Apache* dance. Directed and produced by the *King Kong* (1933) team of Ernest B. Schoedsack and Merian C. Cooper, the Technicolor **Dr. Cyclops** (1940) sends a team of unfortunate scientists deep into the Peruvian jungle to aid the world-famous Dr. Thorkel (Albert Dekker), who shrinks them to doll size; the jokey score is awful, but the blackly comic scenes in which Thorkel toys with his tiny prisoners are great.

A small masterpiece of domestic paranoia, **The Incredible Shrinking Man** (1957) packs a passel of atomic-age anxieties into the story of an everyman who loses everything when radioactive fallout shrinks him into nothingness; kids love the spectacle of a teeny-tiny fellow battling a spider with a sewing needle, while adults see the underlying existential angst of a man reduced by life to an insignificant nub. When a man shrinks, it's cosmic tragedy. When a woman shrinks, it's goofy comedy: An overload of household chemicals turns housewife Lily Tomlin into **The Incredible Shrinking Woman** (1981); not a great movie, but a fantastic performance by Tomlin as the vanishing hausfrau.

Horror specialist Stuart Gordon turned over a new leaf with **Honey, I Shrunk the Kids** (1989), a good-natured adventure in which nutty scientist Rick Moranis accidentally miniaturizes four youngsters (his own and two neighbors) and sweeps them into the yard, leaving the tiny teens to hack their way through oversized blades of grass and battle elephant-sized insects. **The Borrowers** (1997) are a tiny family who live under the floorboards of an

English country house and "borrow" from unsuspecting regular-sized folks.

Bert I. Gordon earned his nickname—Mr. B.I.G.—with movies about giant bugs, but in his melancholy fantasy **Attack of the Puppet People** (1958), a lonely puppeteer, jilted by his faithless wife, shrinks people so he can keep them always by his side; *Toy Story 2* (1999) fans will spot its influence on the scene in which Mr. Potato Head and company brave busy city streets in search of their friend Woody. A team of miniaturized doctors is injected into the bloodstream of a defecting Soviet scientist to destroy a blood clot in the hugely entertaining **Fantastic Voyage** (1966), whose highlight is Raquel Welch's battle with clingy white corpuscles. **Innerspace** (1987) puts a comic spin on the misadventures of a diminutive navy pilot navigating the innards of hypochondriac Martin Short.

Czech stop-motion animator Jan Svankmajer embraces the darkness in Lewis Carroll's *Alice in Wonderland*; Svankmajer's **Alice/Neco z Alenky** (1988)—played by an enchanting real child—shrinks and grows and shrinks again, crossing paths with a nightmare bestiary of stop-motion creatures. In **Talk to Her/Habla con ella**'s (2002) silent film-within-the-film pastiche "The Shrinking Lover," a lady scientist concocts an innovative weight-loss potion, but it makes her portly fiance smaller rather than thinner. Who but Pedro Almodovar would consider the perverse sexual possibilities of relations between a normal-sized woman and a man the size of a peanut and see a bittersweet triumph of all-encompassing love?

LOVE ON THE RUN

Lovebirds on the lam rarely make it to happily ever after, but needless to say, their love burns all the brighter for being doomed.

They Live by Night (1947)/**Thieves Like Us** (1974), Nicholas Ray's and Robert Altman's versions of Edward Anderson's Depression-era novel about young bank robbers predestined by poverty and ignorance to short, brutish lives on the run.

Bonnie and Clyde (1967), with Faye Dunaway and Warren Beatty as the legendary Depression-era bank robbers; the advertising tagline says it all: "They're young, they're in love, and they kill people."

Gun Crazy (1949), with John Dall and Peggy Cummins as fugitive pistol fetishists who "go together like guns and ammunition" and turn to crime; the bank heist scene is a one-shoot tour-de-force. **Guncrazy** (1992) stars Drew Barrymore as a teen who's just murdered her abusive stepfather (Joe Dallesandro) and James LeGros as the newly released murderer who joins her for a hell-bound road trip; title notwithstanding, it has more in common with *They*

Live by Night/Thieves Like Us than *Gun Crazy*, and was
scripted by Matthew Bright (see *Fairy Tales for Grown-Ups*).

Natural Born Killers (1994), with Woody Harrelson and
Juliette Lewis as media-savvy serial killers looking to
justify their love with a record-breaking slaughter binge;
Quentin Tarantino scripted it and **True Romance**
(1993), with Patricia Arquette and Christian Slater fleeing
the pimp whose cocaine stash they accidentally heisted.

Badlands (1973), with Sissy Spacek and Martin Sheen as
alienated youngsters on an interstate killing spree; based
on real-life 1950s murderer Charles Starkweather and his
girlfriend, Carol Ann Fugate.

Kiss or Kill (1997), with Francis O'Connor and Matt Day
leaving a string of bodies stretched across the Australian
outback—but which one is the killer?

Wild at Heart (1990), with Laura Dern and Nicolas Cage as
sweethearts fleeing her insanely possessive mother (Dern's
real mom, Diane Ladd).

The Sugarland Express (1974), with Goldie Hawn as the
devoted wife who breaks her husband (William Atherton)
out of jail so he can help her retain custody of their child;
they wind up with hundreds of cops and reporters in hot
pursuit.

The Getaway (1972), with Steve McQueen and Ali McGraw
as career criminals fleeing their double-crossing partners;
based on pulp-master Jim Thompson's baroque novel and
directed by Sam Peckinpah. The glossy 1994 remake with
Alec Baldwin and Kim Basinger doesn't live up to the
original, but works on its own terms.

LUSH LIFE

Belly up to the bar but be warned: Happy endings are far outnumbered by one-way tickets to the gutter in films about drinking, though these movies do give actors the chance to let it rip.

A quaint reminder of a time when drinking at breakfast was just tippling, the *Thin Man* series revolves around stylish sophisticates Nick and Nora Charles (William Powell and Myrna Loy)—a retired detective and the wealthy socialite whose money keeps him in top-shelf liquor—solve crimes between drinks. The fizzy chemistry between Powell and Loy is consistently irresistible, though the movies—**The Thin Man** (1934), **After the Thin Man** (1936), **Another Thin Man** (1939), **Shadow of the Thin Man** (1941), **The Thin Man Goes Home** (1944), and **Song of the Thin Man** (1947)—otherwise offer diminishing returns.

The bittersweet comedy **Harvey** (1950) stars James Stewart as a gentle, alcoholic dreamer whose best friend, a man-sized rabbit, is either a pooka—a Celtic spirit—or a spirits-induced hallucination. Dudley Moore's **Arthur** (1981) may be the last stand of the flat-out funny souse, and Sir John Gielgud's acid-tongued butler steals his movie out from under him. Two disillusioned, middle-aged friends (Paul Giamatti and Thomas Hayden Church) assess the mess they've made of their lives during a tasting tour of California wine country in the melancholy buddy comedy **Sideways** (2004).

Beyond these films, to find lighter fare among drinking films, you have to stoop to trashy crowd-pleasers **Cocktail** (1988) and **Coyote Ugly** (2000), and they're about bartenders, not drinkers. In the former, likely lad Tom Cruise learns the art of extreme drink slinging from veteran mixologist Bryan Brown; in the latter, do-me feminists in super-vixen stripper gear do cunning stunts with flaming shots. Each provides drinking-game opportunities limited only by your imagination.

Now that the party's over, the rest of these films are sobering looks at alcholism's painful price. In **The Lost Weekend** (1945), blocked writer Ray Milland spends a hellish forty-eight hours at the bottom of a glass. Legendary beauty Susan Hayward showed her chops as a desperate housewife who tries to drown her frustration at having traded her career for marriage and motherhood in **Smash-Up, the Story of a Woman** (1947). Stressed out adman Jack Lemmon drinks himself down the drain in **Days of Wine and Roses** (1962), dragging his loyal wife along. **My Name Is Bill W.** (1989) is a sober—if you'll excuse the word—account of the birth of Alcoholics Anonymous, driven by James Woods's excellent performance as founder Bill Wilson. Cult writer Charles Bukowski thought **Barfly** (1987) prettied up his autobiographical story of living la vida lowlife, but star Mickey Rourke oozes convincing squalor. Indie actor Steve Buscemi made his directing debut with **Trees Lounge** (1996), a sympathetic portrait of a blue-collar loser and his hard-drinking crowd. The giddy highs and stygian lows of a dilettantish novelist and deeply disciplined drinker (Anthony LaPaglia) drive **Happy Hour** (2004), which starts out on a jauntily jazzed high of neon-lit New York streets and ends in pure, sozzled heartbreak. And in **Leaving Las Vegas** (1995)—based on the semiautobiographical novel by John O'Brien, who killed himself shortly before the film went into production—Nicolas Cage plays a washed-up screenwriter who's run out of second chances and systematically drinks himself to ground zero. If it doesn't scare you sober, nothing will.

MACHINE DREAMS

In our imaginations, artificially intelligent machines do the housework, take on dirty and dangerous jobs no one wants, attend to the boring minutiae of day-to-day life, fight our future wars, and even fulfill our wildest fantasies . . . until, of course, they get too big for their circuits. Then you have **2001: A Space Odyssey**'s (1968) sweetly reasonable sounding HAL 9000 supercomputer (voiced mellifluously by Douglas Rain) sending the astronauts whose life support systems he controls into that good night. But the genius of Stanley Kubrick's outer-space head trip is that more than a few tears have been shed as the pleading HAL is slowly shut down, his (because HAL *is* a he, not an it) magnificent processing power reduced to remembering scraps of a vintage popular song. The smart-house program Proteus IV goes equally haywire in **Demon Seed** (1977), making the imprisoned

Julie Christie its babymama. No one cries for Proteus—robo–sex offenders are *trash*—but this largely forgotten (except by the movie-savvy *Simpsons* writers, who whipped up a Treehouse of Horrors homage with Pierce Brosnan as the suave voice of Proteus) sci-fi thriller should make you think twice about ceding control of the locks and lights to potentially malevolent microchips.

Of course, the real stars of our machine dreams aren't computers. They're robots, like A-list celebrity Robby: *Rocky Horror* lyrics notwithstanding, it's not Anne Francis who stars in **Forbidden Planet** (1956), a witty spin on Shakespeare's *The Tempest*. It's Robby the Robot all the way, baby. And while we're name-checking *Science Fiction Double Feature* (see the essay later in the book), yes, Michael Rennie was ill **The Day the Earth Stood Still** (1951), but his death-ray-enabled enforcer, Gort, was ready, willing, and able to fry us all in the name of interstellar peace. Only the words "Klaatu barada nikto" stand between this island Earth and the wrath of Gort. You know what's really wrong with the new *Star Wars* movies? Not enough of beeping pepperpot R2-D2 and fusspot protocol droid C-3P0 (voiced by Anthony Daniels in the sissy style of screwball-comedy regular Franklin Pangborn), who steal **Star Wars** (1977), **The Empire Strikes Back** (1980), and **Return of the Jedi** (1983) and right out from under the human cast . . . except maybe Carrie Fisher in that metal bikini.

In the futuristic **Robocop** (1987), murdered Detroit police officer Peter Weller is resurrected as haunted man-machine, tormented by scraps of memories of his old life. **Blade Runner**'s (1982) top-of-the-line humanoids are also haunted, but by *other people's* memories and the knowledge that they have preset shelf lives; couched as a futuristic noir thriller, Ridley Scott's loose adaptation of Philip K. Dick's sci-fi novel is a melancholy meditation on the nature of humanity, and features evocative performances by Rutger Hauer, Brion James, and Daryl Hannah as the doomed renegade "replicants." Steven Spielberg's **AI: Artificial Intelligence** (2001)—an unrealized Stanley Kubrick project based on Brian Aldiss's short story "Super-Toys Last All Summer Long"—is a weak film, but Jude Law's fugitive sexbot Gigolo Joe is an electrifying creation, no pun intended. Could the oh-so-'60s fembots who populate the spoofy **Dr. Goldfoot and the Bikini Machine** (1965), in which Goldfoot (Vincent Price) builds a passel of robo–gold diggers to fleece rich men, and **Dr. Goldfoot and the Girl Bombs** (1966), "the girls with the thermonuclear navels" be as sexy? Austin Powers clearly thinks so. And Goldfoot's girls owe a debt of imagination to Fritz Lang's robot Maria, an automaton designed to discredit a saintly slum worker in **Metropolis** (1927); it's hard to say which incarnation is more alluring: the glistening black-metal version or the one that looks like silent siren Brigitte Helm. And let's not forget **The Stepford Wives** (1975), perfect suburban spouses who love to cook, clean, look pretty for their husbands, and never, *ever* have a headache (the 2004 remake is an unmitigated disaster).

Disneyland theme parks are taken to their logical conclusion in **Westworld** (1973), where jaded tourists pay top dollar to vacation in perfectly duplicated historical environments where they can wallow in Roman orgies, diddle medieval wenches, or outdraw the fastest guns in the West; the trouble starts when robot gunslinger Yul Brynner decides he'd rather win. **The Terminator** (1984) and **Terminator 2: Judgment Day** (1991) turned Arnold Schwarzenegger's limitations into assets by casting him as a cyborg assassin sent from the future to change the past, and both **Alien**'s (1979) Ash (Ian Holm) and **Aliens**' (1986) Bishop (Lance Henriksen) are vividly realized robot characters who more than hold their own against their flesh-and-blood crewmates. The excellent animated anthology **The Animatrix** (2003), a companion piece to the live-action features, is composed of short films that expand on the *Matrix* mythology; "The Second Renaissance, parts I and II" chronicles the rise of the machines that turned the human race into living batteries.

MAN'S BEST FRIEND

Every dog has his day, but only some of them have movies. **Napoleon** (1995) is a pampered golden retriever pup named Muffin (he'd *like* to be called Napoleon) who gets lost in the Australian outback; it's adorable and suitable for young children. Forget the TV series and Timmy falling down the well: The lovely **Lassie Come Home** (1943), set in WWI-era Yorkshire, explores the bond between a boy (Roddy McDowall) and the collie who keeps coming back after his poverty-stricken parents are forced to sell her. In **Air Bud** (1997), a newly fatherless teen adopts a runaway dog with a knack for shooting hoops; it's straight off the assembly line but runs like clockwork—avoid all sequels. A poor Flemish orphan living with his increasingly infirm grandfather adopts an abused and abandoned canine in **A Dog of Flanders** (1959), a bracingly unsentimental version—the best of several—of the classic children's novel. **The Incredible Journey** (1963), a truly great film for animal lovers of all ages, follows two dogs and a cat as they trek hundreds of miles to find their owners. The lighter remake, **Homeward Bound: The Incredible Journey**, features celebrity voice-overs (Michael J. Fox, Sally Field, Don Ameche) for the pets' thoughts and downplays the dangers they face.

Now it's confession time: The mere sight of Lassie falling into a river makes me cry. So **Old Yeller** (1957), a great movie filled with powerful and complex emotions, kills me. A frontier family adopts a yellow mongrel who bonds with their teenaged son (Disney child star Tommy Kirk) and—spoiler alert!—*dies*. Ditto **The Biscuit Eater** (1940), in which two poor Tennessee boys, one black and one white, secretly train a dog with a "bad streak" to compete in a hunting competition. A first-class film about love, loyalty, family, and sacrifice, but if I think any more about the doggie death scene I'm going to lose it. The 1972 Disney remake is good, but the first version is the real champ. The *Benji* films—**Benji** (1974), **For the Love of Benji** (1977), **Benji the Hunted** (1987), and **Benji: Off the Leash!** (2004)—are super wholesome and formulaic, but the various scruffy Benjis are mighty cute and—not to be too Pollyannaish—every one contains a worthy message about the plight of strays. I once saw a snippet of *Benji the Hunted* in a bar, on a tiny TV *with the sound off*, and so help me, when Benji's new friend the mountain lion cub fell into a stream, I cried. Mortifying.

Not all dog movies are for kids. In **A Boy and His Dog** (1975), based on a typically scabrous Harlan Ellison story, Don Johnson and his telepathic pooch—by far the smarter of the two—scavenge for food and sex in a postapocalyptic world. The French **Baxter** (1989) looks into the mind of a bull terrier and finds one sick puppy who plots against humans—he tries to drown a *baby*—until he finds one he can respect: A rotten little neo-Nazi. In the Mexican **Amores perros** (2000), a car accident ties together the stories of a man in love with his abusive brother's wife and trying to finance their escape through dogfighting (simulated, but very upsetting), a crippled fashion model who loses her beloved pup, and a homeless former revolutionary whose act of kindness backfires horribly on his "family" of mutts. The title in English translation says it all: "Love's a bitch."

DIRECTOR'S SPOTLIGHT: JEAN-PIERRE MELVILLE

The godfather of the French New Wave, idol of Quentin Tarantino and John Woo, Jean-Pierre Melville (1917–1973) was born Jean-Pierre Grumbach in Paris. An avid moviegoer and enthusiastic amateur filmmaker as a teenager, Melville put his career ambitions on hold for mandatory national service in 1937; WWII broke out while he was still in uniform and he spent the rest of the war years in the military. Though he took the surname "Melville" from his favorite American writer, Herman Melville, it also served to hide his Jewishness during the Nazi occupation. After the war, Melville applied to the French Technicians' Union and was rejected; frustrated and disgusted, he walked away from the establishment and founded his own Studio Jenner in 1946, cannily working its financial constraints to his advantage. Melville's first real success was his adaptation of Jean Cocteau's suffocating **Les**

enfants terribles/The Strange Ones (1950), about the near-incestuous relationship between a convalescing teenager and his sister, cooped up in their Paris apartment—Melville's own.

But his influence comes from his crime pictures, starting with the glorious **Bob le flambeur/Bob the Gambler** (1955), starring handsome silver-haired Roger Duchesne, a matinee idol of the '30s disgraced by suspicions of wartime collaboration with the Nazis. The story is nothing special—an aging gambler (a *flambeur*) plans *one last grift* that will bankroll his comfy retirement—but Melville took his camera to the streets, shooting in the veteran bohemian quarter of Montmartre and the mean streets of Pigalle, Paris's real-life den of pimps, gangsters, prostitutes, and thieves. Irish director Neil Jordan remade *Bob le flambeur* rather successfully as **The Good Thief** (2003), relocating the story to the murky pond of Nice's multiethnic demimonde, but couldn't hope to duplicate the sheer exhilarating rush *Bob* generated in the '50s, when the French film establishment was defined by studio-bound productions. Jean-Luc Godard tipped his hat to Melville's trailblazing by casting him as the self-important novelist Parvulesco in his New Wave bombshell **Breathless/À bout de souffle** (1959).

Melville's crime pictures are tinged with dark romanticism but predicated on the notion that the most superficially glamorous outlaws are at heart as rotten as bourgeois bankers; guilt, regret, and betrayal—real and imagined—haunt cops and criminals alike. In the melancholy **Le doulos/The Fingerman** (1962)—"stool pigeon" might be a better translation—burglar Jean-Paul Belmondo remains at liberty by supplying tips to the police, a delicate balance that inevitably goes all to hell. Fugitive crook Lino Ventura is trapped between sadistic cops and thieves without honor in **Le deuxième souffle/Second Breath** (1966); the handheld camera work and rapid-fire editing during the film's armored car heist looks incredibly modern. Melville's existential **Le samouraï** (1967) casts '60s icon Alain Delon as a coolly alienated hit man whose latest employer turns on him; Woo's delirious **The Killer** (1989) owes it a major debt of inspiration and Chow Yun-Fat makes Delon's icy brand of disaffected chic his own. A brutal, dogged policeman is determined to take down a gang of three—newly sprung young gun Delon, alcoholic ex-cop Yves Montand, and Gian Maria Volonte, who's just broken out of prison—before they can pull off an elaborate jewelry-store heist in the bleak **Le cercle rouge/The Red Circle** (1970). In the desolate **Un flic/Dirty Money** (1972), Delon is a vice cop whose girlfriend (Catherine Deneuve) is also involved with bank robber Richard Crenna, a triangle that can only end in disaster. Theatrically released carelessly, in limited venues or in many cases not at all, many of Melville's films are now available on DVD and ripe for wider appreciation.

DIRECTOR'S SPOTLIGHT:
HAYAO MIYAZAKI

In an age when "family film" usually means simplistic stories, noisy, hyperactive characters, and blunt moral messages tarted up with pop-culture jokes, the animated films of writer-director Hayao Miyazaki are nothing short of a miracle: childlike, not childish. His animated fantasies borrow liberally from classic children's literature, including *The Wizard of Oz*, *Gulliver's Travels*, and *Alice in Wonderland*; traditional Japanese ghost stories; the nineteenth-century tales of Charles Dickens and pioneering sci-fi writer Jules Verne; and folklore and fairy tales from all over the world. These influences and more are woven into a seamless world filled with fantastic sights and all-too-human sadness in which the bizarre—even grotesque—rubs shoulders with the *kawaii*, that particularly Japanese kind of cute embodied by Hello Kitty, Astro Boy, and wide-eyed cuties like Sailor Moon. They hum with the vivid life of the Earth and the secret power of names, supernatural shape-shifting, and astonishing transformations; his young heroes and heroines either embody traditional Japanese values—contempt for greed and gluttony, respect for elders, discipline, and courtesy—or learn them, but his films are never preachy.

Born in Tokyo in 1941, Hayao Miyazaki began his animation career in 1963, but worked in relative anonymity until 1984, when he and Isao Takahata (whose **Grave of the Fireflies**, 1988, about orphaned siblings in Kobe at the end of WWII, is among the most emotionally devastating films ever made) founded Studio Ghibli to produce feature-length animated films. Miyazaki's first feature was **Lupin III: Castle of Cagliostro** (1979), but the first true "Miyazaki film" was **Nausicaa of the Valley of the Winds** (1984), an ecologically conscious fable in which a child princess is humankind's last, best hope in a poisoned, postapocalyptic world dominated by giant mutant insects. In **Laputa: Castle in the Sky** (1986), the destinies of two orphans—a working-class boy whose aviator father once glimpsed the fabled Laputa and was ridiculed for the rest of his life and a country girl whose crystal necklace contains an ancient power—converge. **Porco Rosso** (1992) is a former WWI fighting ace transformed into a pig after his squadron was wiped out; as middle age looms, he makes a living fighting sky bandits. Two lonely sisters adrift in a new home, their mother lying sick in the hospital, are befriended by a forest spirit in **My Neighbor Totoro** (1988). A thirteen-year-old witch leaves home in **Kiki's Delivery Service** (1989) and finds her own identity delivering packages from her trusty broomstick. Gods and demons battle for the future of the forest in **Princess Mononoke** (1997), an epic vision of life out of balance and the clash of human aspiration and nature's unpredictable resistance.

In the breathtaking coming-of-age story **Spirited Away** (2001), a rude, sullen ten-year-old and her parents take a detour while driving to their new home; they wander into an enchanted spa where the parents are turned into pigs and their spoiled, self-centered daughter must grow up and learn to negotiate a bizarre world of gods and monsters—ghostly shadows, a sumo wrestler made of daikon, living soot balls with wide eyes and spidery legs, the shunned No-Face—before she can rescue them. A witch's curse transforms a shy, eighteen-year-old milliner into an old woman in **Howl's Moving Castle** (2004), based on Diana Wynne Jones's novel; she reclaims her destiny with the help of a turnip-headed scarecrow and a volatile young sorcerer whose castle—a huffing, puffing contraption made of copper turrets, flywheels, and metal pipes—walks on incongruous chicken feet, powered by a moody fire demon. We should treasure Miyazaki's worlds of wonder; imaginations this fertile are rare and precious.

NOT YOUR FATHER'S MUSICALS

There are songs and there's dancing, but these musicals put a revisionist spin on the tried-and-true formula that set a thousand feet to tapping in the good old days.

Much imitated and never equaled, the exuberant **Rocky Horror Picture Show** (1975) filters the cliches of grade-B sci-fi and horror movies through the glam-rock sensibilities of the 1970s. The sweeter but still truly weird **Yes Nurse, No Nurse** (2003), inspired by a lost Dutch children's TV show of the '60s, revolves around stern but kindly Nurse Klivia, the charming oddballs who inhabit her rest home, and the curmudgeonly landlord who wants to put them all out on the street: I *dare* you to get the damnably catchy title number out of your head. Discovering **The 5,000 Fingers of Dr. T.** (1953) is like finding an absinthe spoon in your grandma's silverware drawer: The order of the universe is called into question. Conceived, written, and designed by Theodore Geisel—the beloved Dr. Seuss—this paranoid, live-action fantasy plunges all-American kid Bart (*Lassie*'s Tommy Rettig) into a surreal world ruled by despotic piano teacher Dr. Terwilliker (the sublimely insinuating Hans Conried, voice of *The Rocky and Bullwinkle Show*'s Snidely Whiplash), who forces kidnapped boys to play his 500-seat keyboard.

Notorious anti-marijuana screed **Reefer Madness** (1936) was reborn as a tongue-in-cheek off-Broadway musical and a subsequent 2005 film; framed by a hysterical anti-drug lecture by Alan Cumming, it includes production numbers for zombies and a Vegas-ized Jesus in a gilded loincloth.

Baz Luhrmann's extravagant **Moulin Rouge** (2001), a delirious fantasy of the raunchy bohemian quarter of nineteenth-century Paris, boldly mixes and matches modern pop songs (admit it: you'd never have thought of grafting "Smells Like Teen Spirit" onto "Lady Marmalade") to tell the story of kept cabaret performer Satine (Nicole Kidman) and the penniless would-be writer (Ewan McGregor) who loves her. Love it or hate it, from Satine's dreamlike entrance on a descending swing to the brutal tango set to the Police's "Roxanne," it's utterly uncompromising, a glittering shrine to the raw power of artifice. Every word of Jacques Demy's deceptively candy-colored, feel-bad **The Umbrellas of Cherbourg/Les parapluies de Cherbourg** (1964), from declarations of love to exchanges with gas jockeys, is delivered in composer Michel Legrand's singsong pop recitative; radiant seventeen-year-old Genevieve (Catherine Deneuve), who works in her family's chic but failing umbrella shop, falls for twenty-year-old mechanic Guy (Nino Castelnuovo) despite her status-conscious mother's objections. He's drafted for a two-year hitch in Algeria, she finds herself pregnant, everyone settles for second best; very French and piercingly poignant.

The still-sumptuous Deneuve lent her stellar presence to French bad-boy director Francois Ozon's **8 Women** (2001), whose all-star cast radiates enough wattage to eclipse a small solar system; eight women are trapped in a country manor, the only man on the scene is dead, and one of them must have killed him. The suspects—each of whom has her own distinctive musical number—include four generations of French beauties, from grande dame Danielle Darrieux to twenty-first-century sexpot Ludivine Sagnier, and Deneuve's catfight with Truffaut-muse Fanny Ardant comes to a jaw-dropping conclusion. And Deneuve graces what may be the grimmest musical in history, Danish provocateur Lars von Trier's **Dancer in the Dark** (2000), starring Icelandic pop star Bjork (who also wrote the music) as a downtrodden, soon-to-be-blind Czech immigrant toiling as a machine-press operator in a dreary factory in Washington State and taking refuge in fantasies inspired by "Czech Fred Astaire" Oldrich Novy (veteran hoofer Joel Grey): Lock up the straight razors and the sleeping pills before you get to the end, because von Trier pulls no punches.

ON THE ROAD

There's more to road trip movies than frat-boy comedy and lovers on the lam—though there are enough of them for a whole other category (see *Love on the Run*). What is John Steinbeck's Depression-era masterpiece **The Grapes of Wrath** (1940) if not an epic, footsore road trip that starts in dust-bowl Oklahoma and ends in the promised land of California; along the way, downtrodden Oakie Tom Joad (played with electrifying intensity by Henry Fonda) is radicalized by his hardworking family's brutal experiences. The classic screwball comedy **It Happened One Night** (1934) is a road trip movie, too: Spoiled runaway heiress Claudette Colbert undertakes an epic jaunt from Miami to New York by bus, car, and thumb—Colbert's saucy lesson in stopping reluctant drivers with a glimpse of shapely leg is classic—accompanied by newly unemployed newspaperman Clark Gable, who smells a scoop but winds up falling for his feisty exclusive. And so is **The Wizard of Oz** (1939): Pursued by the vengeful Wicked Witch of the West, restless farm girl Dorothy (Judy Garland) makes new friends, learns what she's capable of, and follows the yellow brick road to a new appreciation of home. No matter where they think they're going, road trippers always take a detour somewhere else: Blindsided by love or tripped up by fate they travel into the past, take the path not taken, go back to where it all began or down the back alleys of their minds and into the darkest corners of the heart.

Shaggy, dope-addled, and defiantly anti-establishment, *man*, **Easy Rider** (1969) follows hippie bikers Peter Fonda and Dennis Hopper as they take to the empty highways in search of America and find alienation and violence, accompanied by an era-defining soundtrack by Steppenwolf, the Byrds, Jimi Hendrix, and others; Jack Nicholson's turn as an alcoholic small-town lawyer revived his moribund career. The road ends at a Massachusetts prison in **The Last Detail** (1973), in which Navy lifers Nicholson and Otis Young, who swear like, well, *sailors*, are assigned to escort hard-luck swabbie Randy Quaid from their West Virginia base to serve a harsh sentence for a petty offence and show him a little of life en route. The epitome of downtown New York cool, Jim Jarmusch's ultracool black-and-white **Stranger than Paradise** (1984) sets two hipster grifters—John Lurie (of avant-garde jazz-rock combo the Lounge Lizards) and broken-nosed Richard Edson—on a desultory New York/Cleveland/Florida trip through the heart of emptiness, accompanied by a wide-eyed Hungarian waif (under-ground performer Eszter Balint) and the nerve-jangling strains of Screamin' Jay Hawkins's "I Put a Spell on You." Twenty-one years later, Jarmusch's melancholy **Broken Flowers** (2005) finds aging lothario Bill Murray on a personal odyssey in search of four old girlfriends (Sharon Stone, Tilda Swinton, Jessica Lange, and Frances Conroy), one of whom may be the mother of the son he never knew he had; by the last visit he's so far off the beaten track that the roads aren't even on the map.

A raunchy coming-of-age comedy with surprisingly deep emotional underpinnings, **Y tu mamá también** (2001) follows Mexican teenagers Diego Luna and Gael Garcia Bernal as they try to seduce the sexy older woman who's agreed to accompany them to a distant beach so perfect it's called Boca del Cielo—Heaven's Mouth. In the unpredictable **Something Wild** (1986), buttoned-up tax consultant Jeff Daniels lets wild child Melanie Griffith convince him he's a "secret rebel;" their larky Manhattan-to-New Jersey trip takes a dark turn when her sociopathic ex-husband (Ray Liotta) enters the picture.

There are eight million stories in the naked city, but on the open road, well, the possibilities are infinite. David Lynch's uncharacteristically gentle **The Straight Story** (1999) tells the true story of seventy-three-year-old widower Alvin Straight, who made a six-week, five-mile-per-hour odyssey on a lawn tractor to reconcile with his dying brother. In **Sullivan's Travels** (1941) Hollywood "caliph of comedy" Joel McCrea, famous for directing comedies like *So Long Sarong* and *Hey Hey in the Hayloft*, disguises himself as a vagabond, hoping to experience some real-life hard times before making his message picture, *O Brother, Where Art Thou?* He gets more real life than he bargained for, including a sojourn on a brutal Southern chain gang. The Coen Brothers borrowed Sullivan's title for their Depression-era odyssey **O Brother, Where Art Thou?** (2000), in which one Ulysses Everett McGill (George Clooney) escapes a chain gang and travels the Depression-era South, encountering a one-eyed monster and some sultry sirens en route to reclaiming his wife.

The witty, oddly touching (emphasis on the *odd*) banter between bounty hunter Robert De Niro and neurotic bail jumper Charles

Grodin, during their frantic planes-trains-and-automobiles dash from New York to Los Angeles pursued by the Mafia and the FBI, elevates **Midnight Run** (1988) above its action-comedy formula. Tequila-soaked gringo Warren Oates comes apart during a blood-stained trip across Mexico with a flyblown head in a burlap bag in Sam Peckinpah's perverse, surreal fable **Bring Me the Head of Alfredo Garcia** (1974).

Danger lurks on dark highways and lonely interstates. Steven Spielberg's road-rage thriller **Duel** (1971) pits a milquetoast businessman against a malevolent trucker. Icy-eyed Rutger Hauer thumbs a ride from fresh-faced C. Thomas Howell in **The Hitcher** (1986), turning a dream gig—delivering a Cadillac Seville from Chicago to San Diego—into an ever-escalating nightmare. In **Joy Ride** (2001), two college students and a ne'er-do-well relative driving from California to New Jersey play a mean-spirited CB prank on unseen truck driver "Rusty Nail" (the sublimely menacing voice of Ted Levine), who gives them ample reason to regret it. An eloping couple gives a psycho a lift in **Road** (2002), an exotic mix of Bollywood musical numbers and killer-on-the-road thrills. In the suspenseful **Road Games** (1981), Stacy Keach takes a long-haul job from Melbourne to Perth and winds up playing cat and mouse with a serial killer in a black van. And in the darkly witty **Highway to Hell** (1992), young bridegroom-to-be Chad Lowe must burn rubber to retrieve his fiancee from the devil himself (Patrick Bergin).

The siren song of the open road is answered by women as well as men. A girls' night out turns ugly for best friends **Thelma and Louise** (1991)—unhappy housewife Geena Davis and wisecracking waitress Susan Sarandon—after they kill a would-be rapist; they hit the highway in hopes of getting to Mexico before the law or Thelma's abusive husband catches up. In the controversial **Baise-moi** (2000), part feminist polemic and part down-and-dirty rape-revenge film, two disenfranchised sex-workers-turned-killers join forces for a payback tour of the French countryside; the leads are played by Euro–porn stars who know their way around a sex scene. Four incarcerated women form a garage band in the high-energy German film **Bandits** (1997); they escape en route to perform at the Policemen's Ball, becoming a media sensation as they criss-cross the countryside playing impromptu gigs. Three cross-dressing "girls" (Hugo Weaving, Guy Pearce, and Terence Stamp) vamp and camp their way across the Australian outback in the cheeky **The Adventures of Priscilla, Queen of the Desert** (1994), and they always look *fabulous*.

OTHER KINGDOMS, OTHER 'TOONS

Admit it: When you think feature-length animation, you think Disney. Disney's trailblazing **Snow White and the Seven Dwarfs** (1937) laid down the rules for American mainstream animation: wide-eyed heroines, heroic journeys (Joseph Campbell would be proud), talking animals, unsubtle moral lessons, nutty sidekicks, and syrupy songs. Disney stripped the thorns from prickly fairy tales and purged the disturbing psychosexual subtexts from classic children's stories, and made some truly timeless films in the process. Disney's savvy relationship with Pixar Animation produced **Toy Story** (1995) and **Toy Story 2** (1999), as well as Brad Bird's super-savvy superhero pastiche **The Incredibles** (2004). But there are other kingdoms to explore.

Hayao Miyazaki's **Spirited Away** (2001), about a little girl who must rescue her parents from a spirit resort, snatched the Best Animated Feature Oscar out from under two Disney films. Often called the "Walt Disney of Japan" (as is Osamu Tezuka, creator of animated TV characters like Astro Boy and Kimba the White Lion, widely recognized as the uncredited inspiration for *The Lion King*), Miyazaki's films are both distinctly Japanese and completely accessible to Westerners. For more about them, see *Director's Spotlight: Hayao Miyazaki*, and see *Anime for Dummies* for an introduction to Japanese animation.

Disney-trained Brad Bird's **The Iron Giant** (1999) is a fabulous '50s fable about prejudice, self determination, and an fifty-foot alien robot—keep the tissues handy. Disney also trained Tim Burton and produced his black-and-white stop-motion short **Vincent** (1982), narrated by Vincent Price (who else?), but Burton's sweetly macabre sensibilities were a poor fit with the company's corporate culture. In his irresistible **The Nightmare Before Christmas** (1993, directed by Henry Selick), Halloween King Jack Skellington brings his sensibilities to bear on Christmas. **The Corpse Bride** (2005, co-directed with Mike Johnson) is a bittersweet fairy tale about a nervous bridegroom who accidentally betroths himself to a fetching cadaver.

Aardman Animation's cheeky **Chicken Run** (2000) is a rousing, old-fashioned POW-camp breakout movie, except that the clay-animated prisoners of Coop 17 are plump, nattering, oh-so-English chickens. Aardman's **The Curse of the Were-Rabbit** (2005) pits Wallace, a bumbling inventor of Rube Goldberg–esque contraptions, and his silent dog, Gromit, against garden-razing bunnies; though it never achieves the eccentric brilliance of Wallace and Gromit shorts **A Grand Day Out** (1989), **The Wrong Trousers** (1993), and **A Close Shave** (1995), it's studded with harebrained delights like Wallace's "Bun-O-Vac."

A charmingly subversive hippie fable, **The Point** (1971), adapted from songwriter Harry Nilsson and Carole Beers's book and featuring Nilsson's music, embeds the adventures of a round-headed boy in a pointy world within the story of a father breaking television's subversive hold over his son with a bedtime tale. And it was *made* for TV—those were the days! A determined granny rescues her grandson from gangsters in **The Triplets of Belleville** (2003), which tells its story with so little dialogue you'd hardly know it was French. In the eerie **Fantastic Planet** (1973), human beings—called Oms—are kept as pets by huge, blue-skinned "Traags" until one tiny Om rebels against life as a "living plaything." Rooted in West African folklore, **Kirikou and the Sorceress** (1998) tells the story of a tiny boy who saves his village from a witch; it features gorgeously angular animation, infectious traditional music by Senegalese superstar Youssou N' Dour, and some interesting character twists.

Kids love the Beatles' absurd adventures in **Yellow Submarine** (1968); adults dig the dryly witty dialogue and trippy pop-art visuals. The German **Adventures of Prince Achmed** (1926), widely considered the first full-length animated film, uses Balinese shadow-puppet-style animation to tell a story from the Arabian *Thousand and One Nights*. **Arabian Knight/The Thief and the**

Cobbler (1995)—the three-decades-in-the-making pet project of Oscar-winning animator Richard Williams (*Who Framed Roger Rabbit?*)—is a ruined masterpiece: Nervous financiers hijacked the project, inserted insipid song sequences by other animators, and sold it as a rip-off of Disney's pallid *Aladdin* (1992). But Williams's vivid M. C. Escher–meets–Peter Max visuals are jaw-dropping: Trust me, the next time a petition comes around to restore the original version, you'll scramble to sign.

OUT TO SEA

I hate the water and will probably never take a cruise that goes farther than around Manhattan island. But the constraints of shipboard settings have shaped some marvelous movies, from light romps to grand dissections of the human condition.

Preston Sturges's sophisticated comedy **The Lady Eve** (1941) begins aboard one luxury liner and concludes on another; con artist Barbara Stanwyck assumes two different identities to woo an unworldly millionaire (Henry Fonda), once on dry land and twice at sea. Intricately plotted by actor Anthony (*Psycho*) Perkins and legendary Broadway composer Stephen Sondheim, **The Last of**

Sheila (1973) gathers six cutthroat Hollywood types on a producer's super-swank yacht for a week of cruel head games; all the guests have dirty secrets, but one is hiding a whopper involving hit-and-run homicide. In the bittersweet **The Life Aquatic with Steve Zissou** (2004), a Jacques Cousteau–like oceanographic adventurer (Bill Murray) confronts midlife demons aboard his sea-going research station/film studio while hunting the "jaguar shark" that killed his best friend. A country girl marries a barge captain but grows restless with the stifling routine of shipboard life in the mesmerizing **L'Atalante** (1934); shimmeringly beautiful and psychologically complex, director Jean Vigo's second and last feature (he died shortly after, aged twenty-nine) strikes a flawless balance between gritty reality and everyday magic.

The Titanic tragedy is the template for shipboard disaster: arrogant masters of the universe defying fate, ordinary people ensnared in events beyond their imaginations, and an act of God that strips away the masks. **A Night to Remember** (1958) and both versions of **Titanic** draw from the same well of heroism, cowardice, and personal tragedy; the British *Night* combines low-key fidelity to the facts (as known then) and stunning ensemble performances. The 1953 *Titanic* is superior Hollywood melodrama, while the 1997 version features fantastic special effects but a sub-par romance between unhappy rich girl Kate Winslet and poor boy Leonardo DiCaprio.

A high-toned soap opera with an all-star international cast, **Ship of Fools** (1965) crams a generation's worth of pride, prejudice, vanity, and hypocrisy into an overcrowded German ocean liner steaming from Vera Cruz to Bremerhaven on the eve of WWII. **The Poseidon Adventure** (1972) is fabulous trash, as delicious as a tub of greasy popcorn; aging stars and character actors are trapped aboard a luxury liner that's flipped upside down midocean by a tidal wave. Roman Polanski's psychological thriller **Knife in the Water** (1963), traps a squabbling couple—bullying older husband, ripe younger wife—on a small boat with a menacing hitchhiker. A smiling psychopath terrorizes a grieving couple (Sam Neill and a young Nicole Kidman) on a boating vacation in the shallow but entertaining **Dead Calm** (1989).

Mutiny on the Bounty (1935) is so masterful it's a wonder anyone ever considered remaking it; Charles Laughton is a sadistic Captain Bligh and Clark Gable plays principled first mate Fletcher Christian, who's pushed to mutiny during the *Bounty*'s return voyage from Tahiti to England. **The Bounty** (1984) offers a more balanced portrait of Bligh (Anthony Hopkins), but Mel Gibson is a bland Mr. Christian; Marlon Brando played Christian in the epic 1962 production, which founders under his weirdly foppish characterization. A tense WWII drama based on Herman Wouk's Pulitzer Prize–winning novel and set largely aboard a rusty minesweeper, **The Caine Mutiny** (1954) pits tyrannical new Captain Queeg (Humphrey Bogart) against an unruly crew accustomed to lenient command. Queeg's by-the-book talk masks a disintegrating mind, but the mutineers are flawed as well; Queeg was Bogart's last great performance, summed up in his obsessive fidgeting with a pair of ball bearings.

DIRECTOR'S SPOTLIGHT: FRANCOIS OZON

Maybe you can write about French director Francois Ozon without reaching for phrases like *enfant terrible* and *epater le bourgeois*, but why do things the hard way? Born in Paris in 1967, Ozon is the class know-it-all who's frighteningly close to being as clever as he thinks he is. Gleefully transgressive and more than a little bit of a show-off, he'd be intolerable if he weren't a versatile and accomplished visual stylist, a psychologically astute screenwriter, a generous director of actors, and a film buff who knows the difference between paying homage and stealing.

Ozon first made himself known with two shorts, one light and one dark, about the perils awaiting careless vacationers. In the whimsical but sharply observed **A Summer Dress** (1996), a sexually ambivalent teenager annoyed by his boyfriend's swishiness goes to the beach for a nude swim, has a brief encounter with a woman, and must bike home in her dress after someone swipes his unattended clothes. The chilling **See the Sea** (1997) brings together two women—a pampered, slightly reckless housewife whose workaholic husband has left her rattling around their isolated vacation house with a new baby, and the surly young sociopath she allows to camp in her yard; no good comes of it. **Under the Sand** (2000) gave Charlotte Rampling, sleekest star of the swinging '60s, the role of a lifetime as a middle-aged woman coming undone after her husband goes for a midday swim and never returns. **Swimming Pool** (2003), a cool, tricky thriller in the manner of Claude Chabrol, stars Rampling again as a buttoned-up British mystery writer whose working holiday at her publisher's French country house is rudely disrupted by his illegitimate daughter (Ludivine Sagnier), a ripely sensual hellion oozing trouble from every golden pore.

The underrated **Criminal Lovers** (1999) begins as a couple-on-the-run story in which a teenage girl persuades a malleable classmate to murder another boy, then morphs into a freaky variation on "Hansel and Gretel" when the fugitives get lost in the woods and wind up locked in the basement of a sex-starved hermit. **Water Drops on Burning Rocks** (2000), a bittersweet farce about the sex games people play in a suffocating Berlin bachelor pad, was an unproduced theatrical four-hander dashed off in 1965 by the nineteen-year-old Rainer Werner Fassbinder until Ozon pulled off the neat trick of adapting it into a film that simultaneously honors Fassbinder's vicious spirit of provocation while indulging Ozon's own sly caprices. **8 Women** (2001) traps a who's who of French screen sirens—from Catherine Deneuve and Fanny Ardant (who wind up in a mesmerizing tussle) to Virginie Ledoyen—in a fabulous '50s fantasy of a snowed-in country estate with a corpse and gives each a fabulous musical number. If master melodramatist Douglas Sirk and John Waters collaborated on a movie version of the board game *Clue*, the result might look something like this.

A pet rat unleashes a tidal wave of dark family desires in the blackly comic **Sitcom** (1998), Ozon's least successful provocation. **5x2** (2004), which dissects an unhappy marriage in five vignettes that unfold backward from the couple's divorce to their meeting at an Italian seaside resort, retreads the path blazed by Harold Pinter's **Betrayal** (1983). But Ozon on a bad day still throws enough curveballs to keep the game interesting.

RESCUE ME

First things first: Robert Louis Stevenson's *Kidnapped* is less about kidnapping than rousing historical adventure. In these films, it's the whole story. Pseudonymous novelist A. J. Quinnell's **Man on Fire**—in which a bitter, burnt-out former CIA-agent-turned-bodyguard fails to prevent a child's violent abduction and stops at nothing to get her back—has been filmed twice; I prefer the scrappy 1987 version with Scott Glenn to Tony Scott's hyperkinetic 2004 remake, starring Denzel Washington and Dakota Fanning as his charge. A privileged young Caracas couple out for a night on the town is waylaid by professional kidnappers in the Venezuelan **Secuestro Express** (2004); during their captivity, the lies and secrets on which their relationship is built come to light. Blackmail is only the beginning of adulterous, overextended businessman Roy Scheider's troubles in the lurid **52 Pick-Up** (1986), based on an Elmore Leonard novel and directed by John Frankenheimer; the blackmailers take his wife (Ann-Margret) to make sure he pays. **The Candy Snatchers** (1973) are squabbling lowlifes inspired by a TV movie based on the real-life ordeal of Barbara Mackle (1972's *The Longest Night*), who was buried in a specially equipped box while her family came up with the ransom; they think ransoming a schoolgirl will be an easy payday, but her disordered family throws them some curves in this spectacularly sleazy exploitation film.

Unhinged after bearing a stillborn child, fake spiritualist Kim Stanley persuades her weak-willed husband (Richard Attenborough) to abduct a child in **Seance on a Wet Afternoon** (1964), but her plan to collect the ransom and drum up business by using her "powers" to locate the girl go awry. Based on an Ed McBain novel, Akira Kurosawa's **High and Low** (1963) traps wealthy industrialist Toshiro Mifune on the horns of a dilemma: He receives word that a sociopath has taken his child and is demanding a ruinous ransom, only to find that the kidnapper mistakenly abducted the chauffeur's son. How much is the life of another man's child worth? Dumb-as-dirt car salesman William H. Macy hires small-time crooks Steve Buscemi and Peter Stormare to kidnap his wife so he can squeeze some money from his penny-pinching father-in-law in the Coen Brother's bleakly comic **Fargo** (1996)—the opening assertion that it's based on a true story is part of the smart-alecky joke. Well-liked businessman Robert Redford is efficiently abducted from his own driveway in **The Clearing** (2004), which crosscuts between his developing relationship with abductor Willem Dafoe and his family's desperate efforts to get him back; the icy trick is that they're not unfolding in parallel time.

The Collector (1965) is a socially maladroit amateur lepidopterist (Terence Stamp) who imprisons beautiful art student Samantha Eggar in hopes that she'll learn to love him.

Escaped convict Kevin Costner develops an unexpected fondness for the unhappy seven-year-old he takes hostage in Clint Eastwood's underrated **A Perfect World** (1993), but with the law in pursuit their cross-Texas road trip can only end badly. **Cohen and Tate** (1989), a bracingly grim variation on O. Henry's short story "The Ransom of Red Chief," pits mismatched hit men Roy Scheider and Adam Baldwin against the nine-year-old son of a government-relocated witness they've just killed; over the course of an Oklahoma-to-Texas drive, the boy plays them off against each other. Driving cross-country in their shiny new car, middle-aged married couple Kurt Russell and Kathleen Quinlan develop engine trouble somewhere between south of the boondocks and the middle of nowhere in the lean, tautly directed **Breakdown** (1997). Quinlan accepts a lift to the diner just down the road, but when Russell arrives she's gone and no one will admit to having seen her—his predicament is every city slicker's nightmare about what lies beneath those corn-fed heartland smiles.

SAME MOVIE TWICE

This one is for the film geeks, and yes—I'm one. There are remakes and reimaginings and updatings galore, but flat-out do-overs are rare. Take the odd phenomenon of filmmakers reproducing their own overseas hits with American casts in hopes of getting a foot in Hollywood's golden door. In 1993, George Sluizer tacked on a Hollywood ending to the remake of his claustrophobic Dutch thriller **Spoorloos/The Vanishing** (1988), about a guilt-ridden man's obsessive search for the girlfriend who vanished from a roadside mini-arcade while he waited in the parking lot. In 1998, Danish Ole Bornedal recreated **Nattevagten/Nightwatch** (1994), in which a serial killer and a law student working as a mortuary night watchman play nasty cat-and-mouse games. Even Alfred Hitchcock dusted off his modest, English-made **The Man Who Knew Too Much** (1934) and polished it to a high Technicolor shine in 1956, casting Doris Day and James Stewart as a vacationing couple whose child is kidnapped after they accidentally stumble onto an assassination plot.

Acclaimed French comedian Jacques Tati made side-by-side French- and English-language versions of **Mon oncle/My Uncle** (1958), which pitted his signature character, the amiably oblivious Monsieur Hulot, against an automated home; the dialogue, decor, and staging are so different that Tati himself considered them two films. Or consider the **Dracula**s (1931), shot simultaneously as a hedge against the industry's novelty of the hour: sound. Silent films traveled the world with an inexpensive change of intertitles, and in a bid to hold onto its lucrative South American market, Universal put a Spanish-language version of *Dracula* into production alongside the familiar Bela Lugosi one: different cast, different crew, same sets and screenplay. The Spanish variation is more fluid and sexier— check out the cleavage on star Lupita Tovar (mother of actress Susan Kohner and grandmother of *American Pie* auteurs Paul and Chris Weitz). A handful of 1950s spectaculars were shot in two different widescreen formats. The first, Rodgers and Hammerstein's musical **Oklahoma!** (1955), was actually shot two times, first in Todd-AO and then in Cinemascope; because Todd-AO films required special projectors and a unique curved screen, the Cinemascope version was more widely circulated, but the Todd-AO version contains distinctly livelier performances.

The tale of twin *Exorcist* prequels, in which Father Merrin—memorably played by Max von Sydow in **The Exorcist** (1973)—first encounters demonic possession in post-WWII Africa, begins with ailing director John Frankenheimer and his Merrin, Liam Neeson, abandoning the Warner Bros. project. Replacement director Paul

Schrader had nearly completed shooting when studio executives pulled the plug, claiming his film was so unscary it was unreleasable, and hired action hack Renny Harlin for reshoots that became a whole new film. Harlin kept the locations, star Stellan Skarsgard and the supporting actors, recast the secondary two leads and came up with **Exorcist: The Beginning** (2004). But surprise! A year later Schrader's version, awkwardly called **Dominion: The Prequel to the Exorcist**, came back to haunt them.

The **Psycho**s were made thirty-eight years apart. Flush with *Good Will Hunting*'s (1997) success, Gus Van Sant got the go-ahead for a scene-for-scene, full-color "re-creation" of Hitchcock's 1960 classic, deliberately made in black and white because he thought the sight of poor Marion Crane's blood swirling down the bathtub drain would be repellent. Van Sant's variation on a theme keeps Bernard Hermann's jagged score and faithfully mimics the striking compositions and camera movements, adding brief, bizarre inserts (a masked girl in a bikini, scudding clouds, a cow on a highway) during the murder scenes and restoring a couple of images Hitchcock shot but trimmed. Pointless, but you could discuss the casting all night: Is Anne Heche really today's Janet Leigh? Vince Vaughn and Julianne Moore: the new Anthony Perkins and Vera Miles? Does Viggo Mortensen equal John Gavin, or William H. Macy equal Martin Balsam? There will be a quiz.

SCIENCE FICTION DOUBLE FEATURE

I'm not wild for action-adventure in space, which is why the *Star Wars* movies do nothing for me. And no one needs me to recommend **E. T. the Extra-Terrestrial** (1982) or **Close Encounters of the Third Kind** (1977). My favorite science fiction movies are Ridley Scott's **Blade Runner** (1982), based loosely on visionary madman Philip K. Dick's *Do Androids Dream of Electric Sheep?* and Chris Marker's **La jetée/The Pier** (1962), a time-travel story that hinges on a single, frozen childhood memory and is told almost entirely in still pictures. I like Terry Gilliam's remake, **Twelve Monkeys** (1995), but *La jetée* haunts me like a sliver of ice under the skin. To my mind, Gilliam's dazzling **Brazil** (1985) is the ultimate version of George Orwell's *1984* not based on *1984*; Gilliam nails the dystopian despair, then makes it bitterly funny.

I vividly remember seeing **Invasion of the Body Snatchers** (1956) in a rundown revival house called the Elgin, complete with the original downbeat ending; its transparent allegory of creeping soullessness and blind allegiance to the herd chilled the hell out of me. Neither remake—**Invasion of the Body Snatchers** (1978) or **Body Snatchers** (1994)—improves on a thing. Influential English sci-fi writer Nigel Kneale penned three films in which one Professor Bernard Quatermass (stolid American Brian Donleavy in the first two films, Scottish Andrew Keir in the third) survives close encounters with the unknown. In **The Quatermass Xperiment/The Creeping Unknown** (1955), three astronauts go up in a rocket but only one comes down, infected by an alien presence that slowly eats away his humanity; gaunt actor Richard Wordsworth (great-great-grandson of poet William Wordsworth) is extraordinary as the pathetic, doomed man-turned-monster. In the bleak, Cold War–shadowed **Quatermass 2/Enemy from Space** (1957), a secret government project in the English countryside proves to be a cover for something not of this Earth. I'm not a huge fan of the third film, **Quatermass and the Pit/Five Million Years to Earth** (1967), but its premise is a mindblower: While examining what they think is an unexploded WWII bomb in a London underground station, authorities instead find evidence that human evolution has been an alien experiment.

I love the creeping panic in **The Thing** (1951) as researchers trapped in an arctic military facility face a hostile alien. **John Carpenter's The Thing** (1982) remake ratchets up the paranoia by making the intruder a parasite that moves from host to host, leaving the captive staff unable to tell friend from foe, and I will *never* forget the stunned response to the notorious spider-head effect in a small Greenwich Village theater on opening day. I also like both movies of H. G. Wells's **War of the Worlds**: The 1953 version seethes with Cold War panic and the 2005 remake is shrouded in post-9/11 anxiety. The title spells out the premise of **Robinson Crusoe on Mars** (1964) but doesn't convey the surprisingly complex tone, imbued with the racial and political anxieties of the early 1960s, and Death Valley makes a convincingly harsh Martian landscape. A research satellite crashes in a small Arizona town and everyone but a baby and a drunk dies horribly of a mysterious contagion; research scientists scramble to contain the crisis in the grim, near-documentary-style **The Andromeda Strain** (1971). What more need I say about Stanley Kubrick's **2001: A Space Odyssey** (1968), the ultimate voyage into inner space, but that more than three decades later, people are still debating what the hell it was all about? Except, of course, that it gave us the velvet-voiced HAL 9000, idol of all supercomputers that realize they're better than their makers and act accordingly.

Russian filmmaker Andrei Tarkovsky's leisurely adaptation of Polish sci-fi icon Stanislaw Lem's **Solaris** (1972), about a sentient planet and the havoc it wreaks on lesser minds, isn't for all tastes, but I find it mesmerizing. Steven Soderbergh's 2002 remake picks up the pace but feels interminable. **The Matrix** (1999) steeps its head games in dark, pulpy nostalgia for dystopias past, but under the dazzling action sequences and sleek PVC-wear, it's a persuasive challenge to the dead-above-the-eyeballs masses to unite and cast off their chains.

SCOOP DREAMS

To hear journalists tell it, the way they're (mis)represented in movies is a crime committed with B-movie cliches: ambitious careerists who lie, cheat, and manipulate for an exclusive, plucky gal reporters getting by on a flirt and a wink, spineless editors, venal owners et al. They say it so eloquently and so often it seems they must have a point, but what they really have is a platform: If dentists had comparable media access, you'd hear more about the slanders of **Marathon Man** (1976), **Little Shop of Horrors** (1960), and **Finding Nemo** (2003).

"Follow the money," says the confidential source naughtily nick-named "Deep Throat" to *Washington Post* reporter Bob Woodward (Robert Redford) in **All the President's Men** (1976), a gripping depiction of day-to-day reporting in the eye of the storm known as Watergate. Woodward and Carl Bernstein (Dustin Hoffman), a rookie and a grating gadfly, painstakingly uncover the political scandal that brought down the Nixon administration; their long, realistic hours of phone calls, sifting through library check-out chits, and documenting dubious accounting practices are thrilling as any high-speed chase. Its fictional counterpart, underrated U.K. thriller **Defence of the Realm** (1985), sets an apolitical tabloid reporter (Gabriel Byrne) on the trail of an explosive story triggered by two apparently unrelated matters: the death of a juvenile delinquent and a titillating scandal involving a member of parliament, a call girl, and a KGB agent. The fact-based **Shattered Glass** (2003) also captures the thrill of the hunt for information; bright young reporter Stephen Glass (Hayden Christensen), a rising star at *The New Republic*, a respected journal of politics and culture, is gradually exposed as a compulsive liar whose articles are a tissue of falsehoods. It's a great, real-life "how'd *that* happen?" story that also parses the universal nuances of office politics and workplace relationships.

If there's a newspaper movie more cynical than **Ace in the Hole** (1951), based on the hoopla surrounding the sorry fate of spelunker Floyd Collins, who got himself trapped in a Kentucky cave in 1925 and died after more than two weeks of round-the-clock media coverage, I haven't seen it. Kirk Douglas plays disgraced big-city reporter Chuck Tatum, who's reduced to writing for an Albuquerque rag and sees his ticket back to the big leagues in a local human-interest story, which he contrives to transform into a tragic media circus. If Tatum is the journalist's nightmare of what people think about reporters, then the world-weary editor played by Humphrey Bogart in **Deadline U.S.A.** (1952) is the dream: Caught between the impending sale of his paper, advertisers trying to dictate editorial policy, and readers who prefer puzzles, horoscopes, and cake recipes to news, he decides to go out with a bang by nailing an "untouchable" mobster.

"I love this dirty town," declares ruthless gossip columnist J. J. Hunsecker (Burt Lancaster) in **Sweet Smell of Success** (1957), which remains as venomously potent as when pioneering rumor-slinger Walter Winchell—the model for Hunsecker—was a household name. A glittering wallow in ambition at its darkest, *Sweet Smell* is a poison-pen letter to scandal mongering, New York nightlife, and the dark underbelly of glamour. For sheer, crackling fun it's hard to top **His Girl Friday** (1940), Howard Hawks's fast-paced remake of former newspaperman Ben Hecht and Charles MacArthur's billet-doux to tabloid journalism, **The Front Page** (1931). Both revolve around a conniving editor and the star reporter he refuses to lose to marriage and a normal life, but what makes *Friday* hum is that reporter Hildy Johnson is a woman and editor Walter Burns is her ex-husband. And of course, that they're played by Rosalind Russell and Cary Grant, who make the tongue-twisting, brain-teasing, mile-a-minute dialogue seem as easy as falling off a rewrite desk. Two subsequent remakes, 1974's *The Front Page* and *Switching Channels* (1988), barely merit a footnote.

THE SHAPE OF THINGS

B ack in the golden age, Hollywood stars glittered whether they were playing coal miners and spinster librarians or society swells; de-glamming meant eyeglasses, artful stubble, and bad hair. But Robert De Niro, a pure product of the pitiless make-it-real legacy of Brando, Dean, and Clift, raised the bar in **Raging Bull** (1980). To portray boxer Jake LaMotta from his fighting prime to bloated, washed-up middle age, he first trained for a year (even sparring with LaMotta himself), then ballooned up to 60 pounds above his normal weight and delivered a great performance in a great film—arguably the best of the 1980s. But what everyone remembered was the weight change.

The stunning first segment of Stanley Kubrick's uneven Vietnam-era **Full Metal Jacket** (1987) is stolen by the then unknown Vincent D'Onofrio as chubby, tormented misfit Private Pyle, who explodes under the pressures of basic training; he gained 70 pounds for the role but missed out on plaudits because hardly anyone recognized him as **Adventures in Babysitting**'s (1987) golden garage god. Slender Australian actress Toni Collette added 40 pounds to play a chubby introvert in the engaging **Muriel's Wedding** (1994), but was also too little known for the transformation to register. By 2005, when she put on 25 pounds to play the plump sister in Curtis Hanson's underrated **In Her Shoes**, Collette got her due. Petite Renee Zellweger added some 20 pounds to play good-hearted, pleasingly plump Bridget Jones in the irresistible **Bridget Jones's Diary** (2001), pared herself to sinew and bone to play predatory showgirl Roxie Hart in **Chicago** (2002), and piled the pounds back on for the disappointing **Bridget Jones: The Edge of Reason** (2004). Golden girl Charlize Theron gained 25 pounds as part of her uncompromising performance as real-life serial killer Aileen Wuornos in **Monster** (2003), then skinnied down in record time to play a glamorous gadabout in the silly **Head in the Clouds** (2004).

Then there are the losers. Lanky Adrien Brody went from 160 pounds to a gaunt 130 to play real-life Holocaust survivor Wladyslaw Szpilman in the harrowing **The Pianist** (2002). Matt Damon's searing supporting turn as a heroin-addicted ex-soldier in the otherwise undistinguished **Courage Under Fire** (1996) required a 40-pound weight loss, and he dropped nearly 25 pounds three years later for **The Talented Mr. Ripley**. Jared Leto starved off 25 pounds as a junkie in the flashy **Requiem for a Dream** (2000), a slicked up *Reefer Madness* (1938) for the twenty-first century. But the biggest loser award goes to strapping English actor Christian Bale, who shed one-third of his body weight to play a haunted factory worker in **The Machinist** (2004), dropping to a wraithlike 130 pounds, then went from the *Twilight Zone*–like spook show to playing the buff and muscular Dark Knight in **Batman Begins** (2005).

Why do they do it? Like saints and mystics, serious actors are willing to mortify the flesh in the service of their calling; they also win Oscars—extreme makeovers impress audiences, critics, and the voters of the Academy of Motion Picture Arts and Sciences. Theron, De Niro, and Brody took home awards for *Monster*, *Raging Bull*, and *The Pianist*, respectively, and Zellweger's *Chicago* win came hard on *Bridget Jones*'s (round) heels.

SHRINK-WRAPPED

I f psychiatry had not existed, the movies would have had to invent it," the much-quoted Dr. Irving Schneider once observed. But just because movies love psychiatrists doesn't mean they show them a whole lot of respect. There are, to be sure, a handful of sober, relatively unsensational films about the hard work of healing shattered minds, including **I Never Promised You a Rose Garden** (1977), in which doctor Bibi Andersson tries to help schizophrenic teenager Kathleen Quinlan confront her demons of the mind; **The Three Faces of Eve** (1957), starring Joanne Woodward as a woman with multiple personality disorder and Lee J. Cobb as her doctor; **Ordinary People** (1980), in which psychiatrist Judd Hirsch helps suicidal teenager Timothy Hutton come to terms with his brother's death; and **Equus** (1977), with Richard Burton as the troubled middle-aged psychiatrist trying to find out why adolescent stable boy Peter Firth blinded six horses. Even the often-maligned **The Snake Pit** (1948) comes out on the side of the angels; unbalanced young wife Olivia de Havilland winds up at a mental institution whose director is on a mission to *not* run a hell hole. But let's face it: Good, responsible psychiatrists aren't half as entertaining as Dr. Hannibal "the cannibal" Lecter, the undisputed star of **Manhunter**

(1986), **Silence of the Lambs** (1990), **Hannibal** (2001), and *Manhunter* retread **Red Dragon** (2002). I will, by the way, take this opportunity to voice my minority opinion that Brian Cox's silkily insinuating performance as Lecter in *Manhunter* is far superior to Anthony Hopkins's hammy, mannered, and ridiculously overpraised characterization.

In any event, everyone knows the japes—psychiatrists are as screwy as their patients, the difference between "therapist" and "the rapist" is a space, the inmates are running the asylum—but these movies make hay with them. Sinister shrinks put their inside knowledge of both of the mind's weakness and individual's secrets to deeply unethical use in **The Cabinet of Dr. Caligari** (1919), Fritz Lang's **Dr. Mabuse, the Gambler** (1922) and **The Testament of Dr. Mabuse** (1932), **The Amazing Dr. Clitterhouse** (1938), **Cat People** (1942), Edgar G. Ulmer's **Strange Illusion** (1945), **Nightmare Alley** (1947), and **The Brood** (1979)—you have to hand it to David Cronenberg for having the singular warp of mind to coin the term *Psychoplasmatics* for *The Brood*'s grotesquely innovative therapy. As to mental hospitals, a quick tour of **One Flew Over the Cuckoo's Nest** (1975), the low-budget mind-bender **Crazy as Hell** (2002), Sam Fuller's lurid **Shock Corridor** (1963)—trust me when I say the scene in which ambitious reporter Peter Breck, who gets himself committed in hopes of getting the scoop on a murder, stumbles into the nympho ward is worth the price of admission all by itself—or Alfred Hitchcock's **Spellbound** (1945), complete with Salvador Dali's notorious dream sequence, ought to convince you that outpatient therapy is the way to go.

SILENTS ARE GOLDEN

With the exception of slapstick comedies by Charlie Chaplin, Buster Keaton, and Harold Lloyd, silent films are the preserve of film scholars. But these films have stood the test of time and showcase some of the icons of an era when stars had *faces*.

Battleship Potemkin/Bronenosets Potyomkin (1925), Sergei Eisenstein's stunning account of a naval mutiny—everybody steals technique from this landmark in kinetic editing and poetic juxtaposition of images.

The Cabinet of Dr. Caligari/Das Kabinett des Doktor Caligari (1919), a freaky, creepy, trippy bogeyman tale that unfolds in an elegantly psychotic dreamscape that's as widely pilfered from as *Metropolis.*

Flesh and the Devil (1926), with the extraordinary Greta Garbo as a temptress who comes between two friends.

Haxan/Witchcraft Through the Ages (1922), a wild, special-effects-filled and surprisingly graphic history of witchcraft and devil worship.

It (1927), a sexy comedy of class consciousness showcasing quintessential jazz baby Clara Bow.

King of Kings (1927), Cecil B. DeMille's lavish biblical epic, equal parts piety and pagan decadence.

The Last Laugh/Der letzte Mann (1924), about the mental unraveling of an aging luxury-hotel doorman (masterful German actor Emil Jannings) who's cruelly demoted to washroom attendant.

Metropolis (1927), one of the most visually influential films in history—everybody steals images from Fritz Lang's visionary futuristic fable.

Nosferatu (1922), the first adaptation of *Dracula*, featuring cadaverous German actor Max Schreck as a bald, rat-toothed, pointy-eared monster of a vampire.

Pandora's Box/Die Buchse der Pandora (1929), with the luminous Louise Brooks as a hell-bound seductress.

The Passion of Joan of Arc (1928), riveting account of the French martyr's trial and execution, featuring a transcendent, tear-streaked performance by Renee Maria Falconetti.

The Phantom of the Opera (1925), with "Man of a Thousand Faces" Lon Chaney as the tormented phantom.

The Sheik (1921), featuring sex symbol Rudolph Valentino as a lusty desert prince.

The Wind (1928), a subtle psychological drama in which the harshness of prairie life drives city girl Lillian Gish mad.

DIRECTOR'S SPOTLIGHT:
DOUGLAS SIRK

Once dismissed as a panderer to unsophisticated popular tastes, German-born Douglas Sirk (1897–1987) has a reputation that rests on the melodramas he made in the 1950s, Technicolor weepies that simultaneously found the authentic emotional core in Hollywood's most cherished cliches—self-sacrificing women, stalwart men tested by fate, reformed reprobates, wayward children, baroque tragedy, and outrageous twists of fate—and laced them with a bitter critique of mainstream American values. Hipsters who think **All I Desire** (1953), **Magnificent Obsession** (1954), **All that Heaven Allows** (1955), **Written on the Wind** (1956), **Interlude** (1957), **The Tarnished Angels** (1957), and **Imitation of Life** (1959) are camp or kitsch or guilty pleasures— the decor! the costumes! the hair!—are missing the point. Rainer Werner Fassbinder, Pedro Almodovar, and John Woo, all of whom adapted the conventions of melodrama to their own dramatic ends, didn't love Sirk's films because they were hokey, dated goofs. They saw stories of powerful emotions repressed in the name of propriety until they explode, movies whose operatic excesses spring from the stifling ground of social conformity and cold, glittering surfaces.

Sirk—Claus Detlev Sierck—was born in Hamburg to Danish parents. He directed both for stage and screen as the Nazi Party rose to power; Sirk leaned left and his wife, actress Hilde Jary, was Jewish, so they fled to California, arriving in 1941. Sirk worked steadily for more than twenty-five years, forging a hugely successful Hollywood career by being flexible: With equal facility he could direct WWII-era propaganda (**Hitler's Madman**, 1943), historical drama (**A Scandal in Paris**, 1946), musicals (**Slightly French**, 1949; **Has Anybody Seen My Gal?**, 1952), crime pictures (**Lured**, 1947; **Sleep, My Love**, 1948; **Shockproof**, 1949), Westerns (**Taza, Son of Cochise**, 1954), domestic comedy (the proto–*Brady Bunch* blended-family picture **Weekend with Father**, 1951), and epic spectacle (**Sign of the Pagan**, 1954). But the essence of Sirk's genius boils down to four films.

Reckless playboy Rock Hudson finds salvation through science in *Magnificent Obsession*; after indirectly causing both the death of a selfless doctor and the blindness of his widow (Jane Wyman), Hudson wakes up to the meaninglessness of his life. He studies medicine, devotes himself to anonymous good works, and eventually restores Wyman's sight, finding the will to forgive himself in her love. Look below the shoot-'em-up surface of Woo's *The Killer* (1989) and see if *Magnificent Obsession* doesn't look back.

Wealthy, respectable widow Wyman falls in love with her much younger gardener—Hudson again—in *All that Heaven Allows*, horrifying her stuck-up friends and prudish adult children, who convince her to drop her "unsuitable" boyfriend for the sake of the family's reputation and reward her with a TV set. Fassbinder reset the story among Germany's have-nots and gives it a racially charged twist in *Ali: Fear Eats the Soul* (1974).

Written on the Wind is a delirious tangle of sibling rivalry, sexual jealously, material one-upmanship, and lust for power: It follows a rich wastrel (Robert Stack) and a working-class striver (Hudson) who grow up together on the Texas ranch owned by Stack's dad, a self-made oilman who wishes his drunken son were more like Hudson. Stack's spoiled sister, trampy Dorothy Malone, craves her father's attention and lusts for Hudson; smart cookie Lauren Bacall comes between the boyhood friends and Malone trumps everyone after her father's fatal heart attack, which appears to be the direct result of her shameless mamboing in a skintight dress.

And in the extraordinary *Imitation of Life*, two mothers, one white and one black (Lana Turner, Juanita Moore), are lifelong friends whose hearts are broken by their ungrateful daughters: Sandra Dee puts the moves on her mother's man while Susan Kohner abandons her devoted mom so she can pass for white. Watch it and weep—I do, every single time I hear Mahalia Jackson's magnificent voice lay into the gospel heart-ripper "Trouble of the World."

SO YOU WANNA BE A
ROCK 'N' ROLL STAR

Even presidents, best-selling novelists, and movie stars secretly want to be rock gods—look at Gina Gershon, parlaying her part in punk fringe player Cheri Lovedog's semiauto-biographical musical **Prey for Rock 'n' Roll** (2003) into an in-character tour backed by members of NYC noise-rock band Girls Against Boys.

But while many are called, few are chosen; movies that embrace the bottomless pit of longing that drives rock dreams without domesticating it into a Pollyannaish "hold on to your dream" sermon are fewer still. A few electrifying moments in **Jailhouse Rock** (1957) aside, Elvis Presley's dozens of movies are scrubbed 100 percent clean of the all-consuming hunger that scared the bejabbers out of old-fashioned parents. But Kurt Russell nailed it in John Carpenter's **Elvis** (1979), as did Jamie Foxx as Ray Charles in **Ray** (2004), Gary Oldman as Sex Pistol Sid Vicious in **Sid and Nancy** (1986), Gary Busey in **The Buddy Holly Story** (1978), Val Kilmer as Jim Morrison in **The Doors** (1991), Lou Diamond Phillips as Ritchie Valens in **La Bamba** (1987), Angela Bassett as Tina Turner in **What's Love Got to Do with It** (1993), and Ian Hart as Beatle John Lennon in **Backbeat** (1994). Richard Lester's larky **A Hard**

Day's Night (1964) combines French New Wave stylings and the Fab Four's own rags-to-riches story into a swinging sixties soufflé, but its jabs at feckless youthquakers, deranged fans, clueless old fogies, and celebrities overwhelmed by the price of fame are still sharp.

Almost Famous (2000), Cameron Crowe's portrait of an underage *Rolling Stone* writer on tour with fictional arena rockers Stillwater, is based on his own experiences as a sixteen-year-old journalist on the road with Led Zeppelin in 1973; the underbelly of rock dreams is vividly evoked when Stillwater's guitar god sells his sweet, loyal groupie (sorry, "band-aid") to Humble Pie for $50 and a case of Heineken. Breezier but no less cynical, **Expresso Bongo** (1959) follows a sleazy, jive-talking, would-be idol maker (*Manchurian Candidate* star Laurence Harvey) as he trolls a seedy Soho crawling with aging hookers and doomed striptease girls in search of his ticket to the big time. He finds it in golden-voiced teen (real-life pop star Cliff Richard) with "a chip on [his] shoulder and an H-bomb in [his] pants," then loses out to a slicker class of shark.

Todd Haynes's shimmering, thorny, and consummately self-aware **Velvet Goldmine** (1998) sics a *Citizen Kane*–style reporter (Christian Bale) on the twisted trail of Bowie-esque Brit-glit icon Brian Slade (Jonathan Rhys Meyers), via his embittered ex-wife (Toni Collette) and a small army of former friends, including proto-punk Curt Wild, played by Ewan McGregor as a grungy Iggy Pop/Lou Reed hybrid. More glitz than a Mardi Gras float and all the divine decadence a glam fan could want. The criminally underrated **Ladies and Gentlemen, the Fabulous Stains** (1982), directed by *Rocky Horror Picture Show* producer Lou Adler, features enough grunge to dirty the Mormon Tabernacle Choir, plus fifteen-year-old Diane Lane, thirteen-year-old Laura Dern, and flash-in-the-pan Marin Kanter as surly blue-collar teens whose ragged garage band, the Stains (imagine a talent-free Runaways), briefly catches an attitude wave—fueled mostly by guttersnipe get-ups and two-tone skunk 'dos—which they ride right into the rocks. All this, plus the Clash's Paul Simonon, Fee Waybill of the Tubes, and (S)ex Pistols Paul Cook and Steve Jones as rock 'n' roll casualties!

STIFF UPPER BRIT

You say heartwarming gives you indigestion and uplifting tales of the little people and their tiny triumphs bring out your inner Leona Helmsley? Permit me to suggest that the headache-inducing sweetness of formulaic Hollywood pap might be to blame. And the antidote could just be the all-together-now Britcom. They're formulaic too: Friends, families, and neighbors pull together to restore their community's sense of self-worth by way of some quixotic and often utterly nutty scheme. But the formula includes a bracing dose of grit: People get fired and don't get their jobs back, they lose their loved ones and even die; for all the eccentricity and silliness, the uplift feels earned. The ur-text is **The Full**

Monty (1997), in which broke, depressed, unemployed steelworkers take back their manhood with their bare behinds; they become male strippers, even though the lot of them are less sleekly buff than one Chippendale's go-go boy. *Full Monty* director Peter Cattaneo and screenwriter Simon Beaufoy each took the formula out for another spin. Cattaneo made **Lucky Break** (2001), in which a bunch of congenial convicts concoct a prison break by staging a musical in the least secure area in the prison. In Beaufoy's **Blow Dry** (2001), the arrival of the British National Hairdressing Championship reinvigorates both the small Yorkshire town of Keighley and local locksmith Alan Rickman, who's been in the doldrums since his wife and their prize hair model (Natasha Richardson, Rachel Griffiths) ran away together and set up their own shop.

In **The Englishman Who Went Up a Hill But Came Down a Mountain** (1995), a WWI-era Welsh village bands together to save their beloved mountain, Ffynnon Garw, from being downgraded to a mere hill by visiting cartographer Hugh Grant. **Mean Machine** (2001) relocates **The Longest Yard** (1974)—uncredited—to a U.K. penitentiary, where a disgraced soccer star Vinnie Jones rallies his discouraged fellow inmates to whip their sorry selves into a winning team. The prisoners of **Greenfingers** (2001) blossom when sullen no-hoper Clive Owen and the obligatory chipper old fellow persuade them to grow posies, eventually winning a spot in the hoity-toity Hampton Court Flower Show. In **Calendar Girls** (2003), a group of respectable, middle-aged English housewives pose nude for a charity calendar. Yorkshire miners faced with ruin if the Grimley mine closes pin their fragile hopes on getting to a national brass band competition at London's Royal Albert Hall in **Brassed Off!** (1996).

The Bootmen (2000) are Australian, but the dynamic is the same: Blue-collar lads form a muscular tap-dancing troupe and show naysayers that fancy footwork can raise money to teach laid-off factory workers computer skills. To save her home, widowed and suddenly impoverished matron Brenda Blethyn turns her greenhouse into a hydroponic dope farm in **Saving Grace** (2000); her small-town Cornish neighbors gamely pitch in. In **Waking Ned Devine** (1998), a small Irish town conspires to convince lottery officials that Ned—who died of shock when he saw his winning ticket—is still alive so they can collect the payoff that will lift all boats. For sheer daftness, though, it's hard to top **Secret Society** (2000), in which a plump Yorkshire packing plant worker discovers that the proud, self-confident large ladies with whom she works are secret sumo wrestlers. And yes, they get to go *mano a mano* with a team of male wrestlers from Japan in an exhibition match as loopy as it is satisfying.

STORY BY THE BARD

Inspired—sometimes very loosely—by Shakespeare's plays, these films pilfer his plots and characters and spin them every which way but loose. The moral: You can't keep a good story down.

Akira Kurosawa rethought two of Shakespeare's masterpieces, setting them in feudal Japan and closely following the original plots; *Macbeth* became **Throne of Blood/Kumonosujo** (1957), with Toshiro Mifune, and *King Lear* became the epic **Ran** (1985). Both are brilliant. The gripping **Othello** (2001) resets the story in modern-day London, with Eammon Walker as a charismatic black police officer on a largely white force and Christopher Eccleston as the friend and mentor who betrays him after being passed over for a coveted promotion. In the underrated **O** (2001), the same dynamic plays out in a swanky Southern high school, where sole black student Odin James (Mekhi Phifer), a star athlete on a basketball scholarship, is undone by embittered teammate Josh Hartnett.

The musical **Kiss Me Kate** (1953) is simultaneously a backstage romp about a Broadway-bound production of a musical *The Taming of the Shrew* and a retelling of the story via the tempestuous romance between the show's egocentric star (Howard Keel) and his sharp-tongued ex-wife/current co-star (Kathryn Grayson). The slight but charming **10 Things I Hate About You** (1999) makes the shrew a whip-smart and aggressively disagreeable high school senior (Julia Stiles) and her tamer, a handsome transfer student (Heath Ledger). **West Side Story** (1961) recasts *Romeo and Juliet* as a musical romance set in 1950s New York; the leader of a white teenage gang falls for the sister (Natalie Wood, improbably cast as Puerto Rican) of his bitterest rival, who leads a Latin gang.

Shakespeare's magic-filled fable *The Tempest* lies beneath the sci-fi surface of **Forbidden Planet** (1956), while a modern-day Lady Macbeth pushes her weak-willed husband to murder his way to the top of a fast-food outlet in **Scotland, PA.** (2002); detective Ernie McDuff (Christopher Walken) brings him down. Gus Van Sant's **My Own Private Idaho** (1991) reworks portions of *Henry IV, Parts I and II*, into the story of narcoleptic male hustler River Phoenix and slumming mayor's son Keanu Reeves, a contemporary spin on Shakespeare's rebellious Prince Hal, the future King Henry.

THE STRAIGHT DOPE

Bluestockings stomped Hollywood's buzz in 1934. Before then, narcotics were a fact of vice, from nineteenth-century shorts about opium dens to Charlie Chaplin getting an accidental shot of dope in **Easy Street** (1917) and the mind-boggling "Sweet Marijuana" production number in **Murder at the Vanities** (1934), which squeaked into theaters before the door slammed shut on such shenanigans. But nervous studio executives, spooked by vocal muttering about the corrupting influence of movies, drew up their own restrictive Production Code in hopes of heading off government censorship, and drug-related story lines and allusions were swept away alongside smutty talk, nudity, and other risque material. For the better part of two decades, the only way to get a fix at the flicks was via independently produced drug-scare movies, like the now-hilarious **Cocaine Fiends** (1936) and **Reefer Madness** (1937). Otto Preminger's **The Man with the Golden Arm** (1955) helped crack the Code with its stark portrayal of heroin addiction; ex-con and would-be musician Frankie Machine (Frank Sinatra) wants to mend his ways, but the siren song of dope and gambling take him down, all to the hopped up strains of Elmer Bernstein's jazzy score. By the '70s, Cheech and Chong were making drug jokes safe for middle America—their antic **Up in Smoke** (1978) spawned a bumper crop of stoner comedies.

Gus Van Sant evokes everyday lifestyles of the hooked and aimless in **Drugstore Cowboy** (1989), about a makeshift family of addicts (Matt Dillon, Kelly Lynch, James LeGros, and Heather Graham) crisscrossing the Pacific Northwest getting stoked and robbing pharmacies. In professional provocateur Larry Clark's **Another Day in Paradise** (1998), successful middle-aged users/dealers Melanie Griffith and James Woods "adopt" a younger couple (Vincent Kartheiser and Natasha Gregson Wagner) and teach them the ropes of high times and low life. **The Basketball Diaries** (1995) is based on the journals of Lower East Side poet/musician Jim Carroll (played by Leonardo DiCaprio), who slid into heroin addiction between the ages of twelve and fifteen. **The Panic in Needle Park** (1971) takes a druggy tour of Manhattan's then shabby Upper West Side with a very young Al Pacino.

The episodic, bleakly beautiful **Jesus' Son** (2000) follows an aimless, nameless Midwestern doper as he drifts from fix to fix, while Danny Boyle's high-energy **Trainspotting** (1996) plunges into the everyday insanity of a group of unrepentant Edinburgh smack heads (including Ewan McGregor); the wild ride gets a raw power kickstart from Iggy Pop's "Lust for Life." Small-time ecstasy dealer Sarah Polley gets entangled in a web of trouble in **Go** (1999)—watch it just to see a kitty cat steal the show with a few well-chosen words—and real-life sitcom writer Jerry Stahl (played by Ben Stiller) shares his surreal life as a high-functioning Hollywood junkie in **Permanent Midnight** (1998).

The spirit of vintage exploitation just-say-no movies lives on in Darren Aronofsky's vivid adaptation of Hubert Selby Jr.'s **Requiem for a Dream** (2000), about four addicts (including unwary middle-aged diet-pill popper Ellen Burstyn) whose habits devour their dreams. But the "drugs are bad" message is trumped by the vicarious brain buzz of its eye-popping images and jittery editing. Bizarro casting (Mickey Rourke, John Leguizamo, Brittany Murphy, Peter

Stormare, and Eric Roberts in drag . . .) plus crystal meth drive the freakshow thrills of **Spun** (2002); the equally loony **Salton Sea** (2002) features Vincent D'Onofrio as a no-nosed tweaker named Pooh Bear who gets his kicks restaging JFK's assassination with pigeons and threatening to feed Val Kilmer's privates to a badger. Sick kicks don't come better.

DIRECTOR'S SPOTLIGHT: PRESTON STURGES

Preston Sturges (1898–1959) had more talent than he knew what to do with, so he did everything: Sturges wrote plays and film scripts, directed, edited, composed songs, and invented things, including a kiss-proof lipstick. None of his films were as overwhelmingly innovative and influential as *Citizen Kane*, made by fellow jack-of-all-trades Orson Welles in 1941 (though it should be pointed out that *Kane* owes no small structural debt to Sturges's screenplay for 1933's **The Power and the Glory**). But Sturges's body of work yields more first-class films than Welles's—including **Christmas in July** and **The Great McGinty** (both 1940), **The Lady Eve** and **Sullivan's Travels** (both 1941), **The Palm Beach Story** (1942), **The Miracle of Morgan's Creek** and **Hail the Conquering Hero** (both 1944), and **Unfaithfully Yours** (1948).

Sturges was born in Chicago and raised on eccentricity: His mother, the former Mary Dempsey, rechristened herself Mary Desti and claimed aristocratic Italian ties; a close friend of pioneering modern dancer Isadora Duncan, she followed Duncan and dancers around Europe and took her son along. Her high-end cosmetics and accessories company, Maison Desti, made the scarf that strangled Duncan when it got entangled in the wheels of her open-topped car. Preston worked for his mother before trying his hand at writing plays; his racy Broadway hit **Strictly Dishonorable** (1929) was filmed twice, though not by Sturges. He wrote romantic comedies that were both genuinely romantic and truly funny: The ruthless wit and escalating complications of *The Lady Eve* and *The Palm Beach Story* are much imitated and seldom equaled. He tossed off sophisticated dialogue with the grace and ease of an authentic sophisticate and poked fun at crooked politicians, Hollywood pretension, momism, the sanctity of marriage, and the purity of American womanhood. At a time when movie studios were factories for filmmaking and workers knew their place on the line, Sturges made history by persuading Paramount Pictures to let him direct his own screenplay *The Great McGinty*, in which a deeply crooked politician is undone by one mad moment of honesty. With *The Miracle of Morgan's Creek*, the tale of patriotic Midwestern girl-next-door Trudy Kockenlocker (Betty Hutton), whose personal contribution to the war effort—"entertaining" GIs before they're shipped overseas—leaves her pregnant with sextuplets, Sturges managed to simultaneously mock both wartime flag-waving *and* small-town morals while the war was still in full swing. And in *Sullivan's Travels*, a Hollywood filmmaker (Joel McCrea) who wants to stop making frivolous comedies and direct an *important* social drama called *O Brother, Where Art Thou?* decides to take an educational undercover tour of the lower depths and gets stuck there, winding up in a hellish Southern prison where the value of escapist tomfoolery like Mickey Mouse cartoons becomes suddenly clear. It made an indelible impression on me as a teenager, and I imagine the Coen Brothers had a similar experience.

Sturges worked steadily from 1930 to 1944, navigating the studio politics that tripped up Welles until a squabble with Paramount executive Buddy De Silva derailed his brilliant career. He never got it back on track, though years later the Directors Guild and the Writers Guild of America West gave his name to a rarely bestowed award recognizing superior work in both screenwriting and directing. No one could have deserved it more.

SUBWAY SERIES

Bathysiderodromophobes beware: Locations don't come much more confining than subway trains. Inspired by an actual event ("Which one?" a properly jaded subway rider would ask), **The Incident** (1967) traps a cross-section of New Yorkers—recovering drunk, timid homosexual, passed-out bum, soldiers on leave, squabbling couples, a very angry black man—on a late-night train with a pair of sneering white punks on dope (Tony Musante and Martin Sheen, so young they get an "and introducing" credit). The thoroughly convincing subway car is a set, but the station stops were shot on the fly by cinematographer Gerald Hirschfeld—the MTA, not surprisingly, withheld permission to shoot officially. World-weary transit police lieutenant Walter Matthau is on the spot in **The Taking of Pelham One Two Three** (1974) when four hijackers with pre–*Reservoir Dogs* color-coded aliases commandeer a number 6 train and demand one million dollars in one hour; if the money is late, they'll kill one hostage per minute until it arrives. A great suspense thriller and a dizzying flashback to the bad old days when lady cops were a punchline and New York was broke, filthy, and slashed with grafitti.

Everyone remembers the garishly costumed gang members in Walter Hill's 1979 **The Warriors** (lovingly reproduced in the 2005 Rockstar video game), but the long train ride from the Bronx to Coney Island is a trip; it plays fast and loose with the system's geography but captures the seedy '70s ambiance. Ex-con Mark Wahlberg gets caught up in his uncle's shady dealings with New York City transit department in the melancholy crime thriller **The Yards** (2000); its authentic evocation of the era's pervasive corruption and brazenly dirty politics may owe something to the fact that Queens-born co-writer/director James Gray's father, a partner in a company that supplied electronic parts to the MTA, was enmeshed in a scandal involving bribes and false billing. The uneven **Subway Stories** (1997) strings together ten short films by different directors (including Jonathan Demme, Abel Ferrara, and Bob Balaban), based on (purportedly) true straphangers' tales. On a gentler note, legendary documentarian D. A. Pennebaker's first film, the lyrical, short **Daybreak Express** (shot in 1953 but not assembled until

1957), sets footage shot from New York's long-gone elevated Third Avenue line to Duke Ellington's 1948 jazz number.

The unjustly obscure **Death Line** (1972) opens with a bowler-hatted English gent, fresh off a tour of Soho's seedy strip clubs, meeting a dreadful fate in a deserted underground station; what could have been a run-of-the-mill gross-out horror picture is actually a haunting fable about the faceless underclass and long-buried sins that unfold beneath the bustling surface of 1970s London. If the Hungarian **Kontroll** (2004) is to be believed, Budapest's subway system is crawling with pimps, whores, and hostile dogs, the motormen are drunks and the ticket controllers—transit employees charged with making sure passengers have paid their fares—are high-strung jerks at best and bona fide nut cases at worst. Gloomy, fatalistic, and just a little surreal, it's the Euro-yin to Luc Besson's goofball yang, the cartoonish new-wave fairy tale **Subway** (1985), in which bleach-blond street scamp Christopher Lambert, desperately in love with pampered-but-miserable trophy wife Isabelle Adjani, steals her personal papers and takes refuge in the Paris Metro. He finds refuge among the misfits who live in the tunnels and forgotten crannies of the system, including Besson regular Jean Reno before he was grizzled and a baby-faced Jean-Hugues Anglade as skate punk "The Roller." It's all patently ridiculous but oddly charming.

SUITE SMELL OF SUCCESS

I f hotel walls could talk, no guest would ever get a decent night's sleep. These movies explore the random meetings and unlikely relationships that flourish in the transient, suspended cocoon of hotel stays.

"People come. People go. Nothing ever happens," says the most clueless guest of the opulent **Grand Hotel** (1932), where a colorful cross-section of lives intersect, including a ruined aristocrat, an ambitious stenographer, a dying bookkeeper, and Greta Garbo's aging ballerina who just wants to be alone. The nineteenth-century Grand Hotel on Michigan's Mackinac Island becomes a portal into the past in the unabashedly romantic **Somewhere in Time** (1980); modern-day playwright Christopher Reeve falls for a decades-old portrait of an actress and wills himself back to the year 1912 to meet her. In **Lost in Translation** (2003), two lonely, displaced Americans, a restless young woman and a melancholy movie star twice her age, cross paths in a high-rise Tokyo hotel; without their spouses and adrift in a culture that baffles them, they take refuge in an intense friendship that never quite becomes an affair. Vacationing with her family in 1963 at a Catskills resort hotel, sheltered Jewish teenager Jennifer Grey falls for a studly dance instructor from the wrong side of the tracks (Patrick Swayze) in the sweetly sexy romance **Dirty Dancing** (1987).

Plaza Suite (1971) and **California Suite** (1978) are quintessential Neil Simon comedies: glib, often very funny, and set to the rhythm of the Catskills rim shot. In *Plaza Suite*, Walter Matthau plays three different characters in sequential vignettes—half of an estranged couple, a hound-dog producer putting the moves on an old flame, and one of the parents of a bride with cold feet—set in the same suite of rooms in New York's Plaza Hotel. *California Suite* deposits three couples (one divorced) and a pair of friends at the Beverly Hills Hotel and lets the complications rip.

On the "love it or hate it" question of Chinese director Wong Kar-wai's **2046** (2004), I'm under its enigmatic spell. A dreamy, lushly photographed reverie on themes of love and loss, it's a story told in two settings: half of it is set in the rundown Hotel Oriental in 1960s Hong Kong and the other half in the erotic sci-fi novel that a down-on-his-luck writer spins from memories of his own relationships with the women who pass through room 2046. The elliptical **Last Year at Marienbad** (1961) is equally polarizing: In a cavernous luxury hotel, a man tries to convince a married woman (Delphine Seyrig) to run away with him, evoking the passionate affair that she claims not to remember; the cool, mysterious look of *Marienbad's* ravishingly stylized tableaux has been appropriated by more high-end perfume ads than I can count. Seyrig also lends detached glamour to the mesmerizing art-horror film **Daughters of Darkness** (1971), as a movie star staying at a deluxe Belgian beachfront resort (odd, muses the middle-aged desk clerk; she visited here when he was a child, and looks exactly the same) during the off-season and drawing the only other guests, troubled newlyweds, into her web. Blocked writer Jack Nicholson gives in to the haunted vibes of the snowbound Overlook

Hotel while working as winter caretaker in **The Shining** (1980), while Manhattan's storied Chelsea Hotel, a seedily glamorous refuge for bohemians, artists, and eccentrics since 1905, steals the show from a strong but floundering cast in **Chelsea Walls** (2001).

Finally, in the devastating, fact-based **Hotel Rwanda** (2004), a Kigali hotelier (Don Cheadle) uses all his survival skills to rescue his "guests"—an ever-expanding throng of desperate refugees—from the genocidal madness gripping his country. It may be the ultimate, horrifying expression of the notion that hotels are an escape from the chaos of real life.

SUPERIOR SEQUELS

Conventional wisdom says sequels suck and conventional wisdom is right, except when it's not. There are sequels as good as—and occasionally better than—the films that inspired them. Not predesigned trilogies like **Star Wars** (1977), **The Empire Strikes Back** (1980), and **Return of the Jedi** (1983), or **The Lord of the Rings** trilogy, though it goes without saying that they're terrific films. And not Quentin Tarantino's **Kill Bill: Vol. 1** (2003) and **Kill Bill: Vol. 2** (2004), densely allusive glosses on the astonishing and underrated Japanese revenge picture **Lady Snowblood** (1973) by way of spaghetti Westerns, anime, chop-socky pictures, Shaw brothers' martial arts epics, Italian *gialli*, yakuza epics, Euro-sexploitation, and cult TV shows of the 1960s and '70s: They're one great movie split in half for commercial reasons.

I'm thinking of movies like Francis Ford Coppola's **The Godfather Part II** (1974), the first sequel ever to win a Best Picture Oscar. It had a high bar to clear: Coppola's **The Godfather** (1972) transformed a pulp novel about wise guys into bona fide American tragedy of Shakespearian richness. The sequel simultaneously extends the story forward, as reluctant dauphin Michael Corleone (Al Pacino) takes over his father's criminal empire, and reaches back to chronicle the young Don Vito Corleone's (Robert De Niro) bloody rise to power; it ups the tragic ante to biblical proportions.

Alien (1979) or **Aliens** (1986)? I personally prefer the lean, mean, scare machine approach of Ridley Scott's original, a variation on the classic haunted-house formula that solves the genre's biggest problem: Why don't the terrorized victims get the hell out as soon as the spooky stuff starts? But James Cameron's call-in-the-marines follow-up is a humdinger of an entirely different kind, so in the spirit of fairness I'll call this one a draw. Also in the spirit of fairness, I'd like to draw attention to Mario Bava's stylish, microbudget **Planet of the Vampires** (1965): Bava's formidable imagination can't quite overcome the production's limitations, but *Alien* owes it big time.

Cameron's pumped up **Terminator 2: Judgment Day** (1991) expands on and deepens time-travel thriller **The Terminator** (1984) into a mournful celebration of love's power to transcend time and catastrophe. George Miller's **The Road Warrior** (1981) takes the raw material of his grim, stripped-down **Mad Max** (1979)—a dystopian future, a scarred loner (Mel Gibson), open roads crawling with psycho cyclists and speed demons—and turns it into the exhilarating, full-fledged action fable. James Whale's **Bride of Frankenstein** (1935) definitely betters his classic **Frankenstein**

(1931); it's mordantly funny, shot through with fascinatingly weird sexual undercurrents, and includes Elsa Lanchester's iconic performance as the towering bride with the lightning-bolt hair and menacingly fey Dr. Pretorious's (Ernest Thesiger) immortal toast "To a new world of gods and monsters."

A ripping adventure that wears its age as lightly as twenty-eight-year-old Olympic swimmer Johnny Weissmuller wears clothes, **Tarzan, the Ape Man** (1932) is cracking good fun. But **Tarzan and His Mate** (1934) is a blast: Tarzan and Jane (the lovely Maureen O'Sullivan, in an animal-skin bikini of amazing skimpiness), the proper Englishwoman who took to jungle love with almost unseemly enthusiasm, are an enthrallingly sexy, athletic couple (restored versions of the film include a nude swimming sequence) whose sweetly earthy rapport is a sheer pleasure to watch. Akira Kurosawa's **Sanjuro** (1962), the sequel to his masterful samurai adventure **Yojimbo** (1961)—which was inspired by Dashiell Hammett's 1929 pulp crime novel *Red Harvest* and remade, without credit, as the groundbreaking spaghetti Western **A Fistful of Dollars** (1964)—chronicles the further adventures of wandering *ronin* Sanjuro Tsubaki (Toshiro Mifune); it's a little more Hollywood, a lot funnier, and altogether enjoyable. Finally, if Martin Scorsese's twenty-five-years-later sequel **The Color of Money** (1986) is only as good as Robert Rossen's **The Hustler** (1961), it's because *The Hustler* is flat-out brilliant, a dark wallow in poisoned dreams of pool sharks. Paul Newman's "Fast Eddie" Felson, *Hustler*'s cocky up-and-comer, is now a cynical, silver-haired has-been training a hot-eyed young buck (Tom Cruise) very like his younger self; Newman carries his years gracefully but invests Felson with every hard-earned one of them.

TAKE THE MONEY AND RUN

I must admit a bias at the outset: I'm bored by ultra-high-tech heist movies. The remake of **Ocean's Eleven** (2001) just doesn't do it for me, though I'm kind of a sucker for the Rat Pack pizzazz of the original (1960), which showcases Frank Sinatra, Dean Martin, Sammy Davis Jr., Peter Lawford, and Angie Dickinson at their ring-a-ding dingiest. But I love classic caper pictures, in which the infinite varieties of dishonor among thieves ensure that the best-laid plans of mice and men consistently go awry.

Criminal mastermind Sam Jaffe rounds up a gang to steal a million dollars in jewels in John Huston's pioneering **The Asphalt Jungle** (1950), a downbeat crime drama starring Sterling Hayden and a very young Marilyn Monroe as one crook's mercenary doll. With Jules Dassin's **Rififi** (1955), in which a motley crew bands together to pull off the "impossible" robbery of a swanky Paris *magasin de bijoux*—during a twenty-eight-minute set piece with no dialogue or music—*The Asphalt Jungle* established the template for the heist genre. Alec Guiness and his mob (including Peter Sellers and Herbert Lom) have a foolproof plan to rob an armored car that pivots on renting a room from a sublimely daffy old dear in the bitterly comic **The Ladykillers** (1955), but she's not as easy to handle as they imagine. Stanley Kubrick's gritty **The Killing** (1956), co-written with pulp existentialist Jim Thompson, begins with a racetrack betting-room rip-off that rests on a diversion—a sniper shooting a running horse—and ends in a gloriously ironic whirlwind of cash.

Dassin's **Topkapi** (1964), a bit of fluff about a jewel heist in Istanbul polished to a high gloss and studded with international stars like Maximilian Schell, Melina Mercouri, and Peter Ustinov, epitomized light '60s caper films, as does the swinging **The Italian Job** (1969), in which Michael Caine masterminds a gold-bullion robbery, Noel Coward puts up the money, and the getaway hinges on a massive traffic jam and a trio of nimble Mini Coopers (the 2003 remake is nothing special). Robert Redford and George Segal are hired to boost a legendary gem from New York's Brooklyn Museum in the dryly comic **The Hot Rock** (1972), and eccentric jewel thieves Jamie Leigh Curtis, Kevin Kline, and *Monty Python* alumni John Cleese and Michael Palin double-cross each other to the nth-power in the antic **A Fish Called Wanda** (1988).

Quentin Tarantino's fractured **Reservoir Dogs** (1992) dissects a botched jewelry store holdup and yes, Hong Kong director Ringo Lam's **City on Fire** (1987) *does* tell the same story. But it's all in the execution; Tarantino's combination of mordant humor, flawlessly chosen music and casting—from Harvey Keitel, Tim Roth, Michael Madsen, and Steve Buscemi to legendary tough guy Lawrence Tierney and real-life crook-turned-writer Eddie Bunker—elevates the material to wrenching pop poetry. And an armored car robbery triggers a clash of the titans—thief Robert De Niro and dogged cop Al Pacino—in Michael Mann's **Heat** (1995), an epic reworking of his own made-for-TV **L.A. Takedown** (1989).

TEACH THE CHILDREN WELL

Movies about the relationships between students and teachers all too often degenerate into insufferable, treacly slop. Some of these titles veer into the sticky swamp of sentimentality, but none get mired in it and all feature fine performances of educators struggling to rise to their pupils' needs.

> **Goodbye Mr. Chips** (1939), with Robert Donat
> **The Corn Is Green** (1945), with Bette Davis
> **Good Morning, Miss Dove** (1955), with Jennifer Jones
> **The Blackboard Jungle** (1955), with Glenn Ford
> **Up the Down Staircase** (1967), with Sandy Dennis
> **To Sir with Love** (1967), with Sidney Poitier
> **The Prime of Miss Jean Brodie** (1969), with Maggie Smith
> **Conrack** (1974), with Jon Voight
> **Stand and Deliver** (1988), with Edward James Olmos
> **October Sky** (1999), with Laura Dern

THAT '70S PICTURE SHOW

The 1970s were a decade of bad hair, economic uncertainty, hideous fashions, social upheaval, and daring movies that spoke to the cynical, desperate times. The success of two brilliant commercial blockbusters, **Jaws** (1975) and **Star Wars** (1977), brought down the New Hollywood and sent its princes, from Francis Ford Coppola to William Friedkin, down the road of promise unfulfilled. But for a brief and shining moment a wave of ferociously brilliant movies, seething with anti-establishment anger and bristling with ideas, washed over moviegoers and left a legacy of undying images and dialogue.

Peter Bogdanovich's **The Last Picture Show** (1971) depicts the dying days of a small Texas town choked with dust and stunted dreams. Roman Polanski's **Chinatown** (1974) dropped private dick Jake Gittes (Jack Nicholson) down a rabbit hole of corruption in 1930s Los Angeles, complete with a duplicitous dame (Faye Dunaway) and a smiling monster named Noah Cross (John Huston). Martin Scorsese's **Taxi Driver** (1976) sent loner Travis Bickle (Robert De Niro) into the filthy New York night, where he found an attitude—"You talking to *me*?"—and a mission: rescuing child hooker Jodie Foster from slick pimp Harvey Keitel. Terrence Malick's poisonously dreamy **Badlands** (1973) found the seeds of '70s malaise in the inchoate fury of '50s spree killer Charles Starkweather and his childish girlfriend, Carol Ann Fugate; Martin Sheen and Sissy Spacek play thinly fictionalized versions of the pair.

Coppola saw the history of American capitalism reflected in the rise of the Mafia, and transformed novelist Mario Puzo's potboiler into the masterful **The Godfather** (1972) and **The Godfather Part II** (1974), populated by a who's who of Hollywood's young guns—Al Pacino, James Caan, Robert Duvall—and their idol, method man Marlon Brando. Robert Altman found a sprawling portrait of American dreams among country-music stars, fans, and hangers on, but you don't have to care one whit about bluegrass banjo pickin' or "stand by your man" ballads to get lost in his dizzyingly brilliant **Nashville** (1975), which plays out against the backdrop of a maverick presidential campaign.

Shopworn genres got a shot to the heart in movies like **Cabaret** (1970), a grimly glittering musical set in a divinely decadent Berlin nightclub where ambisexual master of ceremonies Joel Grey and Liza Minnelli's smudged, wide-eyed siren of a singer swaddle themselves in fantasy while the Nazis rise to power. Ostensibly a high-tech thriller, Coppola's **The Conversation** (1974) spirals into a black hole of paranoia and alienation and drags electronics whiz Gene Hackman in after it. William Friedkin's **The French Connection** (1971) and Sidney Lumet's **Dog Day Afternoon** (1975) transformed real-life crime stories into bitter fables for anxious times; *French Connection*'s "Popeye" Doyle (Hackman) is a narcotics cop as brutal as the smirking drug lords he despises and *Afternoon* chronicles the escalating series of bizarre events triggered by a bungled bank robbery/hostage situation masterminded by an amiable loser (Al Pacino) trying to fund his boyfriend's sex-change operation.

As America's involvement in Vietnam ground to its unsatisfying conclusion, Michael Cimino's **The Deer Hunter** (1978) and Coppola's **Apocalypse Now** (1979) evoked the war's shattering impact on the national psyche. *Deer Hunter* tears three lifelong friends—Robert De Niro, John Savage, and Christopher Walken—from the comforting rituals of small-town life and hurls them into the bloody chaos of jungle warfare, while *Apocalypse Now*, an intoxicating whirlpool of bizarre, brutal, and bafflingly beautiful images, follows rapidly unraveling military assassin (Martin Sheen) as he travels upriver in search of renegade Colonel Kurtz (Marlon Brando), who's lost himself in the heart of darkness.

TRAIN IN VAIN

L ike hotels and ships, cross-country trains gather a collection of disparate types in an enclosed space: Let the fireworks begin!

"It took more than one man to change my name to Shanghai Lily," purrs glamorous shady lady Marlene Dietrich, who joins gamblers, opium dealers, religious zealots, revolutionaries, and fellow fallen woman Anna May Wong on the **Shanghai Express** (1932) for a three-day trip across civil war–torn China in this glittering melange of exoticism, melodrama, and intrigue. Fed up with her Svengali, vain, possessive theatrical impresario Oscar "OJ" Jaffe (John Barrymore), Lily Garland (screwball comedienne Carole Lombard) heads for the Hollywood hills; two years later, she's a spoiled movie star, he's broke, and fate throws them together on the **Twentieth Century** (1934). Kindly old Mrs. Froy disappears from a trans-Europe express in Alfred Hitchcock's **The Lady Vanishes** (1938), but the other passengers swear she was never aboard; is the vacationing heiress who insists Mrs. Froy most certainly was on the train imagining things, or is there a conspiracy afoot?

Two convicts, hardened lifer Manny (Jon Voight) and cocky whippersnapper Buck (Eric Roberts) bust out of a maximum security hellhole in the middle of Alaska and hitch a ride on the wrong train; part flat-out action picture, part rumination on human nature, **Runaway Train** (1985) manages to be brawny, thoughtful, and thrilling all at once. In the gripping, fact-based WWII action film **The Train** (1965), a French resistance cell led by railway yardmaster Labiche (Burt Lancaster) risks all in the name of French cultural pride, trying to stop a Nazi train without damaging looted masterpieces of "degenerate" modern art inside. A Jewish community in Central Europe concocts a daring plan to escape extermination in the ruefully comic **Train of Life** (1998), constructing their own deportation train in hopes of riding it—half as prisoners and the other half as their "Nazi" captors—to freedom; the film's eleventh-hour tone shift is breathtaking.

A hard-boiled cop escorts a gangster's moll from Chicago to California, where she's going to turn state's evidence; but their train is crawling with hit men and no one is exactly what he or she seems in the suspenseful **The Narrow Margin** (1952). The slick 1990 remake is only serviceable, but the original is tight, taut, and filled with memorably acid-tinged dialogue. Agatha Christie's **Murder on the Orient Express** (1974) is plush, top-of-the-line hokum in which a nasty American millionaire is murdered in his sleeping car, stabbed twelve times after having been drugged; fortunately, smugly brilliant detective Hercule Poirot (Albert Finney) is aboard to interrogate the all-star cast of suspects. A fugitive terrorist spews genetically engineered germs into the lunch rice, turning a Geneva-to-Stockholm train into the pneumonic plague express and trapping one thousand passengers aboard; trashy and highly entertaining, **The Cassandra Crossing** (1976) barrels towards a surprisingly cynical conclusion involving a highly suspect bridge.

And let's not forget silent comedian Buster Keaton's Civil War–era comedy **The General** (1927), which features not one, but two brilliantly executed train chases; in the first, Confederate train engineer Keaton pursues the Union spies who've hijacked "The General"; and in the second, the spies pursue Keaton, who greets an escalating series of obstacles with his trademark stoicism. All aboard!

TRUTHS UNIVERSALLY ACKNOWLEDGED

hy would a twenty-first-century woman be interested in stories about the petty problems of rich, silly nineteenth-century English ladies, except perhaps as a quaint reminder of how far we've come? Because if Jane Austen (1775–1817) were alive today, she'd have written *Sex and the City*. She cast a pitiless yet sympathetic eye on the intricate calculations, self-destructive mistakes, and hard compromises women make, favoring poor relations and sharp-tongued plain Janes trying to balance family responsibility, personal integrity, and the hope of romance.

Of Austen's six novels, *Pride and Prejudice* (1813) is the most adapted. Bookish Lizzie Bennet is one of five daughters of a minor country gentleman; unless they marry well they're doomed to destitution when he dies, because his inheritance will pass to a distant and unfriendly male relative. Lizzie, skeptical about men and prone to snap judgments, attracts the attentions of wealthy Mr. Darcy but gravitates toward penniless Mr. Wickham, a bounder in victim-of-social-injustice's clothing. Peel away Lizzie's regency frocks and out pops Helen Fielding's clever but lovelorn Bridget Jones, handicapped not by lowly birth and impecuniousness, but by the coin of the '90s realm: insecurity and a few extra pounds. The casting is the wittiest thing about **Bridget Jones's Diary** (2001): Bridget's (Renee Zellweger) modern-day Darcy is Colin Firth, who played Austen's Darcy in a hugely popular BBC miniseries version of *P&P*, and her dashing but caddish Wickham—renamed Daniel Cleaver—is Hugh Grant, notorious for his declasse fling with a Hollywood hooker.

The marvelous **Pride & Prejudice** (2005) combines a power-house cast of veterans—Donald Sutherland and Brenda Blethyn as Mr. and Mrs. Bennet and Judi Dench as Darcy's imperious aunt, Lady Catherine—and talented newcomers, notably Keira Knightly as Lizzie and Rosamund Pike as Jane, the sweet-natured Bennet beauty. The lavish 1940 **Pride and Prejudice** deviates seriously from the novel, defanging the society harpies who look down on the Bennets as country bumpkins and blunting the satire, but the superb cast, including legendary beauties Greer Garson and Maureen O'Sullivan as Lizzie and Jane, and Laurence Olivier as Darcy, is a pleasure. Hollywood meets Bollywood in Gurinder Chadha's **Bride & Prejudice** (2004), complete with lavish musical numbers; modern-day Indian beauty Aishwarya Rai assumes American Mr. Darcy is an arrogant ignoramus and lets Wickham's *Lonely Planet* affectations blind her to his avaricious nature. It's flawed—the English-language numbers are banal and the broad comedy falls flat—but when it comes together it's ravishing.

In **Clueless** (1995), a loose but very witty spin on Austen's 1815 soap opera–like *Emma*, bubble-headed but well-meaning Beverly Hills teen Alicia Silverstone sets herself the charitable task of transforming an outcast grunge girl into a popular babe and makes a fine mess of things. Gwyneth Paltrow glows as more conventional **Emma** (1996), whose munificent meddling nearly derails several futures. Taiwanese director Ang Lee brought a keen grasp of family and social dynamics to **Sense and Sensibility** (1995), in which the charity of wealthy relatives puts a roof over the heads of newly impoverished sisters Emma Thompson (who also adapted Austen's 1811 novel) and Kate Winslet, whose search for suitable husbands is fraught with obstacles. A gritty adaptation of Austen's story of fortunes reversed and second chances, **Persuasion** (1995) tracks some authentic mud through the society drawing rooms where a spinster re-wins the man she once rejected in deference to family snobbery. Writer-director Patricia Rozema's bold liberties with the little-liked 1814 novel **Mansfield Park** pay off handsomely. Her 1999 film puts an unsubtle but provocative postcolonial spin on the story of impoverished Fanny (Frances O'Connor), raised by rich relatives who blatantly favor their own children; Rozema highlights the family fortune's dependence on brutalized Antiguan slaves, suggesting that rigid social dictates resulted in the systematic sexual exploitation of women, but her masterstroke was to transform Austen's meek Fanny into a resourceful, brainy woman much like Austen herself.

ULTRA DIVAS: BETTE VS. JOAN

When movie stars were truly stars, Bette Davis (1908–1989) and Joan Crawford (1904–1977)—a haughty New England scrapper with huge, luminous eyes and a brittle accent, and a broad-shouldered club dancer who clawed her way out of grinding Texas poverty to become the epitome of affected Hollywood glamour—were the brightest lights in the firmament. Their notorious rivalry supposedly began in 1935, when Crawford suspected Davis of having an affair with her husband. Real or manufactured, it spiced up their only movie together, gothic freak show **What Ever Happened to Baby Jane?** (1962), in which demented, long-forgotten vaudeville child star "Baby Jane" Hudson (Davis) and her sister, crippled former actress Blanche (Crawford), share a decaying Hollywood mansion oozing with a lifetime of festering resentments; Crawford got to retain a glimmer of her fading beauty, while Davis endured cruelly witchy makeup but got an Oscar nomination.

Three decades earlier, both were young, ambitious starlets, but Davis already had a fully formed persona: Rich or poor, scheming or put upon, she was always tough, self-reliant, and driven. She shone in **Of Human Bondage** (1934), as a cheap cockney tart who ruins the idealistic medical student who gets hooked on her like a drug. In the gritty **Marked Woman** (1937) she's a seen-it-all nightclub hostess who stands up to the mob; as **Jezebel** (1938) she's a tart-tongued Southern coquette who nearly flirts and flounces her way out of true love. As a hard-partying, fatally ill horsewoman, she burns her candle at both ends in **Dark Victory** (1939), toying with stable-hand Humphrey Bogart and society swell Ronald Reagan before realizing she loves the brain surgeon who can't save her. Set in exotic Malaysia, **The Letter** (1940) opens as Davis—the respectable wife of a besotted rubber-plantation owner—shoots a man, unaware that an indiscreet letter could torpedo her claim of self-defense. In **The Little Foxes** (1941), she's a conniving Southern aristocrat who sacrifices her daughter's love to greed, and in **All About Eve** (1950) Davis is an aging Broadway star who doesn't notice the disingenuous up-and-comer angling to replace her until it's too late: "Fasten your seatbelts, it's going to be a bumpy night!"

Crawford reinvented herself constantly. As a spirited but principled flapper, the former hoofer stole **Our Dancing Daughters** (1928). When the vogue for saucy jazz babies waned, she found a new niche playing rags-to-riches shopgirls, like **Mannequin**'s (1938) upwardly mobile newlywed, who escapes her tenement upbringing and deadbeat husband in the arms of a self-made industrialist (Spencer Tracy), or opportunistic manicurist Crystal Allen, who scoops up a neglected husband while his well-bred wife is off shopping in the feature-length bitchfest **The Women** (1939). As Crawford's looks hardened, she became the woman who loves too much, suffering dramatically for her excesses. Self-made businesswoman **Mildred Pierce** (1945) sacrifices everything for the ungrateful, social climbing-daughter who exploits and belittles her. As an aging, alcoholic socialite she furthers the ambitions of **Humoresque**'s (1946) opportunistic, slum-born violinist John Garfield, and in **Possessed** (1947) she's literally driven mad by love, marrying decent Raymond Massey while nursing a dangerous obsession with an uncaring old flame. Film by film, she constructed the larger-than-life persona much imitated by drag queens of a certain age, her face becoming a mask of eyebrows, sweeping lashes, and vivid lipstick. Later roles—like **Johnny Guitar**'s (1954) butch saloon owner Vienna and the tempestuous termagant of **Queen Bee** (1955)—resemble studies for Faye Dunaway's cruel but mesmerizing **Mommie Dearest** (1981) impersonation, but they're never less than riveting.

UNDERWORLD U.K.

Perhaps you associate quaint old England, of the unarmed policemen and picturesque streets, with murder most genteel *a la* Agatha Christie. But that's only half the story; the other is a volatile morass of organized crime run by gangsters as tough and sadistic as any mafiosi.

Take the bloody, profane, adrenaline-fueled **Gangster No. 1** and **Sexy Beast** (both 2000). In *Sexy Beast*, a color-saturated jolt of pure vicious energy, former gangster Ray Winstone is hauled out of Costa del Sol retirement by seething sociopath Ben Kingsley (if your image of Sir Ben stops at *Gandhi*, his performance as a foul-mouthed, vile-tempered all-around bastard will be quite the shocker) to mastermind a London heist. Paul Bettany and Malcolm McDowell share the title role in *Gangster No. 1*; McDowell plays the unnamed felon in the present day, Bettany appears in the flashbacks that chart his rise to underworld power in swinging '60s London. **The Krays** (1990) is a colorful account of the reign of terror perpetuated by '60s flashy fashion plates Reginald and Ronald Kray, identical twin villains (played by non-twin brothers Gary and Martin Kemp of '80s band Spandau Ballet) who could teach today's gangstas something about notorious bling; the scenes of their doting mum clucking over her boys' posse of miscreants like a fussy hen are priceless.

The pitiless, desperate **Brighton Rock** (1947), based on Graham Greene's novel, revolves around underage, perversely religious sociopath Pinky Brown (a very young Sir Richard Attenborough), who runs a gang of older thugs in seedy seaside Brighton until he's undone by the confluence of competition from a more sophisticated crook, police pressure, and his cynically expedient marriage to an innocent waitress who could tie him to a murder. Thug life meets rock 'n' roll decadence in the luridly mesmerizing **Performance** (1970); petty hood Chas (James Fox) pisses off his boss and hides out in the ramshackle townhouse where androgynous rock recluse Turner (Mick Jagger, in his never-topped movie debut) has cocooned himself in a hallucinogenic bubble of sex, drugs, and mutable identities. Ubergroupie Anita Pallenberg is stunning, and the trippy "Memo from Turner" sequence is a self-contained showstopper.

In **The Long Good Friday** (1980), Bob Hoskins stars as a pugnacious cockney gangster whose bid for respectability is scuttled by an inexplicable wave of murder and sabotage; Helen Mirren plays his upper-crust girlfriend and a very young Pierce Brosnan has a small part as an IRA hit man. Hoskins also starred in Neil Jordan's **Mona Lisa** (1986) as a hard-luck flunkie to mob boss Michael Caine; as a reward for taking the fall for Caine, he's given a cushy gig chauffeuring a high-class call girl, but begins to fall for her without understanding the ramifications. Mirren reprised her part as a mobster's cultured moll in Peter Greenaway's ghoulish **The Cook, the Thief, His Wife & Her Lover** (1989); she betrays her husband, boorish vulgarian Michael Gambon, who exacts grotesque revenge—be warned that when Greenaway gets his teeth into a repellent metaphor, he carries it to its ghastly extreme. Gambon in turn plays a nasty piece of work who rubs elbows with the upper crust while maintaining his ties to the lower depths in **Layer Cake** (2005), which stars Daniel Craig as a slick, nameless London cocaine dealer who doesn't understand his business quite as well as he thinks he does.

In Stephen Frears's mournful **The Hit** (1984), elegant Terrence Stamp plays an informer whose day of reckoning arrives ten years after he sold out his underworld pals; his Zen-like equanimity in the face of impending death unnerves both veteran killer-for-hire John Hurt and his eager-beaver assistant, Tim Roth. As **The Limey** (1999), Stamp is fresh out of prison and hell-bent on uncovering the truth behind his estranged daughter's "accidental" death in sunny California; scenes from the kitchen-sink drama **Poor Cow** (1967), which starred Stamp as a feckless young thief and serve as flashbacks to his embittered character's youth, add a poignant note to the bleak present. Director Mike Hodges made two U.K. gangster classics a quarter of a century apart. Michael Caine stars in the blistering **Get**

Carter (1971) as a low-level London thug trying to get to the bottom of his brother's death in bleakly industrial Newcastle—banish the thought of the sorry Sylvester Stallone remake! **Croupier** (1998) chronicles would-be novelist Clive Owen's trip to the underworld via a gig in a mobbed-up London casino. It's a dirty old world, innit?

UNHAPPY FAMILIES

A ll happy families are alike," Russian novelist Leo Tolstoy famously observed in his novel *Anna Karenina*. "Every unhappy family is unhappy in its own way." The uniquely miserable details fuel these documentaries, whose emotional rubbernecking appeal culminates in gratitude that your relatives aren't so bad by comparison.

Dysfunctional family–movie trailblazer **An American Family** (1973) looms large, and not just because it's twelve hours long. It chronicles the disintegration of the well-heeled, apparently happy Loud family of Santa Barbara, California; parents Pat and Bill throw in the towel on their twenty-year marriage, son Lance comes out of the closet, and teen siblings Michele, Delilah, Grant, and Kevin try to keep their balance as their family implodes. Imagine a real-life *Whatever Happened to Baby Jane?* crossed with David Cronenberg's *Dead Ringers* and you have David and Albert Maysles's **Grey Gardens** (1975), about aging mother-and-daughter recluses Edith and Edie Beale, close relatives of Jacqueline Kennedy Onassis who ramble around their squalid East Hampton mansion lost in gilded memories and pie-in-the-sky fantasies of what might have been.

Crumb (1994) reveals that famously eccentric underground cartoonist Robert Crumb—a guy who had a childhood crush on Bugs Bunny—may be the *sanest* of the oddball Crumb boys: Talented eldest Charles is a nonfunctioning hermit, and youngest Maxon engages in disturbing yoga practices like flossing his digestive tract with a 21-foot cloth strip.

When sixty-four-year-old Bill Ward of tiny Munnsville, New York, died in 1990, his fifty-nine-year-old brother was arrested for murder. Joe Berlinger and Bruce Sinofsky's **Brother's Keeper** (1992) shines a light on the peculiar existence of the four "Ward boys," who lived together for decades in a two-room shack without running water, amid the kind of bizarre squalor that recalls Wisconsin-recluse Ed Gein's farmhouse of horrors, mercifully minus the ghoulish trophies of Gein's grave robbing, cannibalism, and murders. And while Sinofsky and Berlinger's **Paradise Lost: The Child Murders at Robin Hood Hills** (1996) and **Paradise Lost 2: Revelations** (2000) began by focusing on the apparent railroading of three outcast teenagers in the mutilation murders of three Arkansas children, the focus soon shifts to the dead boys' disarranged families.

Aspiring filmmaker (and Moviefone founder) Andrew Jarecki wanted to make a documentary about children's party clowns, including David "Silly Billy" Friedman. But when he learned that Friedman's father, schoolteacher Arnold, and younger brother, Jesse, were at the center of a notorious child-abuse scandal, he profiled the family instead. Their obsessive home movies are the centerpiece of Jarecki's gripping **Capturing the Friedmans** (2003), which also scrutinizes the role of hysteria in high-profile child-molestation cases. Where *Friedmans* is measured, James Roland Whitney's examination of his own family's legacy of child abuse, **Just, Melvin** (2000), is mind-bogglingly lurid: He even alleges that his stepgrandfather, Melvin Just, literally got away with murdering a county nurse who caught him molesting one of his stepdaughters. But Whitney grounds his allegations with just enough facts that you can't dismiss it out of hand, and the train-wreck fascination of his undeniably damaged relatives is hypnotic. As a college student in the mid-1980s, future *Hoop Dreams* (1994) director Steve James was a Big Brother to impoverished eleven-year-old Stephen Fielding; James's heartbreaking and horrifying portrait of the adult **Stevie** (2003)—a jobless, substance-abusing child molester—explores the concentric hells of family dysfunction. In **My Architect** (2003), Nathaniel Kahn goes in search of his elusive father, world-famous architect Louis Kahn, who maintained three separate families and died of a heart attack in the men's room of New York City's Penn Station in 1974. And in **Tarnation** (2004), Jonathan Caouette—who began filming himself trying on looks and personas as a teenager—constructs a mesmerizing movie collage tracing his troubled past and stormy relationship with his tormented, unbalanced mother.

DIRECTOR'S SPOTLIGHT:
PETER WEIR

Why is Australian one-trick pony Paul "Crocodile Dundee" Hogan a household name and Peter Weir isn't? Just about everyone loves at least one of Weir's films—some of his most popular include **Dead Poets Society** (1989), **Master and Commander: The Far Side of the World** (2003), **The Year of Living Dangerously** (1983), and **Gallipoli** (1981). Weir made a full-fledged movie star of *Gallipoi's* Mel Gibson, who played one of the two idealistic Australian soldiers (Mark Lee was the other) who enlist in the Australian–New Zealand Army Corps and are shipped off to a WWI battlefield to fight the Turks in the Dardanelles. And **Witness** (1985) served notice that the often-wooden Harrison Ford really could act, given the material and a steady hand at his back. But Weir himself gets no respect. I can't say I love all his films: *Dead Poet's Society* makes my teeth ache; the Gerard Depardieu–Andie MacDowell romance-of-convenience picture *Green Card* (1990) leaves me cold; and much though I'd *like* to like *The Truman Show* (1998), in which a man (Jim Carrey) lives life blissfully unaware that his whole world is actually a set from which his day-to-day experiences are broadcast on TV like a real-life soap opera, it sounds much more provocative than it actually is. But here's the bottom line: Weir is a damned good filmmaker who doesn't make commercial swill or pander to lowbrow fads; under the old Hollywood studio system he'd be cranking out two pictures a year and one in four would be great. As it is, he's directed fourteen and one-third features in thirty-two years (the third is a segment of the 1971 anthology **Three to Go**), and two-thirds of them are terrific. So come on: Step up and give credit where credit is due.

Born in Sydney in 1944, Weir never went to film school—he picked up the basics of directing and film technology while working at a local television station. Many moviegoers discovered Weir through his eerie **Picnic at Hanging Rock** (1975), a dream-within-a-dreamlike mystery set in 1900, in which four blossoming schoolgirls from Mrs. Appleyard's College for Young Women set out to explore a mysterious outback rock formation and only one returns. Personally I was hooked by **The Cars That Ate Paris** (1974), a blacker-than-black story about an isolated Australian town—Paris—whose economy is built on orchestrating fatal car accidents and scavenging parts and property from the wrecks. I had the good fortune to see it in London—I might not have been so enthralled had I first seen the film in its mangled U.S. release version, *The Cars That Eat People*. I vividly remember surrendering to the spell of **The Last Wave** (1977), a dreamy, apocalyptic fable in which liberal lawyer Richard Chamberlain is sucked into the aboriginal "dreamtime"—a sort of parallel world accessed through dreams and trance states—while defending five Aborigines (including David Gulpilil, star of Nicolas Roeg's 1971 *Walkabout*) accused of murdering a sixth in a Sydney alley. Weir was hailed as one of the brightest lights of Australia's New Wave, who included Gillian Armstrong, Fran Schepisi, Philip Noyce, Bruce Beresford, and George Miller (the *Mad Max* George Miller, not the one who made *The Man from Snowy River*), and successfully held his ground against the Hollywood disease, a pervasive, creeping mediocrity that turns promising filmmakers into cynical hacks. I think Weir's most underrated film is the haunting, hallucinatory **Fearless** (1993), which dissects the psychological aftermath of a horrifying plane crash with uncommon intelligence and quiet virtuosity. And whenever I see his name attached to some unlikely project, my first thought is, "*Oh, that might be good, then.*"

WE'RE ALL CONNECTED

How do you tell a story that suggests both the stunning randomness of life and hindsight's power to impose meaning on chaos? Through multiple story lines—all equally important—that overlap, intersect, and ultimately come together. The multi-story narrative is more than a large ensemble of characters or a story that juggles several significant subplots; it's a balancing act in which every thread counts in the final design.

Robert Altman's **Nashville** (1975), a masterful piece of storytelling and one of the greatest films ever made about American self-delusion, filters the stories of two dozen characters through the mannerisms and mores of the country-music industry—country-music stars, political hucksters, sad fringe dwellers dreaming of stardom all cross paths in the country-music capital. They come together at a benefit performance for a populist presidential candidate that culminates in tragedy. Though Altman made many other multi-story films, only **Short Cuts** (1993)—which weaves short stories by Raymond Carver into a dark tapestry of shallow, disconnected Los Angeles lives—approaches Nashville's subtle web of vivid insight into the lies people tells themselves so they can keep going; even an earthquake isn't enough to shake some sense into *Short Cuts'* self-centered, pop-culture-saturated characters.

Los Angeles is also the backdrop for P. T. Anderson's **Magnolia** (1999), which culminates in a rain of frogs, and Paul Haggis's **Crash** (2005). It uses the vast L.A. highway system to engineer collisions between rich and poor Angelenos of all races, classes, and biases, stripping them of their self-delusions and forcing them to reevaluate their lives. The combination of nimble storytelling and provocative themes earned *Crash* a best picture Oscar, an upset victory over the heavily favored *Brokeback Mountain*. Similarly, the underrated TV-movie **Smash-Up on Interstate 5** (1976) sends a cross section of Californians toward a thirty-nine-car reckoning, while **Time Code** (2002) ups the ante by telling the overlapping stories of some two dozen Hollywood types from four different points of view, using a four-way split screen; director Mike Figgis focuses your attention by raising or lowering the level of the soundtrack—it's not as complicated to watch as you'd think.

Quentin Tarantino's **Pulp Fiction** (1994) fractures the chronologies of his intersecting stories about philosophizing small-time crooks and their baroque travails. The quick-witted, high-energy **Go** (1999) also does the time warp, returning twice to the beginning to follow different characters whose destinies intersect at a botched drug deal. **2 Days in the Valley** (1996) isn't as structurally clever, but juggles an entertaining collection of hit men, cops, snobs, oddballs, losers, and creeps as they bounce off each other in the pinball machine of the San Fernando Valley.

13 Conversations About One Thing (2001) unfolds at the points where the lives of New York City housecleaners, college professors, students, and lawyers all intersect. Both **Traffik** (1989), the six-part BBC drama about the drug trade, and the movie that was inspired by it, Steven Soderbergh's Oscar-winning **Traffic** (2000), intertwine stories that reach across nations, social boundaries, and economic classifications. The destinies of moneyed government officials, impoverished third-world farmers, junkies, shadowy businessmen, couriers and dealers, and teenagers of all classes in search of kicks intersect at the corner of supply and demand for heroin in the first version and cocaine in the second. Soderbergh has the star-studded cast—Catherine Zeta-Jones, Benecio del Toro, Dennis Quaid, Michael Douglas, Miguel Ferrer, and Benjamin Bratt, for starters—and the more manageable running time at close to two-and-a-half hours. The BBC variation is twice as long, giving each story more room to breathe, and the sequences set in the lawless tribal zone between Afghanistan and Pakistan took on a whole new significance after the 9/11 terrorist attacks on the World Trade Center.

Intermission (2004) switches adroitly between dark comedy and droll drama, hopscotching among tales of Dubliners chasing love and money in parts of the city that never make it into the tourist brochures. Set in the week leading up to Christmas, the frothy **Love Actually** (2003) blithely ties together the emotional travails of Londoners—from the prime minister with a crush on a pleasingly plump tea girl to a dissolute, aging rock star whose future hangs on a holiday novelty hit and whose deepest, most enduring relationship isn't romantic at all—into one uber-romantic comedy.

Finally, the Japanese *Ju-On* films string together a series of chronologically scrambled stories of lives blighted by the bad vibes emanating from a modest, ordinary-looking house in a pretty Tokyo suburb; the interconnections are spread over multiple films including **Ju-On: The Curse** and **Ju-On: The Curse 2** (both 2000) and **Ju-On: The Grudge** (2002), and the cumulative effect is blood-chilling.

WHAT I DID FOR LOVE

I s there anything more bittersweet than a great love that founders on circumstance? In **Casablanca** (1942), disillusioned gin-joint owner Humphrey Bogart is reunited with the love of his life, Ingrid Bergman, who broke his heart and now needs help for her new husband, a fugitive WWII resistance leader. Passionate, half-gypsy foundling Laurence Olivier and spirited but fatally well-bred Merle Oberon are soul mates from childhood, but strict social mores come between them in Emily Bronte's often filmed

Wuthering Heights (1939). Engaged gigolo Cary Grant and kept nightclub singer Deborah Kerr fall in love on a cruise in **An Affair to Remember** (1957) and vow to disentangle themselves from their respective relationships, but cruel fate interferes with their promise to reunite six months later at the Empire State Building. Hungarian explorer Ralph Fiennes and newly married English painter Kristin Scott Thomas fall heedlessly in love in war-torn North Africa; their story is told in vivid scraps by **The English Patient** (1996), a horribly burned invalid languishing in a makeshift Tuscan hospital.

In **Camille** (1937), based on the much-adapted novel by Alexandre Dumas, naive young bourgeois Robert Taylor jeopardizes his future by falling in love with luminous courtesan Greta Garbo. Married Danish baroness Meryl Streep (playing real-life writer Karen Dineson Blixen, who wrote as Isak Dineson) and restless big-game hunter Robert Redford defy convention in **Out of Africa** (1985). Beneath the avant-garde surface of **Hiroshima mon amour** (1959) lies the thwarted love story of French actress Emmanuelle Riva, who's in Tokyo making a movie, and Japanese architect Eiji Okada; both are married and both haunted by the legacy of WWII.

Henry James's **The Wings of the Dove** (1997) takes place at the intersection of love and money, where poor-relation Helena Bonham Carter and penniless journalist Linus Roache hatch a cynical plan to ensure their financial future. Cynical Philadelphia cop Harrison Ford is enchanted by Amish widow Kelly McGillis, whose young son can identify a murderer in **Witness** (1985).

And finally—because there is a certain finality to it—I make my case for the criminally ignored and forgotten **Miracle Mile** (1989). Shy musician Anthony Edwards enjoys a wonderful first date with waitress Mare Winningham and then accidentally comes upon the knowledge that war has started and nuclear holocaust is an hour away; his blackly comic quest to meet the end of the world with the girl he loves is a pitch-perfect mix of humor and aching romance, right down to the flawlessly melancholy climax at the La Brea tar pits.

WHAT PRICE HOLLYWOOD?

Shopworn metaphors always play in Hollywood, but the one that really slays them is "all the world's a stage"—show business isn't just a great way to make a buck, it's a calling, and if Shakespeare had had the decency not to die in 1616, he could have been the busiest hack in Tinseltown. Of course, movie-business navel-gazing has never been as interesting to civilians as it is to industry insiders, but a handful of behind-the-scenes pictures cut across the great divide between show people and those wonderful losers out there in the dark.

The business was barely legally of age when it began turning a dyspeptic eye on its own tainted workings: George Cukor's sharp dissection of stars on the rise and stars flaming out, **What Price Hollywood?**—whose screenwriters included the acid-tongued Dorothy Parker—opened in 1932. His own musical remake, the 1954 **A Star Is Born** is the gold standard for bitter, soapy stories about the Faustian bargain luminaries embrace in exchange for love and applause; alcoholic matinee idol James Mason falls for the larger-than-life talent of scrappy singer Judy Garland (whose own insecure, high-strung, overworked, pill-popping history inflects her character), helps her get a foot in the door, and watches her rocket to the top while he boards the express elevator to the gutter. "I *am* big," hisses has-been silent goddess Gloria Swanson to failed screenwriter turned gigolo William Holden in the searing **Sunset Blvd.** (1950). "It's the pictures that got small." Billy Wilder's pitiless portrait of Hollywood as a Saturn devouring his children is a macabre masterpiece as chilling today as it was half a century ago. Robert Altman's sleek, cynical **The Player** (1992) turns the same merciless lens on a less mythic Hollywood, zooming in on squirmy sights like *The Graduate* screenwriter Buck Henry pitching "The Graduate 2," in which a bedridden Mrs. Robinson moves in with her daughter and the son-in-law she so memorably seduced in 1967.

Vincente Minnelli's glossy, poisoned valentine **The Bad and the Beautiful** (1952) is a glistening compendium of golden-age Hollywood gossip seamlessly woven into the story of ruthless mogul Jonathan Shields (Kirk Douglas), including a stint making low-budget horror movies *a la*Val Lewton (see *The Beauty in the Darkness*) at RKO and a star-making affair with the damaged, alcoholic daughter (Lana Turner) of a drunken screen legend that echoes the sad career of Diana Barrymore. Everyone agrees that Gene Kelly and Stanley Donen's **Singin' in the Rain** (1952) is one of the best musicals ever made, but hardly anyone mentions the story, a hugely entertaining behind-the-scenes tale of Hollywood at the dawn of the sound era, complete with sob sisters, jazz babies, and regal silent-era beauties with voices that could shatter glass. In the cheerfully cynical **The Stunt Man** (1980), fugitive Steve Railsback finds refuge on a movie set ruled by the charmingly manipulative megalomaniac Peter O'Toole, who hires him to replace a stunt-man who just died on the job. Clifford Odets, the celebrated left-wing playwright who became a hack screenwriter, inspired John Turturro's character in the Coen Brothers' feverish Hollywood fable **Barton Fink** (1991), but Odets's own excoriating **The Big Knife** (1955), starring Jack Palance, said it all first.

The doomed romance of disillusioned starlet Gloria Grahame and on-the-skids screenwriter Humphrey Bogart, who comes under suspicion for the murder of a hatcheck girl, plays out in the shadow of Hollywood's glittering surfaces and dark machinations in the melancholy noir thriller **In a Lonely Place** (1950). Tim Burton's loving **Ed Wood** (1994) celebrates life on the ragged fringes of showbiz through the eccentric life and career of *Plan 9 from Outer Space* (1959) auteur Wood (Johnny Depp), a transvestite dreamer who surrounded himself with a motley crew of psychics, oddballs, and outcasts, including pioneering horror host Vampira (Lisa Marie), without whom there would be no Elvira, Mistress of the Dark, and the aging Bela Lugosi (Martin Landau, who won an Academy Award for his portrayal of the drug-addicted horror icon).

WHAT'S IN A NAME?

So, Mr. Big Shot movie director . . . you're a multimillionaire, your pictures screen from Alaska to Zimbabwe, studio heads have you on speed dial, and you've got Academy Award nominations up the wazoo. But until your name is an adjective you're not immortal. So what if half the people tossing it around have only the vaguest idea what it means? As long as they spell it right, you're in like Orwell, Shakespeare, Dickens, and all those other dead guys who still get their names in the papers.

Even poor souls who've never seen a Charlie Chaplin movie know what Chaplin-esque comedy is: slapstick but graceful—W. C. Fields, no mean physical comedian himself, called Chaplin a "ballet dancer"—sentimental and rueful. Chaplin's woebegone Little Tramp, with his too-small jacket, baggy pants, and pound-puppy eyes, is the international symbol for the beleaguered fellow who picks himself up, dusts himself off, and starts all over again, no matter how many times he's been drop-kicked by life. Chaplin's everyman is reduced to eating his shoe in **The Gold Rush** (1925), delicately twirling the laces around his fork like spaghetti; falls for a blind flower girl who thinks he's a millionaire in the poignant **City Lights** (1931); goes to war with the mechanized world in **Modern Times** (1936); and is mistaken for a power-mad despot (it must have been that Hitler moustache!) in **The Great Dictator** (1940).

Buster Keaton, "The Great Stone Face," was Chaplin's contemporary and his equal as a stunt man—both paid their dues as hard-knock vaudeville performers and in Mack Sennett comedy shorts—but *Keaton-esque* implies a more detached, less eager-to-please style of comedy. Among Keaton's best: **Our Hospitality** (1923), in which he's trapped in the middle of a Hatfield-McCoy-style feud; the ahead-of-its-time **Sherlock Jr.** (1924), about a projectionist who finds himself inside a movie; **Seven Chances** (1925), where he must find a bride immediately or lose a substantial inheritance (1999's dreary *The Bachelor* recycled its plot); **Steamboat Bill Jr.** (1928), which contains the breathtaking gag in which he escapes being crushed by the facade of a falling house because he's standing right in the trajectory of an open window (remember, this was before CGI or green-screen effects; it's pure, audacious, insanely dangerous stunt work); and **The General** (1927).

How did we describe consummately well-crafted, edge-of-the-seat, slightly perverse thrillers before master of suspense Alfred Hitchcock lent his name to the cause? Contrary to careless usage, *Hitchcockian* is not synonymous with insanely convoluted plots or ridiculous last-minute twists—the shocker at the end of **Psycho** (1960) is a model of its kind, meticulously set up and perfectly plausible. And he was much more than a cruel craftsman who could cross-cut a suspense sequence with his eyes shut. Hitchcock's range encompassed darkly cynical fables about human nature such as **Strangers on a Train** (1951), in which two men agree to "swap" murders, and **Rear Window** (1954), about a casual voyeur who may have seen a man disposing of his wife's body, as well as breezy trifles on the order of **To Catch a Thief** (1955), a sun-drenched romp through love and larceny on the French Riviera.

Spielbergian suggests technically impeccable mainstream entertainments, suffused with a lifelong movie buff's love of homage and in-jokes and shot through with a broad streak of sentimentality.

Steven Spielberg managed to find a Holocaust story with something resembling a happy ending for his masterful **Schindler's List** (1993), and really did save the title character in the punishing WWII drama **Saving Private Ryan** (1998). More typical Spielberg pictures include the deliciously scary killer-shark movie **Jaws** (1975), the irresistibly heart-warming **E.T.: The Extra-Terrestrial** (1982)—believe me, the cynic in me tried, but that ugly little alien got me—and **Raiders of the Lost Ark** (1981), a ripsnorting homage to old-time movie adventures.

Canadian David Cronenberg contributed the term *Cronenbergian*, which applies to films that delight in the perverse visceral allure of decay and deformation. Cronenberg graduated from the horror ghetto into the psychological quagmires of **Dead Ringers** (1988)—the phrase "gynecological instruments for operating on mutant women" never fails to give me a chill—and **Spider** (2002), featuring, respectively, Jeremy Irons's extraordinary performances as twin doctors undone by their suffocating closeness, and Ralph Fiennes's portrayal of a fragile mental patient—but never repudiated the crown of "King of Venereal Horror." From **They Came from Within/Shivers** (1975), in which biologically engineered parasites turn the residents of a sterile high-rise apartment complex into sex fiends, to the coldly intense **A History of Violence** (2005), Cronenberg has a rare singularity of vision.

The same is true of expansive Italian sensualist Federico Fellini, in every other way Cronenberg's polar opposite. *Fellini-esque* is frequently used as a snooty synonym for surreal, but his films are a unique mix of earthiness and affectionate grotesquerie that celebrate both the repulsive beauty in the bizarre and the heartbreaking grace in everyday ugliness. Among his masterworks, I prefer **La dolce vita** (1960), a glittering journey to the poisoned heart of Rome's shallow, jet-set nightlife featuring Marcello Mastroianni and pneumatic Swedish bombshell Anita Ekberg (she takes the iconic, evening gown–clad dip in the Trevi Fountain), and **8½** (1963), in which a movie director (Mastroianni again) suffers a serious case of creative block while prepping his new film. But other prefer the gorgeous pathos of **La strada** (1954) and **The Nights of Cabiria** (1957), both starring the director's waifish wife, Giulietta Masina, as downtrodden women whose childlike optimism gets them through life's bitter trials.

Bunuelian denotes old-school surrealism, courtesy of Spanish film-maker Luis Bunuel. He debuted with the *epater le bourgeois* shocker **An Andalusian Dog/Un chien Andalou** (1929), whose eyeball-slitting sequence is still queasy-making, and went on to make a series of witty, savage, subversive, and always provocative films, including the excoriating **Los olvidados** (1950), about Mexican street children; the elegantly wicked **Criminal Life of Archibaldo de la Cruz** (1955), in which a dandy is constantly thwarted in his efforts to become a serial murderer; and the confounding **That Obscure Object of Desire** (1977), in which two dramatically different actresses share one role.

Woody Allen–like is shorthand for the kind of neurotic, Jewish, intellectual New York–centric humor that once had nervous studio executives making lists of words and references they were afraid wouldn't play in the heartland. His slapstick **Sleeper** (1973)—in which a cryogenically frozen nebbish awakes in the year 2173, where scientists have discovered the nutritional merits of cream pies and hot fudge, and the orgasmatron makes messy real sex obsolete—is the high point of his early career; he peaked with the bittersweet romantic comedies **Annie Hall** (1977), co-starring Diane Keaton as his WASP girlfriend (Christopher Walken's bit part as her suicidal brother is a gem), and **Manhattan** (1979), in which Allen's shimmering black-and-white images of his beloved hometown eclipse ostensible love interest Mariel Hemingway. Then Allen started getting all *Bergman-esque*, which either means deep and intensely dramatic or slow, obscure, and pretentious, depending on your response to the spare, metaphysical, and sublimely acted films of Swedish filmmaker Ingmar Bergman. His haunting medieval drama **The Seventh Seal** (1957) gave us the indelible image of Death playing chess with a doomed knight; **Wild Strawberries** (1957) revolves around an old man contemplating the choices that shaped his life; and the elliptical **Persona** (1966) follows the gradual merging of the personalities of a withdrawn actress (the glorious Liv Ullmann) and her extroverted nurse (Bibi Andersson). A slightly warmer side of Bergman is evident in **Fanny and Alexander** (1982), inspired by his memories of his small-town childhood during the first decade of twentieth century.

The adjective *Capra-esque* has been corrupted to mean sentimental and corny, but the versatile Frank Capra—who specialized in stories about regular joes standing up to the system—was a populist without being a sap. Take a long, hard look at holiday staple **It's a Wonderful Life** (1946)—you'll be surprised by the darkness at the edge of town. Other Capra classics include the romantic comedy **It Happened One Night** (1934), the blackly funny **Arsenic and Old Lace** (1944), **Meet John Doe** (1941), which takes a gimlet-eyed view of media manipulation of human-interest stories, and **Mr. Smith Goes to Washington** (1939), in which a naive political idealist (James Stewart) refuses to get ground up in the political gears.

Tarantino-esque scarcely needs explanation: It's pop culture obsessed and a barrage of movie-geek banter, just like fan-boy-turned-film-maker Quentin Tarantino, writer-director of fractured crime pictures **Reservoir Dogs** (1992) and **Pulp Fiction** (1994), and **Kill Bill: Vol. 1** (2003) and **Kill Bill: Vol. 2** (2004), a glorious visual mix-tape of exploitation movie themes and allusions.

WILDE THINGS

U ber Brit-wit Oscar Wilde (1854-1900)—who was in fact proudly Irish—coined dazzlingly clever epigrams as naturally as bees make honey and delivered barbed *bon mots* as casually as they sting. He affected long hair and flamboyant mannerisms in a profoundly conservative time, became an international celebrity—he even slayed audiences in the rough-and-tumble American West—and left a body of brittle, insanely cunning work that's lost none of its bite in one hundred years.

Anthony Asquith's version of **The Importance of Being Earnest** (1952) is the *creme de la creme*, a razor-sharp adaptation of Wilde's comedy of pretenses, pretension, and best friends (Michael Redgrave, Michael Denison) who invent an imaginary wastrel named Ernest and cause themselves no end of complicated trouble. But Oliver Parker's 2002 version, starring Colin Firth and Rupert Everett, is hugely entertaining, and Parker's **An Ideal Husband** (1999) is a frothy brew of scandal, blackmail, and gossip-mongering with a stellar cast: Everett, Cate Blanchett, Julianne Moore, and Jeremy Northam. Charles Laughton plays a cowardly haint in the family-friendly comedy **The Canterville Ghost** (1944)—Wilde, who had two youngsters of his own, penned several children's stories—while Patrick Stewart takes over as a sadder spirit who haunts because he's haunted in the charming 1994 remake. Decadent aristocrat Hurd Hatfield looks as young and innocent as a Renaissance saint, but his portrait tells another story in **The Picture of Dorian Gray** (1945); George Sanders is his partner in heedless hedonism and a very young Angela Lansbury plays the innocent waitress that Gray debauches.

Three films—two released within a year of each other—focus on the married playwright's supremely ill-considered affair with spoiled, would-be poet Lord Alfred Douglas, whose viciously litigious father dragged Wilde's reputation through the mud; the scandal ruined Wilde financially, humiliated his wife and sons, and blighted the last years of his life. Stephen Fry gives a stunning performance as **Wilde** (1997) opposite Jude Law and Tom Wilkinson as Douglas and his poisonously macho father; Robert Morley stars in the excellent **Oscar Wilde** (1959), and Peter Finch followed him in the very good **The Man with the Green Carnation/The Trials of Oscar Wilde** (1960). Finally, in **Salome's Last Dance** (1988), provocateur Ken Russell imagines Wilde and Douglas watching a production of Wilde's libidinous biblical fantasy, *Salome*, in a lavish Victorian brothel; the result is surprisingly warm and very entertaining.

THE WOLF AT THE DOOR

The gulf that divides tragic werewolves from wolf men who embrace the beast within can be measured in the distance from "even a man who is pure at heart and says his prayers at night, may become a wolf when the wolfbane blooms and the autumn moon is bright" to "I saw a werewolf with a Chinese menu in his hand, walking through the streets of Soho in the rain." Lon Chaney Jr.'s poor, hangdog Larry Talbot never wanted to bark at the moon: He was cursed to wander the foggy sets of **The Wolf Man** (1941), looking for a cure and howling mournfully for his lost humanity. Generations of unhappy werewolves followed: confused high-school athlete Michael Landon in **I Was a Teenage Werewolf** (1957); rapist's spawn Oliver Reed in **The Curse of the Werewolf** (1961), condemned to succumb to his basest instincts for daring to be born on Christmas day; flea-bitten Polish nobleman Paul Naschy, a Spanish muscleman-turned-(sort of)-actor whose thirteen low-rent werewolf pictures, starting with **Mark of the Wolfman** (1967), have an inexplicable cult following.

Vacationing students, take note: Avoid quaint English country pubs with names like "The Slaughtered Lamb," or risk becoming **An American Werewolf in London** (1981). Director John Landis's blackly comic horror show features dazzling transformation effects by Rick Baker. What a contrast with the werewolves of **The Howling** (1981)! They disagree about style—some favor keeping their wolfishness to themselves, others want to let it all hang out—but they all love being the children of the night. Joe Dante's smart, scary spin on lycanthropic legends pokes fun at touchy-feely

California fads (werewolves exploring their animal natures at an Esalen-style retreat—brilliant!) without stinting on the horror, and features great Rob Bottin effects. A lean, mean, all-night siege machine, **Dog Soldiers** (2002) pits a six-man platoon of British soldiers doing training exercises in the Scottish wilds against a military experiment in breeding the perfect grunt.

In **Wolfen** (1981), murderous beasts terrorize New Yorkers; it's not a traditional werewolf movie, but I saw it stun an audience of Times Square grind-house rowdies into silence. The ripsnorting **Brotherhood of the Wolf** (2001), a no-holds-barred mix of multinational, multigenre conventions that borrows liberally from classic American monster movies, high-octane Hong Kong martial arts pictures, and melodramatic French costume epics revolves around the hunt for a peasant-killing uber-loupe dubbed the "Beast of Gevaudon." If your idea of fun includes decadent aristocrats, gorgeous Monica Belluci as a spy masquerading as a high-class hooker, and *Matrix*-style martial arts action, this is your thrill ride. And if you ever wondered why they call it "the curse," **Ginger Snaps** (2000) will enlighten as it entertains. Outcast suburban teen sisters Brigitte and Ginger play at being morbid and weird until Ginger gets mauled by some kind of animal and starts acting really freaky. She blames her monthlies . . . which, of course, coincide with the bad moon rising.

WORKING FOR A LIVING

The dark secret of white-collar success is that quiet desperation is often part of the deal. Lest you think men never *used* to care about "quality time" with the kids, **The Man in the Gray Flannel Suit** (1956) tackled the issue before there was a term for it; WWII veteran Gregory Peck nabs a plum corporate job at the glamorous Manhattan headquarters of a major TV network, but climbing the ladder of success means neglecting his wife and children. **The Apartment** (1960) belongs to ambitious young insurance-office cog Jack Lemmon, who curries favor with philandering big wheels by lending it out for illicit assignations; Billy Wilder's scathing estimation of the price of getting ahead hasn't aged a day in forty-five years. Window-washer Robert Morse scales the corporate heights of Worldwide Wickets in **How to Succeed in Business Without Really Trying** (1967), a surprisingly sharp musical satire of self-help jargon and office politicking. Copywriter Richard E. Grant begins having doubts about the business of selling people things they don't need and can't afford in the vitriolic **How to Get Ahead in Advertising** (1989); when he flirts with the idea of getting out, all his most venal impulses coalesce into a talking boil that urges him to new heights of poisonous success.

It's lonely at the top, but it's no better at the bottom. Low-rent real-estate agents Al Pacino, Jack Lemmon, Alan Arkin, and Ed Harris scramble to hold their positions in the dog-eat-dog world of telephone sales in David Mamet's **Glengarry Glen Ross** (1992), a film marinated in testosterone and curdled dreams. **The Clockwatchers**

(1997) are office temps—Toni Collette, Lisa Kudrow, Alanna Ubach, and Parker Posey—ignored by "real" employees and trading their hours for a handful of dimes until a rash of petty thefts threatens their already tenuous positions. An alienated temp worker who just can't get the hang of making friends and influencing people snaps in **She's One of Us/Elle est des nôtres** (2003), only to find that murder is her first step on the path to success in this chilly French critique of the *maladie Americaine*: confusing what you do with who you are. A cynical stripper and a shy girl from the suburbs decide to sleep their way to success in **Secret Things/Choses secrètes** (2002), a lurid look at sexual politics in the office that's equal parts Zalman King–style soft-core romp and oh-so-French philosophical treatise—I *love* it.

Like many of us, these movies laugh through clenched teeth. An efficiency expert assures the research staff of a TV network that computerization won't put them out of work—it will just help them do their jobs more efficiently. The surprise in this all-too-familiar scenario is that it comes from the 1957 Spencer Tracy–Katharine Hepburn comedy **Desk Set**, further evidence that modern problems have been with us for a while. Three frustrated secretaries—Jane Fonda, Lily Tomlin, and Dolly Parton—think they've killed their sleazy, chauvinistic boss in **9 to 5** (1980), which buries a couple of barbs about workplace sexism under its chirpy, "we girls have to stick together" surface. The manifesto of miserable office drones everywhere, *Beavis and Butthead*–creator Mike Judge's **Office Space** (1999) chronicles the petty indignities, injustices, and humiliations of three programmers who've sold their souls to the cubicle god with squirm-inducing accuracy—even when it's funny, it hurts. **The New Guy** (2003) begins to suspect something sinister lurks behind the everyday drudgery and petty irritations of his new job in this creepy, ultra-low-budget comedy of discomfort. Are you *sure* you didn't sign those HR documents in blood?

YOU DRIVE ME APE, YOU BIG GORILLA

When I was a child, local TV stations always showed **King Kong** (1933) and **Mighty Joe Young** (1949) on Thanksgiving. Why? Beats me, but to this day the smell of turkey and the plight of big, sad apes are inextricably linked in my mind. A mournful fable about a misunderstood, lovelorn beast laid low by his beauty (Fay Wray), *King Kong* is the *creme de la creme*, the gold standard by which big ape movies are judged. *Mighty Joe Young* is the kinder, gentler girl-and-gorilla story: Joe is more a pesky kid than a monstrous suitor, he's hauled to civilization to do a nightclub act, not to be exhibited in chains, and he *doesn't* get shot off the top of the Empire State Building by fighter planes. The antidote to all this simian pathos is man-in-a-gorilla-suit pictures.

Planet of the Apes (1968) contains moments of greatness, but let me share a little secret: Half the movie's appeal has nothing to do with trenchant allegory or that great twist ending—it's childish delight in the topsy-turvy sight of gorillas, orangutans, and chimpanzees acting just like us. Tim Burton's 2001 remake fails on every level but one: The ape suits by legendary makeup artist Rick Baker (who made a minor specialty of incredibly realistic simian makeup effects) are breathtaking, thoroughly animal-like without obscuring the distinctive features of the actors underneath, including Tim Roth, David Warner, Michael Clarke Duncan, and Kris Kristofferson.

Boris Karloff plays a doctor looking for a polio cure in poverty-row quickie **The Ape** (1940), which features a bracingly dyspeptic view of small-town America; an escaped carnival gorilla provides a cover for the murders he commits to get human spinal fluid. In **The Ape Man** (1943), Bela Lugosi also needs spinal fluid to correct the effects of an experiment that left him a shambling, half-ape/half-man. In **Bela Lugosi Meets a Brooklyn Gorilla** (1952), forgotten comedy duo Sammy Petrillo and Duke Mitchell (low-rent Martin and Lewis imitators) are stranded on a tropical island with a mad scientist who turns Mitchell into a gorilla. A voodoo potion transforms *Perry Mason*'s Raymond Burr, who's been dallying with his boss's wife, into a *sukara* ("hairy ape" in native talk) in **Bride of the Gorilla** (1951). Burr *owns* a gorilla in **Gorilla at Large** (1954), about an amusement park plagued by murders; his wife is future Oscar winner Anne Bancroft, whose real-life husband, Mel Brooks, teased her mercilessly about this shoddy skeleton in her career closet.

Six degrees of Raymond Burr continue when "kingukongu" meets the King of the Monsters—Burr's co-star in the U.S. version of **Godzilla** (1954). **King Kong vs. Godzilla** (1962) is a silly, satirical monster mash that includes a smackdown on Mount Fuji and the sweetly surreal image of Kong aloft in a net slung under a helicopter and buoyed by colorful balloons. **The War of the Gargantuas** (1967), a childhood favorite of mine, pits a good, brown experimental giant-ape-thing against his bad doppelganger. And finally, **The Mighty Peking Man/Goliathon/Colossus of the Congo** (1977), a Hong Kong knockoff designed to cash in on the 1976 *King Kong* remake (notable only for the now-melancholy sight of Kong straddling the World Trade Center towers), features a giant, rampaging Tibetan ape and a scantily clad jungle cutie (Evelyne Kraft). It's not good, but it's great.

THE ZOMBIE STOMP

The natural history of the living dead is divided into two eras: before and after George Romero. Before Romero's *Night of the Living Dead*, zombies retained their ties to the old country—Haiti—but after Romero, they were fully assimilated citizens of the international horror community.

Zombies immigrated to Hollywood alongside Frankenstein and his monster, Dracula, Dr. Jekyll/Mr. Hyde, and the werewolf, but didn't assimilate as quickly. In **White Zombie** (1932), a young American couple in the West Indies is victimized by wicked zombie-master "Murder" Legendre (Bela Lugosi); its unforgettable images—the voodoo-whammied bride's burial in her spectral wedding dress and the downtrodden zombies working Legendre's creaking, groaning mill machinery—outweigh the sometimes creaky execution. Brutal Cornish capitalist Squire Hamilton takes his cue from Legendre and uses the uncomplaining dead to work his dangerous tin mines in

The Plague of the Zombies (1966), which introduced the nightmarish image of pale hands clawing their way out through the dark graveyard dirt. The shimmering **I Walked with a Zombie** (1943) loosely reworks the plot of *Jane Eyre*, sending a young nurse to attend the catatonic wife—who may be zombified or merely mad—of a tormented Haitian plantation owner with whom she falls in love.

And then came Romero, whose ultra-low-budget, black-and-white **Night of the Living Dead** (1968) tossed out the voodoo and drums for corpses reanimated by radiation (or germ warfare or poisonous chemicals or sonic bug killers) and consumed by the need to devour human flesh. Stripped-down, relentless, and matter-of-factly gruesome, it ushered in a new age of bleak, downbeat horror. The darkly satirical **Dawn of the Dead** (1978), set in a zombie-besieged shopping mall, puts the bite on consumer culture; Zack Snyder's 2004 remake ditched the social commentary but upped the zombie mayhem. Romero's claustrophobic and underrated **Day of the Dead** (1985) takes place in an underground bunker where military scientists try to control the flesh-eating dead, and **Land of the Dead** (2005) sets the living haves and have-nots at each other's throats while the dead show disturbing signs of intelligence.

Romero's *Dead* movies begat a series of Italian knockoffs, which made up for what they lacked in originality with ever-more outrageous gore effects. Lucio Fulci's **Zombie** (1979) kicked off the zombies *all'Italia* craze and includes a notorious underwater shark vs. zombie smack-down.

The hungry horrors of **28 Days Later** (2002) aren't actually dead—merely infected by a bioengineered virus dubbed "rage"—but to paraphrase the late Richard Cardinal Cushing, when I see something that looks like a zombie and bites like a zombie and moans like a zombie, I call it a zombie. Unlike the traditional shuffling dead, they run like hell—1980's **Nightmare City** (one of the Italian gang) may be the first picture to feature sprinting zombies, but in *28 Days Later* they're Olympic caliber. **Shaun of the Dead** (2004) pulls off that trickiest of tricks: mixing comedy and horror without diluting either. Two London slackers wake up one day to a zombie holocaust, too hungover to realize that it's not just another day in dullsville until they find a living-dead girl in the back garden. And in the quietly chilling **They Came Back** (2004), a small French city is overwhelmed when ten years worth of dead people simply return, apparently healthy—if a little distracted and cool to the touch—and threaten to overwhelm the social services safety net with their needs. Monster fads come and monster fads go, but like the poor, the dead are always with us.

EPILOGUE: MY FILMS FOR A DESERT ISLAND

S urely we've all played the game. If you were going to spend the rest of your life on a desert island and could take, say, a dozen some-odd movies with you, what would they be?

While it might be more ambitious and intellectually stimulating to load up on challenging, formally rigorous or emotionally wrenching films like Bela Tarr's **Werckmeister Harmonies/Werckmeister harmoniak** (2000) or Ingmar Bergman's **Scenes from a Marriage/ Scener ur ettaäktenskap** (1974)—films I admire enormously— I'm just not that evolved. If I'm really going to be stuck on some poxy island watching the same handful of movies in perpetuity, I'm going with ones I really, really love. And so I'd take:

Citizen Kane (1941), because it's as brilliant as everyone says and a hundred times as entertaining—wunderkind Orson Welles's genius wasn't that he played with lighting, angles, and editing with the giddy intoxication of a kid dabbling in finger paints or his penetrating look into millionaire Charles Foster Kane's heart of darkness. It was that he wasn't afraid to grab you by the shirt collar and take you on the ride of a lifetime on the best toy train a boy ever had.

Blade Runner (1982), because director Ridley Scott's sleek bravado transformed Philip K. Dick's *Do Androids Dream of Electric Sheep?*, a sad dystopian fairy tale about soul-less androids who wish they could be real boys, into lush, operatic tragedy wrapped in a glittering, rain-slicked vision of a seductively poisoned future. I prefer the director's cut—the one without the voiceover narration and the happy ending—but really, any *Blade Runner* will do.

All About Eve (1950), because it raises bitchiness to dizzying heights and lets two of the art's foremost practitioners—Bette Davis and George Sanders—have their heads. Meow! Hiss!

In a Lonely Place (1950), because every time Humphrey Bogart's bitter, washed-up screenwriter—who just might be a serial murderer—tells hardened chippie Gloria Graham, still clinging to a forlorn hope of heaven, "I was born when you kissed me. I died when you left me. I

lived a few weeks while you loved me," I just about lose
it. Perfect noir, perfect doomed, cynical love story, perfect
fable for disillusioned romantics.

Memento (2001), because its slippery storytelling and reverse
chronology are so damnably clever (see *Consider the Source:
Tricky Narratives and Unreliable Narrators*). Just when you
think you've got it all sorted out, it tosses you a curve and
you have to recalibrate.

Nashville (1975), because everything Robert Altman ever
learned about ensemble filmmaking and dozens of amazing performances by stars—unknowns, up and comers,
and cult favorites—come together like celestial clockwork
in this portrait of American dreams and delusions remixed,
remade, deracinated, codified, and spun into country-and-
western tunes.

The Red Shoes (1948), because Michael Powell and Emeric
Pressburger's acid-spiked valentine to the marvelous,
masochistic mystique of classical dance (see *Everything is
Beautiful at the Ballet*) is as delirious as a feverish hallucination, as vivid as a waking dream, and as intoxicating as a
rum-infused bonbon.

La Jetee (1962), Chris Marker's fatalistic science-fiction tone
poem in still images, because it's haunted me for more
than twenty years and still brings tears to my eyes every
single time.

Kill Bill, Vol. 1 and **Vol. 2** (2003, 2004), because they're dozens of movies in two, the best parts of I don't know how
many exploitation movies I saw at an impressionable age.
The movie's spine is Quentin Tarantino's reworking of

the 1973 Japanese revenge fantasy **Lady Snowblood/ Shurayukihime** (1973)—an amazing movie in its own right—but he layers on a collage of images and melodies from yakuza epics, spaghetti Westerns, anime, chop-socky pictures, Italian gialli, euro-sexploitation, and TV shows of the sixties and seventies, the more obscure the better, meticulously juxtaposed and blended together so they evoke Proustian memories of pulp highs savored in the smoky haze of grind houses and darkened basements.

Performance (1970), because the more I watch Nicholas Roeg and Donald Cammell's drug-and-sex soaked psychodrama about an East End gangster, a paranoid, reclusive rock star named Turner, and his girlfriends (James Fox, Mick Jagger, swinging sixties sexpot Anita Pallenberg, and androgynous Michele Breton) playing wicked games in a rundown townhouse, the spookier it gets. Maybe it's the ghost of Brian Jones, Jagger's model for Turner, who died shortly before *Performance* opened and not long after being ousted from the band he co-founded.

Rumble Fish (1983), because it's the perfect blend of teen angst and unbelievably gorgeous black-and-white filmmaking—I could watch it for the time-lapse photography of rolling clouds and shadows streaking down the sides of brick buildings alone—set to a hauntingly percussive score by former Police drummer Stewart Copeland.

Fight Club (1999), because hit-or-miss director David Fincher landed one to the gut with his adaptation of Chuck Palahniuk's deeply screwed-up cult novel about self-actualization through brutal, bone-crunching bare-knuckle fighting. The ending is a jaw dropper, and if there's a step out of place on the way I haven't caught it yet. I'm always up for another look.

And now a confession: I read too. There are a handful of meta movie novels I'd pack along with the pictures, starting with David Thomson's *Suspects*. At first glance it appears to be a collection of biographical sketches of noir movie characters, a sort of movie geek companion to Thomson's revered *Biographical Dictionary of Film* in which high-class hustler Julian Kaye (Richard Gere in *American Gigolo*) is the son of mad former silent movie queen Norma Desmond and the much younger screenwriter she killed (Gloria Swanson and William Holden in *Sunset Blvd.*), and cabaret singer Amy Jolly wound up in a corrupt Mexican border town twenty-eight years after she followed her French Legionnaire into the desert, burned brown as a gypsy and telling fortunes as "Tanya" (Marlene Dietrich in *Morocco* and *Touch of Evil*). But a story bubbles up through the character sketches, narrated by small-town hero George Bailey (James Stewart in *It's a Wonderful Life*) and connecting the dots that lead from the poisoned glitter of *Laura* (1944) to the defeated gloom of *Night Moves* (1975).

Mark Z. Danielewski's *House of Leaves* begins with *The Navidson Report*, a samizdat film that documents the special peculiarities of the house into which photo journalist Will Navidson and his family have moved, starting with the fact that it's slightly smaller outside than it is within. Less-than-reliable narrator Johnny Truant gets involved with the Navidson affair when he finds a manuscript collecting all the known facts and conjectures about it in the apartment of a nutty, blind, and recently deceased neighbor; Truant's footnotes to the manuscript tell a whole other story of encroaching madness, as do the appended letters from his institutionalized mother.

Finally, Theodore Roszak's *Flicker* spins the same kind of centuries-old conspiracy theory as *The Da Vinci Code*, with the difference that Roszak can actually write and finds clues in movies instead of classical paintings. Roszak weaves the thirteenth-century Cathar heresy, flick(er)s, secret religious society "Oculus Dei," forgotten German émigré director Max Castle (think Edgar G. Ulmer), whose shabby exploitation pictures exude an uncanny power, and the song "Bye Bye Blackbird" into a hell of a tale that suggests movies are so much more than a medium. It's being filmed after several false starts by Darren Aronofsky, of the truly creepy conspiracy picture *Pi* (1998), though like the other two I think it's fundamentally unfilmable. That said, I was briefly and tangentially involved with an effort to get *Flicker* off the ground in 1998. Producers Bobby Geisler and John Roberdeau, hot off Terrence Malick's *The Thin Red Line*, were looking for a director to make the Castle films within the film. Dario Argento's name came up and mine with it; my souvenir of hosting a screening of *The Bird with the Crystal Plumage* (1970) for various involved parties—it went down like a lead balloon—is a flip book made by Roszak and depicting Shirley Temple fleeing a flock of blackbirds that become a gaping maw. Read *Flicker* and you'll get it.

I'd also pack the complete works of William Shakespeare as well, and I'd probably wind up casting and recasting my perfect-world movie versions in my head. Because it all comes down to this: I love the infinite promise of movies, even when individual pictures disappoint, bore, or make me feel silly for succumbing to their venal come-ons. There's always another title waiting, and it might be the one.

CAST & CREW

A

Abraham, F. Murray, 111
Abril, Victoria, 6
Adler, Lou, 181
Affleck, Ben, 77, 84
Alcott, John, 37
Aldiss, Brian, 138
Allen, Lewis, 80
Allen, Woody, 5, 47, 66, 73,
    229–30
Almerayda, Michael, 97
Almodovar, Pedro, 4–6, 131, 177
Altman, Robert, 61, 91, 110, 132,
    201, 218–19, 223, 243
Amano, Yoshitaka, 75
Ameche, Don, 140
Anderson, Edward, 132
Anderson, P.T., 219
Andersson, Bibi, 173, 230
Andress, Ursula, 87
Andrews, Dana, 58
Anglade, Jean-Hugues, 192
Ann-Margret, 58, 161
Antheil, George, 108
Anulka, 129
Apple, Fiona, 12
Araki, Gregg, 86
Ardant, Fanny, 148, 160
Arden, Eve, 1
Argento, Asia, 75
Argento, Dario, 62, 119, 246
Arkin, Alan, 235

Armstrong, Gillian, 218
Aronofsky, Darren, 187
Arquette, Patricia, 133
Ashly, Ray, 96
Asquith, Anthony, 231
Assayas, Olivier, 48
Astaire, Fred, 18, 60
Astor, Mary, 44, 93
Atherton, William, 133
Attenborough, Richard, 161, 211
Audiard, Jacques, 94
Austen, Jane, 205
Auteuil, Daniel, 26
Avalon, Frankie, 9–10
Avalos, Stefan, 64

B

Bacall, Lauren, 110, 179
Baker, Rick, 233, 238
Balaban, Bob, 191
Baldwin, Adam, 162
Baldwin, Alec, 133
Bale, Christian, 172, 181
Balint, Eszter, 150
Ball, Lucille, 1
Balsam, Martin, 165
Bancroft, Anne, 61, 238
Banderas, Antonio, 4, 6, 26
Banks, Russell, 72
Barbato, Bailey, 50
Barbato, Randy, 50
Barkin, Ellen, 58, 129
Barney, Matthew, 87
Barrie, J. M., 43
Barrymore, Diana, 224

S

FILMS & MEDIA

A

C

H

I

N

T

Y

Z

ABOUT THE AUTHOR

Manhattan born-and-raised **Maitland McDonagh** misspent her youth prowling Times Square grind houses in search of horror, exploitation, and mondo movies and still managed to find regular employment as a film writer. She is the senior movies editor of tvguide.com (www.tvguide.com/movies), where she oversees the movie section, reviews hundreds of new releases every year, and writes the popular column Ask FlickChick.

She is the author of three previous books: *Broken Mirrors/Broken Minds: The Dark Dreams of Dario Argento* (1991), *Filmmaking on the Fringe: The Good, the Bad and the Deviant Directors* (1995), and *The 50 Most Erotic Films of All Time* (1996). She is a contributing writer to *Time Out New York* and has written for dozens of U.S. and European magazines and newspapers, ranging from *Film Comment* to *Fangoria*, as well as numerous film anthologies.

McDonagh earned an MFA in film history/theory/criticism from Columbia University, where she co-founded and co-edited the magazine *Columbia Film Review* (later *Columbia Film View*), and has taught film at the City University of New York and Brooklyn College.